THE EMPLOYER'S GUIDE TO RECRUITING ON THE INTERNET

THE EMPLOYER'S GUIDE TO RECRUITING ON THE INTERNET

Ray Schreyer & John McCarter

IMPACT

Copyright © 1998 by Ray Schreyer and John McCarter

All rights reserved. Printed in the United States of America. No part of this book may be used or reproduced in any manner whatsoever without written permission of the publisher: IMPACT PUBLICATIONS, 9104-N Manassas Drive, Manassas Park, VA 20111-5211, Tel. 703-361-7300, Fax 703-335-9486, or e-mail: *impactp@impactpub-lications.com*

Library of Congress Cataloging-in-Publication Data

Schreyer, Ray, 1958-
    The Employer's Guide to Recruiting on the Internet/Ray Schreyer & John McCarter.
    p. cm
    Includes bibliographical references and index.
    ISBN 1-57023-096-X
    1. Employees—Recruiting—United States. 2.Employees-recruiting—United
States-Computer network resources. 3. Web sites—Management. I. McCarter,
John. II. Title.
    HF5549.5.R44S295 1998
    658.3'111'02854678—dc21   98-3550
                                 CIP

For information on distribution or quantity discount rates, Telephone (703) 361-7300, Fax (703) 335-9486, E-mail (*impactp@impactpubli-cations.com*), or write to: Sales Department, IMPACT PUBLICATIONS, 9104-N Manassas Drive, Manassas Park, VA 20111-5211. Distributed to the trade by National Book Network, 15200 NBN Way, Blue Ridge Summit, PA 17214, Tel. 1-800-462-6400.

We dedicate this book to one of the characters in it. There is a real-life

model, but she prefers anonymity in this context at least.

Susan Sweet (our code for her real name) is the closest thing we could

find to a hero or heroine for this book. She drives Ray to distraction

with her lack of technical insights, and once she pushed the calm and

courteous John to a cold fury with her hectoring over online ad costs,

but we appreciate her diligent application of both good business

sense and online ad services to a financially

rewarding result.

We prize her because she has done what we hope and

expect the readers of this book will do: weigh our

advice carefully and incorporate it into a

successful recruiting plan that fits their goals and

circumstances.

Acknowledgments

Ray Schreyer

I would first like to thank my bride, Gayle, for putting up with me being tied to a computer during our first months of marriage. I promise I will come down from my office and start living again now that this book is finished. Also - I admit - I should have left my portable home during the honeymoon! Your support and understanding has been a blessing in this project.

Special thanks to my partner in crime, John (Billy Bob) McCarter. His wit, wisdom, and humor have made this effort a joy. I couldn't have even considered this project without him.

Thanks to Sharon, Edna, Debbie, Yvonne, and the gang at the big green bank in Charlotte. You all helped me learn this new technology and I will be forever grateful.

My most special thanks is reserved for Chelsey Carter at Landmark Communications. When this book had lost its way you were gracious enough to help it find a new home at Impact Publications.

John McCarter

My first acknowledgement must be to my co-author, Ray Schreyer, the resident alpha geek on this literary project. Without his copious technical expertise, extensive experience, and relentless data collection, the book would have been simply impossible. Ray is the best there is when it comes to making online job advertising work for employers.

A vital element in the success of most people is the confidence of a loyal spouse who believes in you even when your own self image sags. My wife, Sue, possesses all the core competencies for that undercompensated position. She even remained supportive when she suspected that some of the strictly fictional characters in the book are not only real, but are also not-so-distant relatives. Even after thirty years of marriage, she still can't name all of the several hundred living here in the Carolinas.

My daughter Laura and son-in-law Scott Robert have been unfailing in their enthusiasm for the project. My other daughter, Amy, an insightful business person herself, has held me to the strict literary standards I set for her years ago. My son Daniel, a well-stressed teenager, has been encouraging but very concerned that the book not reflect unfavorably on him. I have promised not to associate him with any of its many shortcomings.

A more general round of thanks is due to my extended family for teaching me that a good story is the highest form of communication; to Clemson University for persuading me that I could learn anything; to the United States Navy for a "can do," "take no prisoners" approach to management; to Thorne, Stevenson & Kellog, Canada, and Drake, Beam, Morin (USA) for an outplacement perspective that portrays recruiting from the other side of the coin; to the headhunter who taught me most of what I know about management recruiting, but who will remain nameless here and hereafter because of his sloppy ethics; and to the faculty at the Belk College of Business, University of North Carolina at Charlotte, for their business insights and inspiration.

A real publishing hurrah goes to Ron Krannich, the man with vision at Impact Publications, Manassas Park, Virginia. He had the insight to recognize that *The Employer's Guide to Recruiting on the Internet* is a management book for human resource professionals, not a computer geek training book that lost its way. In addition to purely selfish reasons for welcoming the success of this book, we hope that its economic achievements will serve as a case study for the marketing staff at MacMillan and

Company. Ray and I really would have chosen to see the book on the market a year earlier, but we are delighted with the additions and enhancements that the delay allowed us to incorporate into its pages.

Contents

THE EMPLOYER'S GUIDE TO RECRUITING ON THE INTERNET

Introduction

Internet based recruiting is an enterprise which distinctly resembles the Klondike gold rush of the last century. The opportunities are real, the pitfalls are abundant, scoundrels abound, regulations are non-existent, and there is no reliable "how to" manual for success; except one. *The Employer's Guide to Recruiting on the Internet* is the "how to" manual for human resource professionals involved in recruiting.

Please note that computer science majors will not discover any technical insights that they were not aware of before they started college, that job seekers who search these pages for job leads will soon despair, and that CEO's will be more appalled than enlightened. The book is a down-to-earth, bottom line exploration of the realities of using the Internet to supplement the challenging task of finding the high quality human resources that are so necessary to both short and long term corporate success.

We did have fun writing the book. The fellow human resource professionals who read the book will discover that we have disguised their most infamous peccadilloes with funny stories that illustrate the sins without indicting all the sinners. Humor is an effective way of delivering balm and insights simultaneously.

The Internet can be utilized in human resource recruiting in three major modes. The obvious first is the placement of online job ads in the various Internet based venues, and related promotion of corporate career opportunities with your organization. The recruiting web site is the ugly stepsister of this approach.

The second and often neglected mode is resume research. The hundreds of thousands of resumes available on the Internet can be utilized, but it requires a managed rather than an ad hoc process.

The third mode is Internet research. The vast quantity of raw data about companies, staff, skills, processes, and transactions on the Internet is an underdeveloped resource for recruiting. The inside professionals need to borrow a leaf from the books of the better compensated outside group, headhunters, and develop deeper insights into the industry they serve.

One of the major objectives of this book is to provide a strategy for evaluating the disparate and desperate claims of online job ad vendors for recruiting effectiveness. In an industry with considerable turnover in vendors, their staff, and their operating policies, naming the villain of the week is a futile exercise. Instead, we provide you with valuable insights into the industry and a process for making astute comparisons.

As an example of how Internet sleight-of-hand works, we noted recently that a new evaluation service had named a marginal player as the leading resource in online job advertising nationwide. Rising to the challenge, Ray did a half hour of research into the criteria used, and invested another half hour in adjusting our web site, www.carolinajobs.com. Within one day, our humble site was rated in the top five job sites by that service. Get real!!

Any promising, but unregulated industry attracts scoundrels like roadkill draws flies in August. You need to understand the dynamics of Internet recruiting to avoid having your recruiting budget become roadkill on the Information Superhighway.

Another major objective is to provide a sound basis for integrating Internet recruiting with the broader human resources functions. The biggest early mistake that human resource departments make is to assume that an Internet job ad is just a newspaper ad without the hard copy. Internet job advertising is such a paradigm shift that the recruiting process is permanently altered. It is giving pioneers a significant edge, but the next set of heroes and heroines will be the human resource professionals who lead their peers by using the Internet to reclaim serious recruiting as an internal function, producing dramatic savings for their companies, and demonstrating to corporate executives that the process can and should be managed effectively. The Internet is a recruiting tool that makes it possible, and this book tells the reader how.

We anticipate that the parameters of recruiting will be changed by the Internet in two dramatic ways.

First, aggressive internal recruiting efforts will migrate down to much smaller companies. Any local 300 person company can now afford to perform a nationwide search for a tool engineer without mortgaging the plant, or paying a headhunter more for a job candidate than the recruit will earn for the three months he is settling down in his new job. A strong internal recruiting function is no longer the exclusive province of Fortune 500 companies; one good human resources professional can do it.

Second, the overall level of persons recruited by internal staff will rise significantly in terms of compensation and responsibilities. The justification for engaging retained search, contingency search, and other headhunter categories of outside recruiters will be challenged by the information gathering and communication capabilities of the Internet. More and more senior executives are checking the Internet for career opportunities; that is where they find the ads placed there by savvy headhunters. In today's climate of rapidly evolving technology, does it make sense to invest in an executive or senior professional who is indifferent to, or ignorant of, the Internet?

The headhunter profession will survive, but the market will become much more competitive and those that escape extinction will be the ones whose capabilities extend far beyond simply finding the best candidates. But their biggest protection will come from a general corporate willingness to pay handsome premiums to outside resources while treating internal human resource professionals like senior clerks.

Our ambition for this book is to arm those professionals for a more proactive and high profile role in corporate success. Human resource requirements are a pivotal, strategic issue for all organizations. We designed *The Employer's Guide to Recruiting on the Internet* as a tool for getting the best people for your company.

INTERNET JOB ADVERTISING
The future is here today

Finding talented professionals has always been one of the most time-consuming and expensive endeavors for an organization. In the pre-information era, your options were rather limited: hire a recruiter at 25-35 percent commission to find the needed new talent, or place expensive display ads in local or national newspapers. Both options have positive and negative consequences.

The Sunday want ad section of the newspaper is a mainstay of American life. In every town and city, hundreds of people review this section for the latest career opportunities in their communities. But, is it the answer to finding the folks you need? Well, maybe, sometimes.

Consider the process: On Monday afternoon, you decide you need a new employee. You have developed a job description and a list of the qualifications necessary for success on the job. Your first daunting task is cutting this job description down into a newspaper advertisement. You would like to put the whole job description in the paper, but you know about column inch costs. More often than not, you do your best to balance the ad costs with the right amount of information and the result is usually a terse three lines. Now you have to hurry, so it can be in the newspaper offices by Wednesday afternoon to make the Sunday edition.

Sunday arrives and you see your ad in all its glory. Now you prepare for the onslaught of resumes. They arrive in droves from folks who have qualifications that cover the spectrum from accounting to zoology. But the problem is, very few candidates really match the qualifications you need. Soon you are two (or more!) weeks into the process, and you find that you just can't find the right folks in this local talent pool that read the newspaper.

So now you must decide whether to try the whole process again in another Sunday paper, maybe Chicago or LA will do, (get ready to take out that check book!) or maybe it's time to contact your always eager recruiter friends.

Those recruiter folks can be great to work with. They will meet with your organization, help you clarify and refine your job requirements, and selectively target the talent pool you need to reach. Before you begin, you will need to decide whether you want to hire one on a contingency or retained basis.

A contingency recruiter only gets paid if and when he makes the placement. This winner-take-all approach attracts a lot of recruiter energy to the jobs that are perceived as being easy to fill quickly, and employers often place job orders with more than one recruiter to get best results from their investments.

In contrast, a retained search firm/recruiter is hired to conduct the search and is paid with partial payments up front for their efforts. The typical retained search firm has a long-standing, close relationship with its clients and handles job searches exclusively. The retained search firm also likes to have its operating expenses covered up front by their clients.

Unfortunately, both types of recruiting services can be very expensive. The going rate is 25-35 percent of the candidate's first-year salary, and the time from initial job order to placement can run from several weeks to a year or more, depending on the effort and time individual recruiters dedicate to your job order. Naturally, effort toward the placement really depends on the type of recruiting arrangement you select and the level of expertise the recruiter(s) brings to the table. The profession has low entry thresholds and a broad spectrum of competencies.

Fortunately, a third option is now available. It is the Internet, and it is emerging as the definitive way to match job seekers with employment opportunities worldwide. Its costs are minimal, the response is nearly instantaneous, and it is the recruiting tool of the future.

GROWTH OF THE INTERNET AS AN INFORMATION RESOURCE

The Internet is a network of networks, a collection of hundreds of thousands of computers inter-linked to each other worldwide with the capability to communicate and exchange data and information. The Internet came into being during the Cold War. The U.S. Department of Defense developed a computer network system called ARPAnet (Advanced Research Projects Agency), whose main purpose was to allow military personnel and scientists to communicate, specifically during a nuclear disaster. Time passed, and universities and corporations started to use the technology. In the mid 1990s, use of the Internet exploded with millions of individual electronic surfers and the emergence of a global cybercity with stores, libraries, museums, and magazines. Today, you will find USA Today, MTV, General Motors, and every major and minor rock group online.

It was estimated in early 1996 that over 55 million individuals worldwide used the Internet; this number is expected to nearly double to over 100 million by 1998. The typical Internet user in 1995 was 18-49 years old, college educated, and had a professional/technical career. But this is changing. Online technology is finding increased acceptance in everyday American life for many reasons:

- Computer costs continue to go down, giving consumers more horsepower for their dollar. In the mid 1980s, it was nothing to spend $5,000 for a basic PC. Today, a quality system can be purchased for less than $1,000, and the advent of WebTV gives consumers an exceptionally low price point for Web access at less than $500.

- Computer processor speed continues to rise. Today's Intel Processors are hundreds of times faster than the IBM PC processors of the mid 80's. The horsepower necessary to handle multimedia (graphics, sound, video, and so on) has finally arrived.

- Internet-access costs are going down as more Internet service providers (ISP's) enter the market. AT&T, BellSouth, MCI, and Sprint are some of the names that are now ISP's. Gone are the days when America Online and CompuServe were charging over $3 per hour for access. Today, Internet access fees average in the neighborhood of $20 per month for unlimited access, and free Internet access is often provided at universities and public libraries. On December 1, 1996, America Online announced its plan to offer unlimited pricing plans ranging from $9.95 to $19.95 per month, providing affordable online access for most families.

- Modem speeds continue to rise, giving users faster access to data. It seems like it was only yesterday when we were all excited about our 2400 baud modem and how quickly it allowed us to connect online. Today 56K is the standard, with 128K and beyond waiting in the wings.

- Cable is about to become the preferred mode of Internet delivery, leaving behind traditional telephone technology and adding the bandwidth necessary to capture the richness of Internet multimedia.

- Information placed on the Internet via home pages, databases, and so on, is increasing as the number of Internet consumers increases. Fashion today dictates that you have your own company home page with slick logos and graphics. Everyone from universities to corporations to pizza parlors are opening digital storefronts to offer products and services and to display information about their organizations. Commerce on the Internet is expected to increase hundred-fold by 1999, and organizations are lining up in droves to catch the wave of this much anticipated new marketplace.

- Mainstream acceptance has been reached as major corporations and media organizations proudly display their Internet addresses (www.mycompany.com). These addresses are now on business cards, billboards, magazine ads, and commercials. Before long, you can expect to see it proudly displayed in the yellow pages and on every newspaper ad, both locally and nationally.

THE EMERGING EMPLOYMENT MARKETPLACE

In the beginning, cyberjunkies, engineers, and computer techies were online, and that was basically it. They talked to each other in cryptic text-based messages with lots of weird code at the beginning and end of notes. Words like Gopher, Telnet, and WAIS were part of their Internet vocabulary. If you needed to hire one of these folks to harness the powers of your mainframe for mundane tasks like printing invoices, placing an online job ad for their talents was a good idea. But back then, you had to understand their jargon and have the ability to "play in their sandbox" to effectively communicate.

Initial online job-recruiting efforts generally started by having some HR person with an aberrant techie gene give this new technology a shot. In the early days, ads were placed in the Online Career Center or in Usenet groups, and good systems people were found regularly. It took services like America Online and CompuServe, appealing to a mainstream audience, for online recruiting to evolve. Because of the user-friendly nature of America Online and the World Wide Web, being a computer hacker was no longer a requirement for playing in the online sandbox. Accountants, teachers, social workers, bankers, insurance agents, even bakery supervisors began going online to look for jobs.

Even though ads for system programmers and other high-tech positions continue to dominate online, organizations are now beginning to list jobs that are less technical in nature. This trend will continue as the Internet population begins to more closely mirror the general population in character, education, experience, and skills. Currently, online recruiting represents 20-30 percent of the recruiting efforts in organizations that are pioneering the use of online job ads.

NET NOTE

It happened on August 7th 1996 - newspapers, television, and radio stations nationwide reported the same story: America Online was off-line for 18 hours. Millions of subscribers were left stranded on the Information Superhighway. The headlines reported the lost commerce, the missed e-mail, and the general disruption of business nationwide.

Though it was catastrophic for some, that day had significant impact on online professionals. That was the day the importance of the Internet and the online world was finally recognized! Gone were the days when cyberspace was the realm of hackers; now, real business was being conducted online, and the world's media was talking about it!

WHY DOES INTERNET ADVERTISING WORK SO WELL?

We have all been raised in the newspaper paradigm: The Sunday want-ads contain the job listings for the week. In cities and towns across America, this venue has been the marketplace where we searched out our employment opportunities. But even though newspapers have worked well in the past, they are no match for the Internet as a recruitment vehicle. The Internet is a superior tool due to several factors:

- It substitutes economical electrons for expensive newsprint

- It recognizes the nationwide market for talent and a much more mobile society

- It utilizes technology that greatly enlarges access to a job market

- It enables employers and job candidates to be more specific about their needs

- It raises the standards for intermediaries in the candidate search process.

ELECTRONS VERSUS TREES

When you multiply the space of even the smallest job ad by the circulation totals of a large regional or metropolitan newspaper, you can easily assume that someone had to kill at least one tree to produce that ad. Not only did they have to kill it, but they had to transport, slice, dice, soak, shred, and process it into a large paper roll with other trees. Then they had to deliver it to the newspaper, where a large staff in a capital intensive facility printed thousands of copies for readers who had a level of interest ranging from zero to 100 percent. Many job ads in newspapers go into the recycling bin without being seen.

Internet based job advertising is not a tree hugger response to paper consumption, but it does represent a paradigm shift in the economics of job ad distribution. The online job ad intrinsically costs dramatically less. While the cost parameters for the Internet are shrinking, the mature newspaper industry finds itself the victim of climbing costs and increased reader sophistication.

The newspaper industry is doing a splendid job of reducing the production costs of their publications, but it is an uphill fight. Electrons are not only very economical, they are quite recyclable. The local electric-power utility charges for kilowatt hours in terms of cents. The power consumption of computers and computer printers is so low that a reader can access, record, and print a copy of the individual job ad that interests him at an insignificant cost.

With the costs of computer software, computer hardware, and the telephone lines that connect them shrinking steadily, the online job ad cost is destined to remain low. Competition among providers of online ads is heating up, and the only threat to the high response rates is the sheer volume of job ads that could appear on the Internet.

THE BIG MARKET

Several generations ago, moving across the country to a new job was much more challenging, an ordeal largely reserved for desperate dust-bowl farmers, military servicemen, IBM managers, and persons escaping a bad reputation back home. Since World War II, advances in transportation, communication, commerce, education, and job opportunities have changed to create a much more mobile society. A large chunk of today's job market did not even exist when our parents and grandparents celebrated the victories of World War II, and they are located in places that many of them have never even heard of.

This dramatic pace of change is increasing, not leveling off. On one hand, companies often find themselves in competitive situations that don't allow for the internal training of personnel for critical skills: if the companies are unable to develop, produce, and deliver this year, distinct and substantial market opportunities will have passed them by. In those critical and common circumstances, companies need new people who can provide a competitive edge now. And those companies are willing to move the right people from one end of the nation to another to get their services.

On the other hand, individuals and their families are more tolerant of career changes that involve a geographic dislocation. Sometimes, the job opportunity represents a special professional challenge, a smart career move, and a more secure job. Other motivations are more personal: to be close to relatives, to live in an area that has special appeal, to have great schools, or to enjoy the unique recreational opportunities in the new area.

Whether the motivation is professional or personal, a nationwide job hunt demands a serious investment of time and money if you use regional newspapers. In contrast, online job ads allow people connected to the Internet to casually and conveniently perform either a regionally specific or nationwide job search. Companies with compelling human resource requirements can reach millions who are looking because they are out of work, because they think their skills have a much higher value than their employer does, or because they just like to track who's hiring in the industry.

NOT JUST FOR HACKERS

The perpetual adolescents who wrote machine code while dressed in sandals and blue jeans, and consumed inordinate amounts of caffeine and other unnamed stimulants may still be out there, but they no longer constitute the majority of online job searchers. Using a simple keyword search, hundreds of thousands of people who lack programming talents are discovering thousands of real jobs on the Internet. Some of these people got their feet wet with E-Span, The Online Career Center, CareerWeb, or Career Mosaic.

This job-market accessibility has been a revelation on a par with e-mail, spell checking, and cut-and-paste. For those of you who remain bashful, just give your middle schooler Appendix A of this book (along with a modest incentive) and watch her or him produce stunning results. Most children with even a little Internet experience can find those sites for you within seconds. For the career searcher who can find these job database sites and can think of a few simple words to summarize his work, it is the electronic equivalent of Open sesame!

For employers needing quality job candidates, access is even easier. The baseline skills are using either a fax machine, or e-mail on a convenient computer. For the managers who have staff with those talents, delegate.

One prominent misconception is that one needs to be an Internet expert to be successful with online advertising. In truth, just as you don't need typesetting skills to advertise in newspapers, you don't need computer skills to advertise on-line. Technology has bridged that gap for you.

GUESSING GAME

For generations, the per-line costs of newspaper advertising and a closed end view of human talent have converged to produce bare-boned, terse statements of min-imum requirements in job advertisements. The per-line, per-inch cost constraint is deader than a doornail; most online ad sources will not charge you a nickel more for an ad with twenty column inches than for an ad with one column inch. The valuable job candidate that reads job ads is not attracted to the one-dimen-sional ad that represents staff as simply interchangeable cogs in a corporate ma-chine.

You now have the freedom to sell the job, your company, the career future, the community where the job is located, the working conditions, teamwork, pay, bonuses, retirement, benefits, educational opportunities, and free parking. Your only space limitation is the literary discretion that persuades you to not bore the able job candidate.

With technology taking care of cost, the challenge is now shifted to building a recruiting strategy that is an integral part of a company's human resource goals and is also a secret weapon for aggressive growth. A paradigm shift is already un-derway in many companies as they perceive the hiring, training, retention, and ca-reer-planning functions as interrelated elements of a comprehensive human resource operation. By using computers and professional insights creatively, they can manage their talent needs from drafting an effective, targeted, online job ad to planning the retirement party.

HIRED GUNS

Finding productive, able employees will always be a challenge, and many compa-nies will continue to use outside recruiters, executive search firms, and other in-termediaries for valid business reasons. All companies are not prepared to control the costs and process of personnel recruiting by utilizing online job advertising and their internal staff. But most can implement a simple process that helps them evaluate the quality of service provided.

With online job advertising, employers can:

- Test the job market waters quickly and economically

- Develop and maintain a database of likely job candidates

- Sell their company and its career opportunities aggressively

- Justify the costs of a nationwide (rather than local) search

Online job advertising is not a recruiting panacea, but it does change the cost and accessibility parameters of corporate recruiting. The good headhunters will continue to service clients, but marginal ones relying on luck and resume volume will find themselves replaced by their competitors or competent in-house recruiting staffs. If a headhunter is only setting up appointments for people discovered through online job advertising, the employer can handle that work internally and save the fee.

KEY POINTS

As we shift away from the old newspaper paradigm to the emerging online job marketplace, several points define the value of this new medium:

- The ratio of newspaper-ad cost to online-ad cost is often 10 to 1.

- The response rate of newspaper ads compared to online job ads places newspapers at a severe disadvantage in terms of qualified applicants, but not in terms of response counts. Well-written online ads produce more good prospects and require less work to wade through the resumes received.

- The job seeker, using keyword searches, can find appropriate ads faster and in higher volumes on the Internet

- Because of the column inch constraints on newspaper ads, online ads are considerably easier to read and understand.

- Getting a good resume through an online ad service can cost you as little as $75, but using a recruiter could cost you $10,000 or more ($50,000 first-year salary X 20 percent fee).

The incomprehensible aspect of online job advertising is that so few major employers are effectively using this tool. More understandably, the select minority that do use this tool are cagily guarding their online advertising edge like the government protected the Manhattan project during World War II.

THE DRIVING FORCE: KEYWORD MATCHING

For the job seeker, keyword searches take the mystery and the misery out of finding job opportunities online. This technology is important to employers because it dramatically enlarges the variety and depth of positions that can be effectively marketed online. Beyond using a Windows-type interface that leads job candidates to the keyword-searchable database, the only skill they need to find an appropriate job opportunity is the ability to think of a few words that describe the positions they want.

For example, an engineer who would like to work in California could key in engineer and California and press the Enter key. The database software would then search through tens of thousands of jobs in the database for files that contain those two words, and would provide the job candidate with a list of matching job descriptions. By clicking the titles, the job candidate could examine each in turn, and if interested, could easily print a hard copy for future reference.

The job candidate can broaden the job search by reducing the number of words used, or sharpen it by adding more words or by substituting vague words with ones that focus more on the type of work desired. No in-depth knowledge of how the software works is required, just an understanding that the software search process ferrets out all files that include the words keyed in.

This technology makes it practical for bankers, nurses, carpenters, stock brokers, pilots, plumbers, bakers, musicians, doctors, attorneys—and almost any other kind of trade or profession you can name—to use the Internet for a job search. With terminals being installed in public libraries and employment security offices, the economic threshold as well as the technological barriers are being lowered. Additionally, as online job databases continue to grow and fill up with a wider spectrum of job opportunities, job seekers will in turn seek them out.

By the end of the century, the Internet might even replace newspapers as the main source and repository of employment information and opportunities.

EXAMPLE OF KEYWORD-SEARCH TECHNOLOGY

There are dozens of job search engines on the Internet that utilize keyword search technology. Although there are slight differences between many of the job search engines, all work in a similar fashion. The following steps depict how a job seeker would conduct a typical job search:

1 The first step for any job seeker is to enter keywords to be searched. In this example, you will look for an engineering job. Type the keyword "engineer" into the search-criteria input box and click the Search button (see Figure 1.1).

2 The database will return a list of all the positions that match the keyword. In this case, the computer searches every job ad in the database for the word "engineer". The computer returns a list of the titles of every job listing in the database that contains the word engineer somewhere in its text. As shown in Figure 1.2, over 15,000 jobs that match the criteria appear in the database.

3 Click the job title to access the entire job description (see Figure 1.3).

4 If too many job titles are returned, the job seeker can narrow the search by returning to the original entry screen and entering additional keywords. As shown in Figure 1.4, to look for a mechanical engineering job in California, enter the keywords "engineer", "mechanical", and "CA".

5 When you enter the more specific search criteria (engineer, mechanical, and CA), fewer than 200 job ads (versus the 15,000+ returned on your initial search) are returned (see Figure 1.5). The use of keyword combinations gives job seekers the ability to instantly and easily find the exact type of job in the location they desire.

OVERCOMING THE MAJOR HURDLES: FEAR, CHANGE, AND INERTIA

Nothing feeds the fires of apprehension like a new approach that actually works! Here are some typical excuses people give for not using online job ads, and some measured responses to each:

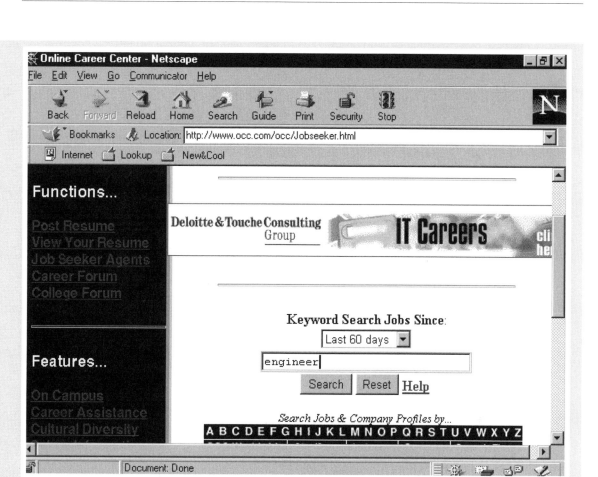

Figure 1.1. Main keyword search page.

I Don't Understand the Internet!

There is nothing about placing job ads online that cannot be learned in less than three hours of guided applications. With this book, a fax machine, and a good online ad service, you can place excellent online job ads the same day you finish the book. If you can produce e-mail, the job is even easier for all concerned.

How Will I Know If It Really Works?

You can determine which online ads are working for you the same way you determine which newspaper is generating the most responses: by including an identifying tag in the ads. Many advertisers direct job seekers to send resumes to "Dept. Internet" or some other appropriate tag whereby response can be measured and tracked.

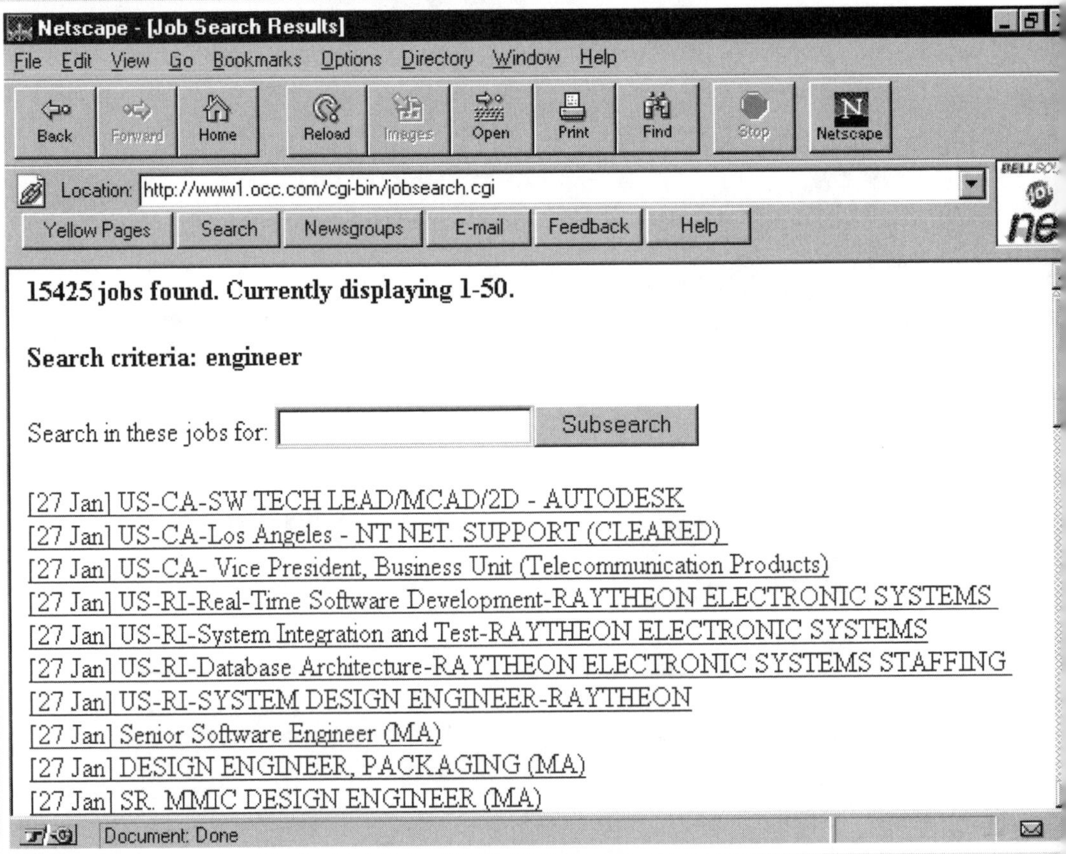

Figure 1.2. Return screen of job titles.

IF I ADVERTISE NATIONWIDE, I'LL GET MORE RESUMES THAN I CAN POSSIBLY READ!

The number and quality of resumes you receive depends as much on how you write the ad as where it appears. As you will learn in Chapter 3, "Writing the On-line Job Ad," well-crafted online job ads can reduce the number of resumes you receive while improving their quality.

WILL ONLINE JOB ADS CHANGE EVERYTHING ABOUT OUR RECRUITING PROCESS?

No. Beyond getting resumes from good candidates, the rest is up to you. Online

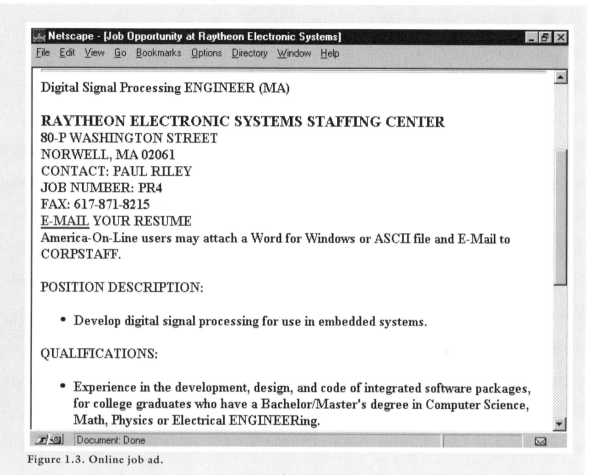

Figure 1.3. Online job ad.

job advertising can improve the quality and expedite the receipt of resumes, and can dramatically lower the costs of obtaining them. Properly applied, online job advertising can significantly improve recruiting by enabling HR departments to more closely control both the process and the cost. This technology can open doors for increased sophistication in human resource management, although the threshold for obtaining quick and substantial results is quite low.

CAN THE IS DEPARTMENT PLACE JOB ADS ON THE INTERNET FOR ME?
Yes, and the Information Systems (IS) folks can also type letters, make coffee, place telephone calls, and adjust chair heights. But beyond setting up an Internet

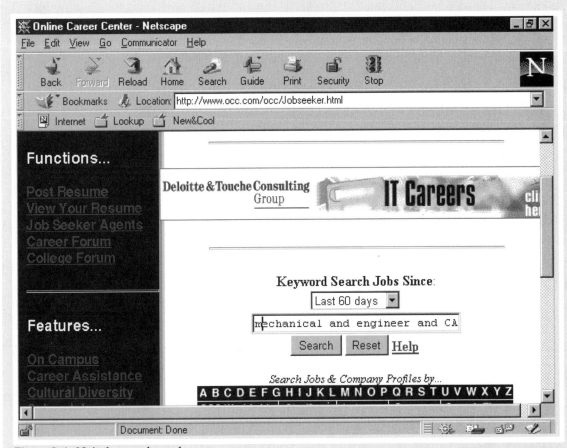

Figure 1.4. Main keyword search page.

connection initially, all possible functions related to placing job ads online can be done equally well, if not better, within the HR department. Please give those hard-pressed, extremely talented folks in Information Systems their due and don't harness them to a task that will not utilize their specialized skills. Drafting effective online job ads is a creative literary challenge, but the technological part of placing them is the equivalent of sending a fax.

Don't confuse technological proficiency with the functions of a marketplace. The online ad services perform two important functions:

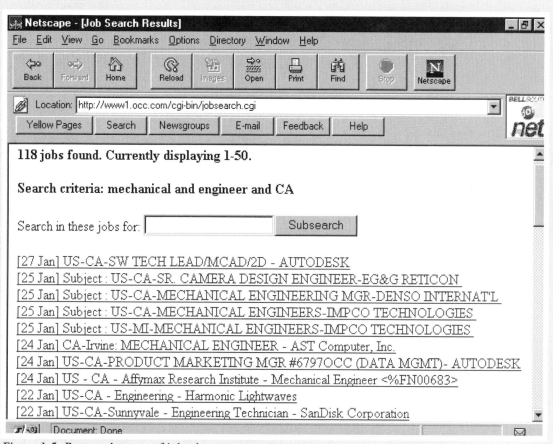

Figure 1.5. Returned screen of job ads.

- **Technological** - The services manage the high tech end of online advertising, enabling both the employers and the job seekers to use the marketplace without understanding the technology.

- **Market Management** - The services create and maintain convenient, efficient markets with enough visibility to attract large numbers of buyers and sellers. Your IS staff can surely create a very attractive and user-friendly Web page for the posting of job openings. However, most of the job candidates will be checking the big commercial online job databases that contain between 1,000 and 50,000 job ads.

A good parallel would be the task of selling 100 shares of Microsoft stock. Would you walk down Main Street with the certificates in hand, offering them to every prosperous looking person you encountered? Or would you direct a stock broker to sell them for you on the New York Stock Exchange, a well-developed market for securities? The point is simple: A large, efficient market can typically handle the transaction at a lower cost to you and get better results at the same time.

NET NOTE

At the end of 1995, representatives from one of the nation's online-ad services signed up one regional office of a large national executive-placement firm (Big Recruiter USA) for a trial run. Within weeks, comments flowed back that they received high quality resumes, and were very pleased with the service. Weeks passed, and other regional offices began to sign up with the online job-advertising service. Everyone was happy until the national office of Big Recruiter USA found out.

Shame on the regionals for thinking out of the box!! A memo was sent to all regional offices forbidding them from doing business with commercial job databases. After all, the national offices of Big Recruiter USA had hired their own Internet experts, and they now had their own slick Web site with fancy graphics, forms, and content. Six months later, the regional offices were sneaking back onto the commercial online employment ad services.

"Damn the national office, we have to run a business and we can't do it without job candidates!" was the cry. It seems that the corporate Web site lacked the key component necessary for recruiting success on the Internet: TRAFFIC. Though the site was successful in terms of reader appeal, functionality, and design, few job candidates knew of its existence.

WHERE DO I FIND THE BUDGET FOR THESE ONLINE JOB ADS?

Start by reviewing your complete recruiting budget, and make a serious assessment of where your advertising and recruitment dollars are going now. Can you determine which newspaper ads are effective in generating resumes? Online job ads are just another form of advertising, and you should have the flexibility to place some trial online ads to test their effectiveness.

If you use the techniques in this book to avoid one placement fee to an outside recruiter, you can finance online job ads for at least three months.

NET NOTE

In 1994, an associate of ours, who happened to work part-time in corporate staffing at Big Bank-USA, approached the head of corporate staffing with a novel idea: He would place all their job ads on the Internet in one of the major databases for a trial period. Buy-in was instant from visionary managers, but the corporate recruiting staff wasn't eager to try this online world. Comments like "The kind of professionals we need are not on the Internet!" and "Take my ads off, I don't want junk resumes!" were the norm. After several months, the few recruiters who were using the service began turning heads with solid recruiting successes, and the program slowly won additional converts. More tangible acceptance came in 1995 when the company CEO announced the new corporate Internet strategy. All the recruiters were Internet friendly after he blessed the Internet.

But the program faded under bureaucratic budget pressures while human resources waited for the corporate Internet strategy, a concept that remained undefined in late 1996. Today, the Big Bank corporate HR department is still waiting to become part of that strategy, and only a fraction of the bank's job openings are finding their way to the Internet, still by the secretive efforts of a few pioneering recruiters.

Amazingly, many talented bankers do find their way to Big Bank through the Internet, but they respond to online job ads placed by outside recruiters who collect five-figure fees per placement for a service the bank could enjoy with an annual four-figure online ad service contract. Such is life in corporate America, and such are the problems with change.

As the saying goes, no one ever got fired by picking IBM. Similarly, no corporate HR person ever got fired for placing an ad in the Wall Street Journal, New York Times, or for hiring an approved executive recruiter to assist in a job search. Yet spending a few hundred dollars on this new Internet recruiting tool scares many HR professionals.

One fact is certain: Many of the executive recruiting firms that corporate America goes to for staffing solutions are already on the Internet placing dozens, if not hundreds, of job ads based on the job orders sent them. They collect the resumes, do some screening, present candidates to their clients, and collect their 25-35 percent fee. The biggest challenge we face is educating corporate HR departments about the Internet. In the meantime, we continue to wish our executive recruiter friends well as they collect their handsome fees - more easily than ever before!

KEY WAYS TO END THE FEAR AND INERTIA, AND INITIATE CHANGE

Since we introduced online advertising to clients in 1994, we have noted how easy it is to convince contingency-based recruiters to try this new technology - after all, these folks are motivated by the income generated from placements. They love any technology that helps them to do their job better. On the other hand, we have also noticed the exact opposite experience from corporate HR departments. Change avoidance is the norm, and anything new is assumed to be ripe with risk and failure. Logic stumbles over fear and timid comfort in "what works well enough" prevents this new technology from being accepted at many organizations. Here are a few suggestions for overcoming this inertia.

- What does the NIKE commercial say? Just Do It! Experiment with an online job ad. With some time and $150, you can place your first ad and assess the results.

- Employees need to see that management is committed to the new technology. If you are a manager, talk about the Internet, show some interest in the new technology, learn how to use it yourself, and in turn show others. Don't rely on your latest college whiz kid to do your Internet research: do it yourself!

- Provide equipment and time for employees so they can use this book to find good candidates on the Net.

- Provide everyone with e-mail accounts and start using them.

- Provide Internet training, specifically on the employment market.

- Develop well-written information sections about your company and community, and other relevant information for each of your online employment ads.

- Listen for feedback and suggestions from your staff.

- Reward employees who think out of the box and who take calculated risks.

NET NOTE

For several months we tried but, to no avail. Big Bank could find no money in their budget to purchase the $4,000 per year Internet recruitment package we were offering. After all, they had high-dollar IS folks, real computer experts, handing their current Internet projects. We left dejected.

A few weeks later, we marketed our online services to Susan Sweet's contingency-based recruiting service that specializes in banking. Susan had no Web pages, no Internet experience, and no IS staff. But she listened, bought our modest job-ad package, and wrote her ads the way we suggested. Within several months, she made over $100,000 in placement fees at Big Bank, and also had big paydays at several other banks across the nation.

S U M M A R Y

Internet employment advertising is easy, inexpensive, and is working decisively today for leading recruiters and pioneering human-resource departments nationwide. You don't need to be an Internet expert or even be online to use this new technology. Internet job advertising is best implemented and maintained by the HR department. Internet job advertising is growing exponentially and currently accounts for 20-30 percent of the hiring efforts at leading organizations. Internet job advertising is the only way to cost effectively reach talented professionals worldwide.

CHAPTER 2

GETTING YOUR FEET WET
First steps in Online Advertising

The perils of online job advertising are grossly exaggerated. Challenged by the prospect of change, the barriers we erect for ourselves include the idea that innovation is either sinful, fattening, insensitive, exploitive, environmentally unsound, politically incorrect, unproved, or just too hard to learn. For anything having to do with computers, the last is the all-time favorite.

But technology is not as intrinsically threatening as it is unsettling. New freedoms attack old excuses and the habits of intellectual laziness.

Online innovation is deceptive because it is wide open to quick minds and venture capital. As a result, new concepts are generated daily to face an intensively paced, Darwinian competition: hundreds fail monthly, and a lucky few reach a ripe old age of success at five years before fading into oblivion. To the discomfort of non-technical onlookers, if a complete understanding of the Internet is considered necessary for Internet utilization, they may have another 50 evolutionary years to wait before it becomes stale and mundane.

Thoroughly American in the constant reinventing of itself, the Internet is a smorgasbord of commercial and intellectual opportunity. Those who insist on examining every morsel before making their first selection may starve to death from the delay.

The deceptive part of online job advertising is its computer-based technology. It is unanchored by a large investment of installed, limited-function hardware, and it is driven ahead by a market obsessed with user friendliness. That term became an overworked cliche before most of the population learned how to use a computer, friendly or not. Future users of the Internet in particular, and computer owners in general, should note with relief that much of the innovation taking place today is in increased functionality, not new applications for computers. The big (smart) money is targeted on making it possible for all of us to use computers effectively.

For the online job advertiser, most of the hard work is already complete. In the compressed world of computers, a generation of progress has been achieved in less than five years.

How much do you really need to know in order to save money and improve the recruiting effectiveness of your company? If you can write a reasonably accurate description of open jobs at your company and read to the end of this chapter, you know enough. If your ambitions are to be a bottom-line hero in the human resources department, you must read the whole book.

This chapter just gets you by, but it's not a bad place to start getting some tangible results. Improvements can come later; this chapter gets your feet wet and helps pay some of the bills.

Perfection takes too long, progress is achieved one step at a time.

QUICK & EASY: CALL THESE FIRMS TO PLACE ONLINE ADS

While there are dozens (if not hundreds) of online advertising services that run ads online for organizations, we have selected several that have a proven track record in providing results for their clients. Call these fine organizations, fax in your ads, and monitor the results. With these organizations, you do not need to be on the Net or even own a computer. Give it a try! If you want some coaching on writing an online job ad, read to the end of the chapter. Chapter 3, "Writing the Online Job Ad," adds valuable insights as well.

CAREER MOSAIC

Career Mosaic is one of the first and one of the best advertising venues on the Internet. Several clients have reported solid success using Career Mosaic over the past few years. Single ads cost $150 and run for 30 days. Volume packages are available. Call 1-888-339-8989 for details.

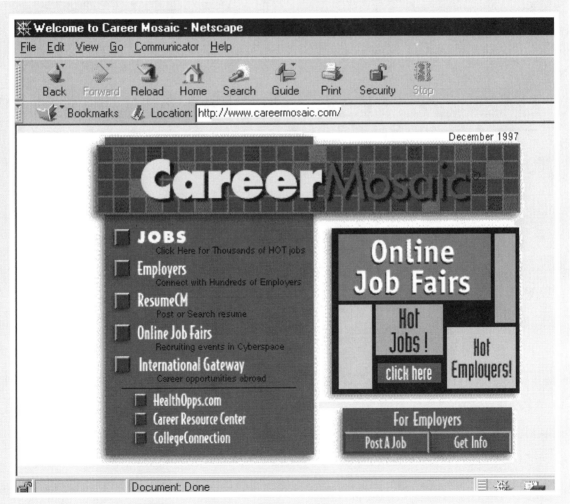

Figure 2.1. The Career Mosaic Web site on the Internet.

CAREER WEB

Career Web specializes in advertising professional, technical, and managerial jobs. Companies have found solid success with their highly professional website and excellent customer service. Single ads cost $135 and run for 30 days. Unlimited advertising packages are available at very reasonable costs. Ad posting includes additional posting to Yahoo. Call 1-800-871-0800 for further details.

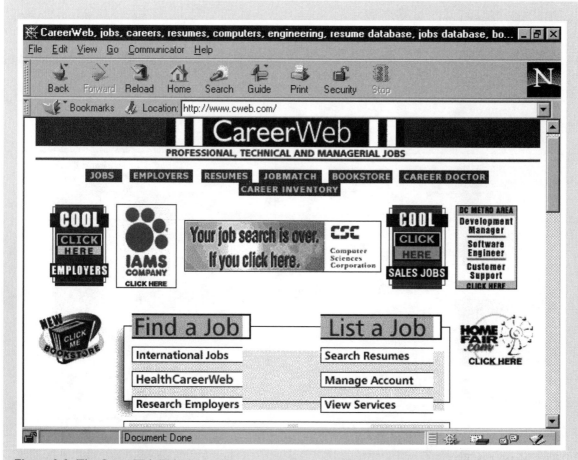

Figure 2.2. The CareerWeb Web site on the Internet.

E-SPAN

E-Span was one of the first online job ad services. Ads appear on CompuServe, where they host the career management forum, and on the Internet proper. Costs are $150 for a single ad. Discounts are available for high-volume ad commitments. Internet Usenet postings are included with ad placement. Call 1-800-682-2901 for further details.

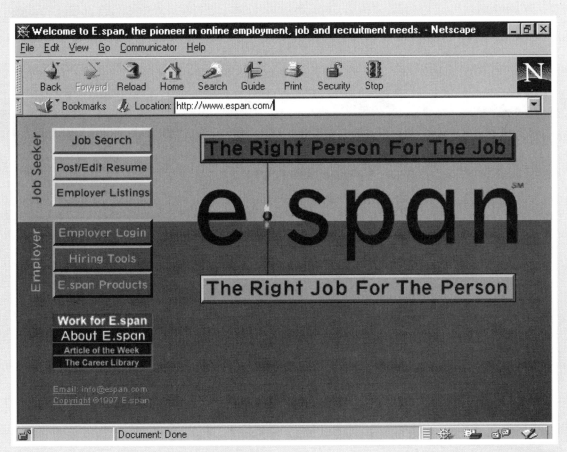

Figure 2.3. The E-span Web site on the Internet.

THE MONSTER BOARD

The Monster Board is one of the offerings of TMP Worldwide, one of the nation's largest employment ad agencies. Single ads start at approximately $175 for 60 days. Volume discounts and special Internet recruitment programs are available. Call 1-800-MONSTER. Choose Option 1 on their automated answering system.

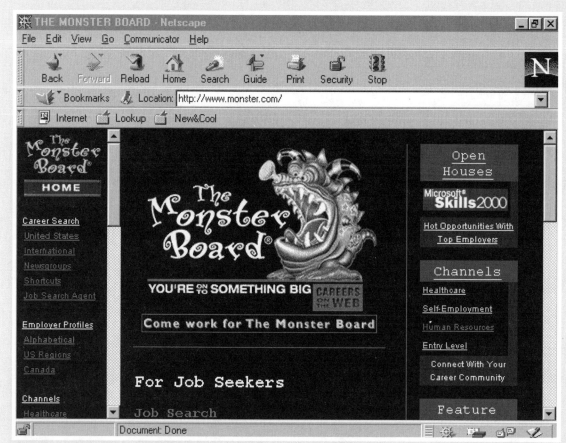

Figure 2.4. The Monster Board site on the Internet.

NATIONJOB NETWORK

NationJob is a real value leader. For $75 an organization is able to advertise an ad for one month in several venues that include: The NationJob database, Yahoo, Headhunter.net, and Americas Job Bank. Three month unlimited packages and monthly budget packages are available. Call 1-800-292-7731 for further details.

❑ ❑ ❑

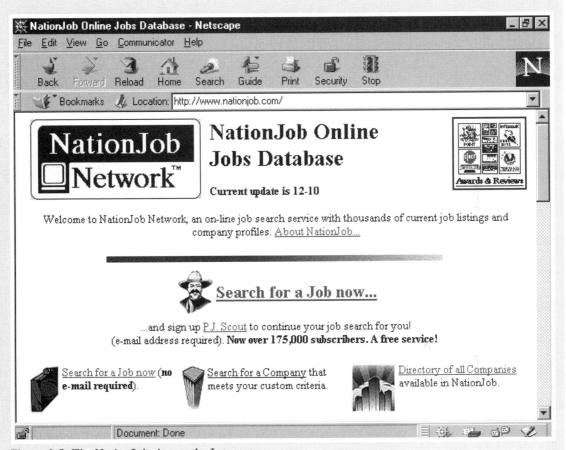

Figure 2.5. The NationJob site on the Internet.

MULTIPLE OPTIONS

A popular option for many organizations is to post job ads to multiple Internet Job venues. Just as is the case with newspaper media placements, agencies that specialize in online media placements are starting to emerge. By using such an agency, one individual manages your ad placement with several services. An example of such an agency is Online Opportunities.

❑   ❑   ❑

Figure 2.6. The Online Opportunities Jobnet Site on the Internet.

ONLINE OPPORTUNITIES

Online Opportunities specializes in helping employers receive maximum Internet exposure for their ads and assistance in managing the results. At the beginning of 1998 they had formed partnerships with several of the leading job database providers. Packages are available which posts jobs to the following leading venues:

- 4Work

- Americas Job Bank

- CareerMagazine

- CareerSite

- CareerWeb

- E-Span

- Headhunter.Net

- JobNet

- JobWeb

- NationJob

- USENET

- Yahoo

In addition to job postings, Online Opportunities offers a Corporate Offsite Resume Database where they gather and manage resume response by email, fax, or mail. Call 1-888-562-6382 for pricing information or visit their website at http://www.jobnet.com.

LITTLE KNOWN SECRET

Before you dash headlong into online advertising, you should know that inadvertently some of your job ads may already be there.

Advertising vendors of all types depend on the responses their customers receive as the source of future business. If no one sends a resume, doubts arise about the effectiveness of the advertising dollars spent. As a result, two interesting online tactics influence the results generated by job ads.

Newspaper publishers, always sagacious regarding income, have purchased the technology and developed alliances that allow them to create an online duplicate of their hard-copy newspaper job ads and distribute them electronically. A good example is The Chicago Tribune; you can purchase a hard copy of that daily or check www.careerpath.com online if you are looking for a job to advance your career.

The double-venue coverage is a value added service that gives a newspaper's column-inch customers more bang for their advertising buck and cements long-standing relationships. This practice is likely to escalate until real cost constraints are encountered. Other newspapers found at www.careerpath.com include

> The Atlanta Journal Constitution
> The Baltimore Sun
> The Boston Globe
> The Charlotte Observer
> The Chicago Tribune
> The Columbus Dispatch
> The Denver Post
> The Rocky Mountain News
> The Detroit News
> The Detroit Free Press
> The Hartford Courant
> Houston Chronicle
> The Los Angeles Times
> The Miami Herald
> The Milwaukee Journal Sentinel
> St. Paul Pioneer Press
> Star Tribune
> The New York Times
> The Orlando Sentinel
> The Philadelphia Inquirer
> The Sacramento Bee
> San Jose Mercury News
> The Seattle Times/Post Intelligencer
> Sun Sentinel
> The Washington Post

This low/no-cost option has a critical shortcoming - it depends on the original paper-based text, and is subject to the quality of the software or the transcriber used to re-create the online version. The end product is a stripped down, color-less, anemic version of what it could be, and it will be in competition with thousands of more well-endowed regular job ads online.

❏ ❏ ❏

The BIG question is, "How much does the newspaper ad contribute to the newspaper/online ad combination? Would the customer buying the ad lose any significant part of the benefits by only running an online job ad?" Companies can use ad tags to collect answers to those questions for themselves. (More on this later.)

NET NOTE

1998 appears to be the year CareerPath (aka "The Newspaper Job Classifieds Site") will begin serious competition with other online job services. 1997 saw the addition of employer profiles and informed sources tell us that a "resume matching service" and "Internet only job postings" are on the horizon. Finally, employers might be able to harness the user traffic of CareerPath without paying the high newspaper column inch rates - or will they? - the world is watching!

QUICK AND UNCOMPLICATED

To write your first rough online job ad, start with the newspaper version to capture the basics about where and how job seekers should send their resume, the salary and benefits that go with the job, start dates, and so on.

Describe the job in considerable detail, followed by a full listing of necessary qualifications and management "like-to-haves". Borrow shamelessly from the last edition of the corporate annual report to tell the job candidate what a good place your company is. Use Chamber of Commerce data about the virtues of the surrounding community. If the accumulated, well-written document is less than a page long, repeat until it fills at least one page. When completed, including a spell and grammar check, you are ready for the next step. See Chapter 3 for the long version of this process.

Do not buy into the deceptive assumption that no one will want to read a long ad. You only want one out of ten browsers to read the whole ad—just the ones who are excited about the job which you describe in the first paragraph. Do you want to wade through the resume of every job candidate who finds four words in a thirty word job ad that she or he can define?

❑ ❑ ❑

Here is a quick example of what a first online job ad might look like:

Job Title: Director of Exceptional Children; TEACCH Certified, Autism
Organization: Norman County Board of Education
Department: Exceptional Children (Also known as Special Education)
Job Code: BDEEx1
Address: 2500 Bass Point Dr. Wylie, NC 28111
Telephone: (704) 555-1234
Facsimile: (704) 555-4321
E-mail: BoardEd@xyz.com
Job Location: Wylie, NC
Status: Full Time
Salaries: $70-$90k per year; based on experience
Benefits: Major medical, dental, North Carolina retirement

DESCRIPTION:

Successful candidate will direct the Exceptional Children Department of the school district, establishing and implementing standards and procedures for the education and care of all children with special needs. Will report directly to the Superintendent of Schools and provide day-to-day direction to principals, teachers, and other staff regarding this special group. Will ensure compliance with federal, state, and local mandates, and serve as an advocate before the board of education, the state legislature, and other concerned parties.

The job also involves developing and implementing a certification program for all special-education teachers and associates, and developing a network of medical professionals and therapists who can serve this population proficiently.

Will be responsible for budgets covering both in-house services and payments to outside consultants and special institutions. Must have excellent communication and negotiating skills, and a talent for working with teachers, parents, school administrators, and outside professionals.

QUALIFICATIONS:

Must have at least 10 years experience as a TEACCH psychoeducational consultant and a Masters Degree in Special Education. The school system also expects a thorough understanding of and proficiency in the drafting of individual education programs. The Exceptional Children Director must be proficient in the following tests:

Psychoeducational Profile-Revised

Adolescent-Adult Psychoeducational Profile

Childhood Autism Rating Scale

Vineland Adaptive Behavior Scale

Woodcock Johnson Psychoeducational Battery (and) Achievement Aptitude Profile

Learning Achievement Profile (LAP)

Early Learning Achievement Profile (ELAP)

An understanding of autism, all levels of mental retardation, physical handicaps, ADHD, Tourettes syndrome, learning disabilities, seizure disorders, speech therapy, occupational therapy, motor skills, and other neurological, emotional, and behavioral difficulties are required. Familiarity with psychological instruments such as the Leiter International Performance Scale, the Bayley Scales of Infant Development, and the Merrill-Palmer Scale of Mental Tests will be a plus.

The person selected must have good presentation skills and proficiency with Microsoft Word in addition to routine office management experience.

COMPANY:

The Norman Board of Education is committed to the education and training that opens up the world of opportunity to all of the students in our county. We prize and support professional standards, personal initiative, and student-centered education. By consistently performing above state and federal standards in all key areas, the school system staff has won the enthusiastic financial support and personal respect of the community it serves. North Carolina's institutions of higher learning and the business community at large endorse our programs by their eager acceptance of our graduates.

COMMUNITY:

The Norman County area has been respected since its inception for a joint commitment to enterprise and education. Excellence in both fuels achievement in the other, and our successes are a source of energy for every other worthwhile endeavor. We support the arts, sports, and civic accomplishments. Lake Norman is an important recreational resource, and the Charlotte metropolitan area and the mountains of North Carolina are a pleasant drive away. Our crime rate is the lowest in the Southeast. The qualified candidate should submit a resume by e-mail, and a second by correspondence with a cover letter to the address above.

❏   ❏   ❏

As you can see, there is nothing high-tech or complicated about this ad beyond the non-computer, non-Internet specifications for the job. It simply makes excellent use of the available space to tell qualified candidates about the job, its requirements, the organization, and the location environment, with some details about salary and benefits. If you can write a similar quality ad about the career opportunities at your company, you can be successful with online job advertising.

Do shorter ads sometimes produce good results? Yes, they often produce even more resumes, but the strong job ad we recommend generates more than enough excellent candidates and less paper. See Chapter 8 for more about the economics of large scale resume results.

After you create the ad using the word-processing system of your choice (Microsoft Word, WordPerfect, Lotus Ami Pro, Wordstar, or a manual typewriter), fax or mail or email the job ad to the online ad service of your choice.

Please note that you can place the ad with few constraints:

- with technology only a little more complicated than a fax machine

- for less than $200

- with no intermediaries between you and the prospective employees

- with no new capital investment

- with no long-term contracts

- with no restrictions on the length or content of text

- without a Computer Science degree

- with the same effectiveness guarantee you get from a good newspaper

Is one online job ad an adequate test of the process? No, there may be no one out there interested in that particular job with your company. And if you haven't read Chapter 3 before you send the ad, you may have missed some of the finer points.

But you do need to see for yourself how easy it is to place an online job ad, and the results may surprise you.

If you work with a local representative of a large nationwide online ad service, you may get some good free advice about your ad for the asking. You can also finish reading this book for a wealth of tips on getting the most from your online recruiting expenditures. However, please remember that most of the vendors in the online ad marketplace have only one product to sell, and many consider the commercial speech standard a license to lie.

S U M M A R Y

The biggest, ugliest secret about online job advertising is that it is not big, ugly, difficult, expensive, or complicated. Knowledge is power, and simple truths are the most certain weapons.

Online job advertising is so good that newspapers use it to boost the response rates of their hard copy job ads. Imagine that the airline industry discovers a vendor who provides them with a new, safe fuel that is even better than standard aviation fuel, but it only costs them 4 cents per gallon; and they leave their airfares at the same level. If you don't believe how good online job advertising is, just check out www.careerpath.com and note all the hard copy ads placed there by its prominent and successful newspapers. If your favorite daily publication has ads online, review your annual newspaper advertising budget.

Online job advertising is so good that recruiters love it. You should surf the net often to determine whether one of your favorite recruiting agencies is already a featured online advertiser. We know you find it hard to believe that one of those nice folks who take you to lunch at fine restaurants and never forget birthdays and anniversaries - would simply take your job order, run an online job ad, and deliver the best resumes to you.

We sympathize, but we also suggest that you place some online job ads of your own and wait at least two weeks before you distribute the job orders to outside recruiters. Also, even if you have no online skills, you can probably find an online-savvy friend to check the job listings for you to see who is advertising for the same kind of position that you need. Better still, have them set up some bookmarks to help you do it yourself in the future. If that seems too technical for you, read the rest of the book and find out how simple it is.

High school dropouts with a telephone, a fax machine, and $150.00 can place online job ads.

What are you waiting for?

WRITING THE ONLINE JOB AD

Before you get cold feet and allow your brain to lock up from writer's cramp, consider the necessary resources for writing an online job ad. One is a functional word processing system such as Microsoft Word, Lotus AmiPro, or WordPerfect. A typewriter and a fax machine will do, but any reputable word processing software system with a modem attachment on your computer and Internet access will make the process much easier. In a pinch, a #2 pencil, a legal pad, a 32 cent stamp, and an envelope will do the job. Look to Appendix E, "Equipment Shopping List," for some advice on the equipment you could use and justify through recruiting savings.

Next, you need verbal literacy at the twelfth grade level. You may need a college graduate staff person to meet that standard, but not necessarily so. A serious but flexible vocabulary is an integral part of this requirement, but 50 cent words are not nearly as important as clarity in describing the job and the work environment. The job candidates are not looking for eloquence, just good job opportunities.

Finally, a healthy supply of courage is imperative. A well-written job ad could be read by more people than some Pulitzer prize winning books, and the tone of the ad is as important as the content. You are selling the job to the best and the brightest; the ad must be honest and upbeat, a call to career adventure and professional challenges.

THE COLUMN INCH PARADIGM

Every tangible and important innovation is complicated by people enamored with the way things were before. People respond to changes by stubbornly dragging as much history along with them as possible:

- The early steam ships had sails, just in case.

- The classic bicycle seat is patterned after a horse saddle, providing much more protection for the nonexistent horse's backside than the bicycle rider's.

- The first automobiles were obviously horse-less carriages.

- For almost 80 years after their invention, submarines looked like destroyer escorts with periscopes

- Computer makers clung to vacuum tubes as long as they could, even after transistors were readily available, and the big mainframes were such an accepted standard that young, brash upstarts outside the industry had to invent the personal computer in garages.

Online job advertising faces a similar dilemma. When the newspapers started selling more than news and slipped into classified advertising, they established a very practical model for charging their customers: the column inch. It works remarkably well, because many costs associated with publishing a newspaper (paper, ink, labor, and so on) can be estimated and tracked on a per column inch basis.

As a result of this superb paradigm, all current generations of human resources personnel involved in recruiting have mastered the art of the short, pithy job ad. The typical ad gives the job title, two or three key requirements, obligatory statements of fair treatment, and a way to contact the employer. Most people in the field can complete an ad with fewer than 50 words, and a few masters actually get resumes with jobs described in fewer than 25 words. If people in human resources cannot document that they are getting the best talent at a fair market price, they can at least show how their short job ads are saving their company money. Here is a representative ad:

Banker, commercial lending, 5 years. exp.

Fax resume & salary. history (704) 543-7317

BUT TERSE IS OUT

Given a choice between the following two job ads, which do you think would be most effective for attracting qualified candidates?

STANDARD NEWSPAPER AD

RESEARCH ASSOCIATE

We are currently seeking a research associate for our Charlotte office. Qualified candidate will possess an accounting or related degree and health care and financial background.

Excellent computer skills and strong organizational skills are essential. Compensation commensurate with experience. Forward resume to Willard Associates, e-mail: recruiter@aol.com.

STANDARD ONLINE AD

Research Associate, Health Care Specialist - Willard Associates, NCWillard Associates

Health Care Recruiter, Dept. RA/INT

5000 Panther Lane

Charlotte, NC 22812

Fax: 704-123-1234

e-mail: recruiter@aol.com

Job Location: Charlotte, NC

Salary Range: $30-$40 K depending upon experience.

Benefits: Major medical, dental, 401(k), retirement.

DESCRIPTION:

Willard Associates, the leading integrated professional services firm in the Carolinas, needs an experienced and resourceful research associate to support our well-regarded health services consulting team in delivering outstanding solutions to a select group of health care management clients. The work involves detailed review of client company populations and their health need profiles, matched against the billing structures and health delivery strategies of contracting providers. You will work with a managing partner, a registered nurse with administrative experience, and an information systems specialist.

QUALIFICATIONS:

Requirements include a working knowledge of hospital and private practice billing systems, Microsoft Office and statistical software, and federal health care reimbursement procedures. Experience in tracking health care costs in a hospital or large group practice will be especially appealing.

COMPANY INFORMATION:

Willard Associates is expanding its already considerable presence in health care management for large corporate clients and is committed to remaining the outstanding consulting resource in this market. We have a large market share and top management focus on excellence. In addition to a compensation package commensurate with experience, we offer outstanding health, retirement, and insurance benefits.

COMMUNITY INFORMATION:

Charlotte is a fast growing center for health care, as well as commerce and banking, in North Carolina. It contains two major health care systems and a large group of associated clinics and practices, attracting health care professionals from the major teaching hospitals both within and outside the state. Charlotte enjoys an excellent and diverse school system, a competitive standard of living, and a strong civic spirit.

To apply please fax, e-mail, or postal mail your resume, cover letter, and salary history to:

Willard Associates
Health Care Recruiter, Dept. RA/INT
5000 Panther Lane
Charlotte, NC 22812
Fax: 704 123-1234
e-mail: recruiter@aol.com

The difference is obvious. The short ad will cost between $200 and $300 in a major regional newspaper, and more if you want it to run in the Sunday edition.

The much longer online ad will cost you $150 or less, and will run for at least one month around the world.

But what will it cost to run the short ad on the Internet? About $150, depending on the online job ad agency you use. No, that is not a typographical error - the cost will be the same for both the short ad and the long ad on the Internet.

What appears to be an anomaly is simply common sense. Most of the cost of online job ads is in the overhead. Their investment is in storage space, fees, computers, telephone lines, staff, and so on, which require significant up-front expenditures. But electrons are so cheap that the additional cost of a 21 inch job ad over a 1 inch job ad is barely significant, unless the service provider receives the ad in a format that requires retyping. Otherwise, the typical cost of providing the extra 20 inches is less than the cost of counting them.

As a result, online job ad agencies across the industry charge flat, per ad fees or provide special volume deals on multiple-ad packages. Under either marketing approach, you pay nothing additional for longer ads. Like everything else on the Internet, that practice is subject to changes next week, but the economics of online advertising will most likely pressure the industry to retain the current standard flat fees.

As a result, the corporate recruiter has a golden opportunity to creatively and aggressively sell the career opportunities within his company. The only effective limit is the patience of the reader; per inch constraints are out, and writing integrity is in.

However, personnel turnover in recruiting may be necessary. Under the old paradigm, the task of writing a job advertisement required creativity that was the rough equivalent of composing the script for a Wanted poster to be mounted at the post office. Writing a good online job ad is more challenging.

THE NEW PARADIGM

The new paradigm lends itself more to the talented short story author than to a law enforcement clerk.

The new challenge is to address the five key aspects of an effective online job ad:

- A persuasive, appealing description of the job: its responsibilities, the working conditions, the colleagues, the growth opportunities, the job security, and so on.

- A complete listing of requirements, including competencies, traits, skills, background, education, experience, training, plus the highly desirable features and some "nice to haves." Those requirements describe the kind of person the company is really looking for.

- A sound, responsible description of the company and its goal statement, management style, advancement policies, status in the industry, prospects for the future, geographic distribution, history, and so on.

- A description of the job's physical location: the community in which the successful job candidate will work and live. Even if mobility is part of the job, the prospective employee needs to know that the company cares about the living conditions and home environment of their employees.

- All of those mundane details, such as salary, benefits, where to send the resume, the contact person, where to discover more about the company (such as the corporate Web page), whether the job is full time or contractual, the target start date, and so on.

For some companies, the transition to the broader horizons of online job ads will not be difficult. Larger companies, especially, have recognized the value of selling the company as well as the job; and their newspaper ads are artfully designed to deliver a consistent, positive image of their organization, usually through display ads.

For small to medium-sized companies, the transition will frequently be a stretch, but one with a handsome cost/benefit ratio. Now they can afford complete, descriptive job ads that explain, in detail, why their open position is the answer to the career anxieties of highly qualified candidates. If they have a good story to tell, they can certainly afford to tell it now. Through online job ads, the Internet is a great leveler of recruiting opportunities.

Before we explore the intricacies of writing good online job ads, one point is worth making well, and even repeating occasionally:

The expanded venue of online job ads does not require the quantity of creative writing as one might think. Key components, such as the company and community descriptions, can be boilerplated and used repeatedly. Similarly, requirements and a well-written job description can be recycled when the same type of position opens again.

An employer might choose to have just one corporate description section, or it might instead have a variety that reflects the diversity of operating principles and prospects of its major divisions under a corporate umbrella. There could be variations among the online ads for recruiting senior management personnel and those for recruiting technical staff or sales personnel within the same division. However varied the choices, the number of company sections to be composed should be significantly fewer than the number of open positions that occur annually within the organization.

We highly recommend the archiving of online job ads. Properly stored and cataloged, the archived ads are an important resource that can dramatically reduce your administrative burden and provide for quick, responsive turnaround when job vacancies occur. A clear, positive, and persuasive job ad deserves to be saved for posterity, and even improved upon occasionally.

Similarly, the community section can have a comprehensive description of the geographic area in which the job exists. The local chamber of commerce and regional travelogues can be gold mines for good reasons for moving to the area from across the nation. The human resources department can create templates for the major cities or regions in which the company's jobs exist.

Because of the uniformity of many benefits packages and other administrative details, the completion of that data will be routine, although it requires considerable attention to the critical aspects of the position. (A $7.50 per hour wage for a senior vice president could be an embarrassing oversight.)

Successful Online Ad Components

Composing a successful online job ad requires that you put together various components that both sell the job and inform the job seeker about the job, the job's location, your company, and how to apply for the position. Following is a sample online ad that contains the various fields (or components) that we have found to be most successful for attracting qualified job seekers. Each field is important in the online world and is discussed in this chapter.

Sample Job Ad

Job Title: Instrument Technician (NC)
Company: XYZ Contract Services

Department: Corporate Staffing

Job Code: IT100 Int.

Address: 2800 Park Dr. Charlotte, NC 28226

Phone: 800-123-4567 Ext. 143

Fax: 800-123-4568

E-mail: Recruiter@xyz.com

Job Location: Charlotte, NC USA

Status: Full-Time Position

Salaries: $18-$20/hr. depending upon experience

Benefits: Major medical, dental, profit sharing, and 401(k)

DESCRIPTION:

Successful candidate will work with industrial instrumentation and controls. Main duties include troubleshooting, repairing, and calibrating PLCs. Will use smart communicators and calibration equipment. Good communications skills necessary. Electrical background a plus.

QUALIFICATIONS:

Associate's degree in Instrumentation via either an industrial or technical school program required. Must be willing to travel. 2-5 years experience in the field a must.

COMPANY:

XYZ was founded in 1983 with the mission to service the process instrumentation needs of industries in the Carolinas and Georgia. We have enjoyed steady growth in volume of business and, at our customers' request, have expanded our services to other areas. XYZ is now organized into four divisions: Engineering Services, Textile Services, Contract Services, and Shop Services. We currently provide technical personnel, both contract and direct, as well as project work throughout the Carolinas and Georgia. Our staff contains engineers, designers, CAD operators, technicians, skilled laborers, and programmers, and provides a broad range of services to the industries we support.

COMMUNITY:

North Carolina offers quality schools, nearby lakes, excellent public and private colleges, a rich history, and graceful residential communities. The beautiful Blue Ridge Mountains are a short distance from Charlotte, and peaceful beaches are accessible for a weekend of fun in the sun. The four seasons, with an extended fall and an early spring, offer diversity and comfort for anyone. The qualified candidate should submit a resume and salary requirements.

THE JOB TITLE

The job title is one of the most important ingredients in a successful online job ad, yet corporate recruiters placing online ads seldom grasp its significance. If you recall how a keyword search is conducted, keywords are entered by the job seeker into an input screen, the command is sent to search the database, and a listing of job titles is returned. Imagine what the job seeker would do if he received 5,000 entries like this in his returned listing of job titles:

Programmer

Programmer

Programmer

Jr. Programmer

Mid-Level Programmer

Programmer/Analyst

Jr. Programmer/Analyst

and so on..

It seems absurd, but this is what really happens. Yes, he is looking for a programming job, but none of the titles attempt to catch his attention. Mostly generic job titles are returned, and often the job seeker gets a long list of thousands of similar titles that have no differentiating feature. Often the job seeker is not enticed to look deep in the list, and your ad remains buried among thousands of other faceless jobs.

Be creative with the job title. In most sites you have about 65 characters to entice the job seeker to look further. Here are a few suggestions to liven up your job title:

- Change it to something catchy: "Need a Web Maestro" or "Entrepreneurial Accounting Leader"

- Add the city/state of the job.

- If you are a company, differentiate yourself from search firms by making comments such as "Major NC Bank" or "Large Southern Utility," or just add your name next to the job title (response rates tend to be much better for companies than for search firms).

- Add the date the job ad was uploaded, which will let job seekers know how current the posting is (several online job ad services automatically do this).

CONTACT INFORMATION

Contact information is the easiest to complete and the most embarrassing place to make an error. Consider using templates to ensure the correct completion of these details and exert positive control for the data that changes from one ad to another.

Response Location and Department: Setting up blind ads (those without names and addresses), as is often done in the newspaper, is not recommended. Job seekers need to see the company name and address to be assured that this is a legitimate ad from a legitimate operation. If all they see is a fax number with only a company name and no location, they might question the legitimacy of the ad. If you do not want to receive resumes by mail, state that in the body of the ad text. Of equal importance, consider carefully where exactly you want to have resume correspondence sent.

Source Coding: We suggest not putting an individual's name in the ad unless that individual is lonely and wants to talk to lots of folks worldwide. If the ad states, "Send resume to Joe Smith - Technical Recruiter," odds are that Joe Smith will receive quite a few calls, especially if your organization is running multiple ads.

All ads should contain source codes to make it easy for you to find out where the responding job seeker viewed the ad. Even if online job ads are your only advertising effort, use a source code to easily separate the advertising responses from the broadcast resumes some job seekers use. The only effective way to ascertain where the best value is for your recruitment advertising dollars is to track and monitor where the candidates come from (the response count) and calculate the final cost per hire for each advertising source.

But be sure not to rely ONLY on response counts as a measurement of success. Our research has found that all things being equal, newspaper advertising generates a larger percentage of candidates that fail to qualify for the position than does online advertising. By its very nature, online advertising contains a more in-depth description of the job, discouraging job seekers from applying if there is a mismatch between their qualifications and the organization's requirements. Also, job seekers generally don't perform wholesale browsing through online ads. They enter keywords descriptive of their skills and qualifications to get a reasonable set of jobs to review rather than trying to read every ad in a 9,000-ad database. Less browsing translates to fewer non-qualified resumes.

Here are some suggestions for job coding, see other options in Chapter 7:

WALL STREET JOURNAL	DEPT. WSJ
ONLINE CAREER CENTER	DEPT. OCC
CAREER MOSAIC	DEPT. CM

Phone Number: Think again before adding your company phone number to the job ad. Do you really want to talk to hundreds of people across America? For positions that are exceedingly hard to fill and that have a very narrow candidate pool, it may make sense to add your phone number to the job ad and to be able to talk with one of these candidates immediately. On the other hand, if your job position is more general in nature and has hundreds of thousands of potential candidates nationwide, BEWARE. Your phone may ring off the hook when the ad goes online.

Fax Number: Definitely include a fax number; it is one of the preferred ways of receiving resumes. Even though we are in the midst of a high tech revolution, faxes are still the most acceptable form of quickly communicating information.

E-Mail: Receiving e-mail resumes is a double edged sword. On one hand, resumes sent via e-mail have several advantages:

- They can be electronically stored and searched for later retrieval.

- They are cost effective to both the company and the candidate by reducing paperwork, mail costs, long distance fax bills, and so on.

- They allow the job seeker to instantly get a resume in the recruiter's hands.

Unfortunately, our experience in conducting e-mail recruiting campaigns has indicated quite a few drawbacks:

- Because it is virtually free for a job seeker to e-mail resumes, the number of junk resumes your organization receives may be substantial. While conducting an online recruiting effort for a major corporation via e-mail, we noted that several individuals sent their resume via e-mail every week for the same position. In another case we noticed that one leading jobs database had made it so easy to apply online (just a few clicks of a mouse) that job seekers were applying to almost EVERY position within the organization. Recruiters were buried in sea of electronic mail.

- The e-mailed resume rarely arrives in a format that is remotely as attractive as the original. Try submitting an e-mail resume to one of your hiring managers for review and see what comments you receive! Let's face it, many managers are not yet attuned to reading text based, poorly formatted, e-mailed resumes. The best practice is to review e-mailed resumes internal to the human resources recruiting function, and ask promising candidates to mail a hard copy resume with a cover letter to obtain complete consideration. For most management jobs, qualified candidates will be sending that correspondence without being asked, regardless, but it will not hurt to ask.

We suggest giving e-mailed resumes a try. If your organization has a means to place them into a resume database for later retrieval, then by all means, e-mail is a good method. On the other hand, if you need to immediately forward resumes to hiring managers, faxed or mailed resumes may be the preferred choice.

BACKGROUND DETAILS

Pride goeth before a fall. And nothing cripples human resources recruiting staff as much as the low key fantasy that thousands of able and eager candidates are desperate about getting the job you have open. Get a life and perform a reality check; you are in the sales business. Most of the resumes received from any source reflect an interest in a job, not the job, and it is your job to acquire the very best candidates, not some minimally acceptable creature.

The fully qualified, three-dimensional job candidate wants to see a full battery of reasons for applying to a new position with your company. Without stretching the truth, you need to use the online job ad to provide them with as much information as possible, and eliminate the excuse that more text will make the ad more expensive. You must find and describe for the job candidate a good selection of reasons to make the switch from their current situation to employment at your company.

Job Location: Defining exactly where the job is located is an important detail for job seekers. Because many organizations hire from locations different from the job site, this clearly needs to be stated on the ad. Additionally, it may be important to state where in a city the job is located if the ad is for an organization in a large metropolitan area - for example, downtown Chicago. If, on the other hand, the job involves travel or is performed at multiple sites, or if the ad is for several jobs at multiple locations, be sure to state that in this section:

Job Location: Throughout Northern Illinois
Multiple positions in Dallas, Chicago, Raleigh
Piedmont Area of North Carolina
North & South Dakota

Status of Position: The status of jobs is important today. Gone is the assumption that all employment arrangements are full-time. Today, some of the common work arrangements between employer and employee are consulting, contract, full-time, internship, part-time, permanent, PRN, and temporary. Be sure the ad clearly states the type of work arrangement your organization has in mind.

Salary: There have always been two schools of thought regarding placing salary figures in job advertisements. One view is that a salary figure creates an expectation in job seekers, either too low or too high, and thereby lessens response. Another concern is that salary ranges lock organizations into a set amount. But work arrangements are really negotiable, based on the skill level and competencies of the candidate.

Although several of these concerns are valid, our recommendation is to include salary information in the job description. Having a salary range gives job seekers an indication that the position is real, and that sparks their interest. A clearly stated salary or salary range also helps the job candidate define how important the job is to your organization.

Benefits: It's a good idea to list the additional benefits an individual will earn when working for the organization. In addition to the traditional retirement, health, 401(k), and profit-sharing plans, be sure to list any secondary benefits the position might offer a candidate: job sharing, flex time, additional education, day care for children, and so on.

The Job Description: The most important principle to remember about online job ads is that the best job candidates will not necessarily spend hours looking for a job on the Internet or have the keyword-search expertise to reduce the number of ads they review to a small set. Like a newspaper story, your lead statement in the job description should catch the attention of a job candidate surfing the Net.

Your target reader may have already looked at 15 online job ads and have 50 yet to go on his current keyword search.

Your job description's lead sentence needs to be clear, high-impact, and directed. It may bear a stark similarity to the incredibly short newspaper ads you once composed. The text should quickly and explicitly capture the two or three features most appealing about this particular career opportunity. Don't worry about apparent redundancies. Few readers will notice, much less be offended, if you elaborate and expand on key aspects of the job later in the job ad. But the hooks to capture their attention need to be there early in the online job ad.

Although the division of job ads into the five major categories described previously helps with the readability of the ad, the job-description part of the ad can legitimately borrow from subsequent sections any key features likely to draw the strong interest of qualified candidates. Job opportunities, qualifications, salary, location, and company key points can be used to seize the initial interest of the online reader.

Beyond that first eloquent description of the job, you need to explain and clarify all the key positive aspects of the position. You can even cite the formidable challenges that will be the foundation of a better career path, along with the justification for the salary you are offering and the prospects of increases to come. Good job candidates relish challenges.

One of the obstacles to be overcome for the human resources professional is a lack of good information about job content. The hiring manager may have simply pointed out a subordinate and said, "Get me another one of those!" The best documentation that the human resources person has might be a short job description that is five years out of date and has never been reviewed by the current hiring manager (if she even knows it exists). But it is a good starting place.

Other valuable resources might include

- Copies of the exit interviews from former job incumbents, combined with their job applications, resumes, and personnel reviews.

- The job applications and resumes of current employees in a similar position, ranked by the recent job evaluation scores and overall tenure.

- Cost justifications for performance increases, grade level changes, and staff size increases for the job under consideration.

- A core competencies profile of the job.

- A quick survey of the incumbents about what they like about the job.

- A comprehensive review with the hiring manager about the specific tasks and goals that she has in mind for the new person. The core competencies profile just mentioned is a good basis for this discussion, but more details will be useful.

- Any Five Factor or Myers Briggs personality data accumulated about successful job incumbents.

The process of drafting an effective job description is a fairly simple proposition after you have accumulated good data about the job itself. The challenge is getting that data, especially if the hiring manager has an incomplete or unbalanced perspective of the job function. However, a good look at the job content and pressing performance needs may produce collateral benefits that add significant value to the department concerned.

The goal is a job description clear and persuasive enough to elicit a "that job is for me!" response from a qualified person reading your online job ad. You are looking for a strong reaction, a career driven, positive response that results in a resume with a cover letter and follow-up telephone calls. Any remotely appropriate ad will prompt the despondent, marginally proficient job seeker to e-mail a resume. The response you want is from the top-of-the-line professional who is looking for career growth, more personal satisfaction, real job security, and maybe also more money. That response requires a top-of-the-line online job ad.

TIP

The well-written, targeted, longer online job ad achieves something special: It tends to attract fewer total resumes and more excellent resumes. The explicit demands for quality performance and reaching specified task objectives tells every Internet viewer:

- *Your company knows exactly what kind of person it wants.*
- *Your company is goals oriented and performance driven.*
- *Your human resources function is able and willing to filter resumes for qualified candidates, and the hiring managers expect that quality performance.*

The well-written job ad compels the Internet surfer to self-select out (not apply) if the job is not a reasonably good fit. Whatever his level of competence for the job you are advertising, the job candidate is likely to be more qualified to perform the filter function than many of the clerical staff in human resources. Let the job candidates filter, and the number of resumes you do receive will be much more manageable; and they will be more promising.

JOB QUALIFICATIONS

Having described and sold the job, the qualifications section of your online job ad covers the meaty details of the talents and experience you want to find in the person to be hired. Don't be bashful. If you are looking for an aircraft pilot with advanced degrees in physics and electronics, combat experience, 3,000 flight hours in jets and 2,000 hours with multi-engine aircraft, and who is 20 years old or less, you might have to trim your expectations later. But if you were informed of the opening early and the ad only costs you $100, you can always run another ad with more conservative requirements. There is a big difference between the cost of an excellent online job ad and a quarter-page display ad in the Wall Street Journal.

Begin your job qualifications with the basic, hard core requirements. If you need a degree in mathematics or computer science, name the degree. If you prefer that the degree come from one of the top universities in the field, state and/or explain your requirements. If there is some combination of training or experience that you will accept instead of that degree, you can include that if the qualifications are not ambiguous.

Throughout the job qualifications section, use numbers liberally. If you want to hire an industrial engineer with MOST (Maynard Operations Sequence Technique) work measurement qualifications, specify how many hours of standards she should have written to qualify for your job. If you seek an architect with hospital design experience, indicate the number of years of experience and the square feet of hospitals designed. For commercial lenders, indicate the dollar size of portfolios generated. Be conscious of numbers when writing the job ad, and review it at least once with the operating manager for untapped numerical potential when completed.

Work from checklists about the job to specify the hard core requirements, the highly desirable, and the bonus features you want to see in a candidate. Create a checklist for the systems or proficiencies she will use on the job. If quality is a big issue, identify or describe the program utilized: TQM, ISO 9000, or whatever. Describe applicable performance reviews, diversity, flex time, and other policies.

For sales management, describe the distribution policies and sales force compensation plans. You want to attract those persons who have parallel, successful backgrounds and discourage those who lack key skills.

Don't be bashful about covering the capital equipment environment, either. If the job involves information systems, relate the kinds of computers the successful job candidate will have available. For an injection molding engineer and manager, name the major kinds of plastics forming equipment, using model numbers, PSI levels, and other salient details. For an overseas construction management job, name the major kinds of heavy equipment used and languages needed. For surgeons, outline the major kinds of diagnostic and treatment facilities that set your hospital apart from others and with which she must be able to work.

Survey the software environment as well. There are differences between UNIX and Windows. Your checklist should include the major operating systems and application software used, and specify the degree of sophistication needed for each kind of software that the successful job candidate will be routinely using on the job. There is a big difference between using Excel to balance your checkbook and applying it to a multivariate systems modeling problem. The job candidate will also need to know whether your computers are networked or free standing, and the kind of support provided. Defining the environment helps your company and the candidate make good decisions.

Consider the non computer environment as well. Is knowledge of foreign languages desirable, because of customers or overseas ownership of the business? Does the accounting department use LIFO or FIFO? Is the prevailing management style hierarchical, management by objective, or team oriented? Are personnel trained using on-the-job, computer based training, on site classrooms, special off site vendors, or community colleges? Does the human resources department use the Myers-Briggs or the Five Factor personality tests? Is the company a single-shift or a multi-shift operation? By pointing out relevant environmental circumstances as well as the hard core requirements, the job opportunity is more fully described.

You should also list some of the extras you would like to have in a job candidate. Would you like to see some practical work experience in the same industry of a prime client? Would an advanced degree give the job candidate more advancement flexibility? Would experience with a special kind of software make your company's transition to it easier? Do you need someone who can guide your company through the qualification process to become a favored vendor in a tough industry? Are there specialized skills missing on your current staff that now compels you to send clients or customers elsewhere?

And the most important qualification of all is the job candidate's readiness for advancement. As a bare minimum, you should indicate what the next step up the ladder is and how soon the job candidate should be ready to move forward in her career. It also would not be a bad idea to explain the criteria that management will use to decide who and when someone will advance.

To summarize, the job qualifications section is a clear, if wordy, exposition of what the company wants in a qualified job candidate. At the same time, it outlines the environment in which the successful job candidate will function and the criteria for advancement. While the job description sells the job explicitly, the job qualification section discourages the faint of heart and the under-qualified. But at the same time, it can help sell the job to candidates with the necessary qualifications and compatible interests.

THE COMPANY

The company section of the online job ad is an obvious selling opportunity. In this general description of your business environment, you explain why the company is a great place to work and becoming even better. You should answer at least some of the following questions:

- What are the principle products and services of the company?

- What distinguishes the company from its competitors and who are they?

- What are the likely sources of corporate growth and prosperity?

- What is the average tenure of personnel for the job being advertised and similar jobs?

- How is the career planning for the job related to the company's growth and prosperity?

- What is the corporate goals statement?

- What is the corporate policy on in-house career advancement and training?

- What new products or services have been introduced recently?

- What are the current employment levels?

- How many persons have been retired, released, downsized in the past year? Three years?

- How many persons are scheduled to join the company in the coming year? Three years?

- What achievements during the past three years are a special source of pride to the company?

- What special achievements are planned for the immediate future?

- What are the corporate commitments on retirement? Disability? Job security?

THE COMMUNITY

The location of the new job is a frequently untapped opportunity for selling the new job. If a likely candidate wades through the job description and the job requirements with undiminished interest, the location can be either real encouragement or a substantial obstacle to the job change. Every community has some strong points unless you subscribe to the idea that some locations are so bad that the citizens there are simply trapped.

The easy way to complete this section is to borrow shamelessly from the literature of the local chamber of commerce, commercial travelogues, old National Geographic issues, Web sites, real estate brochures, and AAA guidebooks. In addition to those resources, check the weekend edition of local newspapers and regional magazines for meaty details of regular events in the community.

But exercise caution and discretion in selecting what you consider the choice attractions of the region. You may even choose to survey some of the successful professional peers on what they and their families like about the neighborhood. As a serious human resources person, you may be delighted with the art, theater, and musical variety in Charlotte, North Carolina, but the mechanical engineer you need to hire may be thrilled instead with the Charlotte Motor Speedway or the two professional sports teams. Do the tree lined streets or abundant churches make a difference? What should you say about the schools?

A good survey should cover such broad categories as:

- housing

- schools

- safety

- recreation, entertainment

- professional associations

- spousal career opportunities

- convenience to other regions, attractions

- education and other opportunities for children

- climate

- cost of living

Don't neglect your exit interviews and other input regarding the location. No matter how many hours a week your employees are at work, some important fraction of their waking hours are spent interacting with the community at large, and the relationship that an employee's family has with the surrounding environment will have a significant impact.

Special note regarding the cost of living: You can sometimes lure a good candidate away from a job where they are making more money than you can offer if the cost of living is significantly lower where you are, and there are other compensating benefits.

LINKING TO MORE INFORMATION

Just when you thought you learned all the tricks about writing online job ads and fully enticing job candidates to your job opening, there is more!

One of the nice features about the Internet is the ability it gives you to hyperlink to another site from anywhere else on the Net. Consider adding links within your job ads to information and data that supports the sale you are making to the job candidate. If your company currently has a home page, you should provide a link to it so that the job seeker can learn more about the organization quickly and easily. Another idea may be to link to a local Web site that provides information about the job location and community (the local schools, housing market, even night life).

With hyper linking, the possibilities are endless. Not only can you link to other Web pages, you can link to application blanks, searchable company databases, company screening tools, and so on. We will address those more advanced discussions in subsequent chapters. But be cautious in your planning: Some commercial online ad services are open to linking, others are not, and some charge dearly for the privilege. Additionally, if you consider linking to additional information from your job ads, make sure the information supports your goal: attracting the right candidates. If your corporate Web site is dull and boring, what message are prospective candidates getting about your organization?

This is how a link appears written in Hypertext Markup Language (the language of the Net):

<A HREF="http://www.xyzcorporation.com">XYZ Corporation</A>

This is how the same link appears when viewed on the Web:

XYZ Corporation

ADDING LINKS TO YOUR JOB ADS

The question asked by most clients who begin to use online employment advertising is, "Can we link to our company's Web site?" The answer is yes, as long as the ad is appearing strictly on the Web. To create a link to your company Web site, simply add your company's site address (http://www.mycompany.com) to the following script:

<A HREF="http://www.mycompany.com">Click Here</A> to visit our Website for more information.

If you don't have an in-house guru to counsel you on HTML, we recommend *Teach Yourself HTML in 24 Hours* by Sams.net

Next, add this script to part of your online ad to create the hyperlink. When this script is added to your online job ad, it will read "Click Here to visit our Web site for more information." The Click Here part of the script will be highlighted. Job seekers only have to place their mouse pointer over those words, click the mouse button, and they will be taken instantly to your company's Web site.

Following is an example of an online job ad's company description with a link script appended to the end:

COMPANY:

XYZ was founded in 1983 with the mission to service the process instrumentation needs of industry in the Carolinas and Georgia. We have enjoyed steady growth in volume of business and, at our customers' requests, have expanded our services to other areas. XYZ is now organized into four divisions: Engineering Services, Textile Services, Contract Services and Shop Services. We currently provide technical personnel, both contract and direct, as well as project work throughout the Carolinas and Georgia. Our expertise is a wide range of industry support includ-

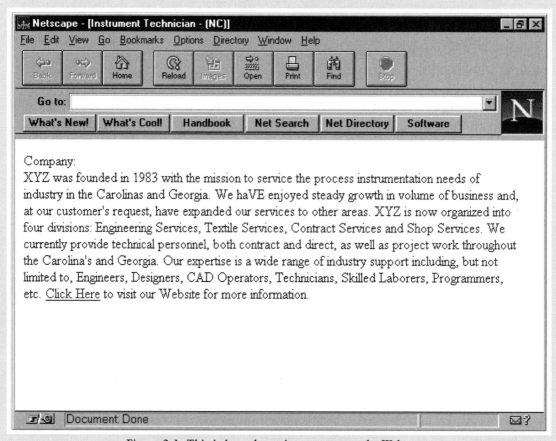

Figure 3.1. This is how the script appears on the Web.

ing, but not limited to, Engineers, Designers, CAD Operators, Technicians, Skilled Laborers, Programmers, and so on.

<A HREF= "http://www.xyzcompany.com">Click Here</A> to visit our Website for more information.

Figure 3.1 shows this company information and link script as they appear on the Web.

Sample Online Job Ads

To help you get your feet wet, the following sample ads were created to provide a glimpse of the potential residing in online job ads. They could have been much longer and would have had much more impact if they were real jobs and not just the passing fancies of fertile imaginations. The real point is that these are sales documents, not unlike those unsolicited bulk mail brochures that arrive in our mail boxes frequently. The purpose is to capture the attention of the right potential buyers and provide enough good information to persuade them to take the next step: contacting us about the job opportunity.

Sample Ad #1

Commercial Lender, Transportation - PowerBank, NC

PowerBank

Corporate Staffing, Dept. CL/INT

1500 Tryon Ave

Charlotte, NC 28209

Fax:	800-123-4567
E-mail:	recruiter@powerbank.com
Job Location:	Charlotte, N.C.
Job Status:	Full Time Position
Salary Range:	$60-$80K depending upon experience.
Benefits:	Major medical, dental, 401K with 6 percent match after 1 yr., standard retirement program, flex-time, health club membership.

Description:

Our Corporate Commerce division needs an experienced and thoroughly professional banker with at least ten years experience, and a significant concentration in rail, barge and trucking industries. The banker selected will be a senior member of a team involved in seven figures plus lines of credit, large leases, and IPOs. Will supervise a staff of four for research work and portfolio management.

QUALIFICATIONS:

Must have an in-depth knowledge of transportation markets east of the Mississippi and their place in international trade. Should now be managing a portfolio of at least eight figures and speak at least one foreign language fluently, preferably German or Spanish. Candidates should be familiar with the Microsoft Office Suite and the Money Sentinel portfolio software.

COMPANY INFORMATION:

PowerBank enjoys a strong reputation for service to the corporate and governmental institutions in the southeastern United States. Conservatively managed, but well invested in regional and worldwide enterprises, the bank supports its customers with excellent guidance and decisive action. We are prepared to expand our lending assets by 10 percent a year for the next five years with a distinct emphasis on infrastructure and high technology growth. Located in Charlotte, North Carolina, PowerBank is an acknowledged community leader in a culture that prizes leadership.

COMMUNITY INFORMATION:

Charlotte is the economic anchor of the Carolinas with a long history of commerce, education, and innovation. Located at the intersection of I-77 and I-85 between Lake Norman in North Carolina and Lake Wylie in South Carolina, the city grows ever closer to the surrounding towns and cities, both nurturing and sharing in strong manufacturing, distribution, banking, and information processing enterprises. The city has a fine reputation in the arts, excellent museums, and a healthy public school system encouraged by several outstanding private schools. Charlotte housing features both traditional tree-lined streets and golf course hugging estates.

To apply, please either fax or e-mail your resume.

SAMPLE AD #2

Industrial Engineer, New Site Planning Manager - Walnut Engineering, NC
Walnut Engineering
Recruiter, Dept. IEPM/OCC
1 Tarheel Drive
Charlotte, NC 28210

Fax: 800-123-4567

E-mail:	recruiter@walnut.com
Job Location:	Charlotte, NC
Job Status:	Permanent Position
Salary Range:	$60-$70K plus bonus potential of 10 percent of salary.
Benefits:	Major Medical, dental, life insurance, 401K with 4 percent match.

DESCRIPTION:

The I.E. planning manager will work with client management and engineers to design, plan, install, and implement high speed machining and injection molding production and assembly operations. The work involves equipment selection, plant layout, materials planning, incentive standards design and implementation, production simulation, just-in-time systems, and quality planning. The planning manager will travel forty weeks per year to client sites in the Americas, averaging 4-5 days onsite each week. Excellent project planning, communications skills, teamwork orientation, and goals orientation is necessary for satisfactory performance.

QUALIFICATIONS:

Requirements include an advanced degree in management or engineering; applicator certificates in MOST, MiniMOST, and MaxiMOST with at least 200 hours of work standards documented; MicroStation drafting qualifications with a portfolio of industrial design; superior Microsoft Office skills; 2 years experience with a leading simulation software package; and an ISO 9000 background. Candidates with a fluency in Spanish and extensive consulting experience will receive special consideration. A familiarity with Okuma and other leading brands of machine tools will be valuable, as will any "plans-to-production" manufacturing construction.

COMPANY:

Walnut Engineering Corporation is a Charlotte-based consulting firm specializing in the management of industrial construction projects, working with clients, construction firms, and equipment suppliers to develop turnkey production facilities that meet the highest standards for both productivity and quality. Our firm consists of forty professionals and an excellent support staff; the average employee tenure is eighteen years. The Charlotte office contains state-of-the-art computer and communications equipment to support our wide ranging and varied operations.

COMMUNITY:

Charlotte is the largest small town in the United States. It is rich in churches, synagogues, and good schools. The citizens take great pride in their enterprise, diversity, and good government. The city is the home to the Carolina Panthers, the Charlotte Hornets, and the Charlotte Motor Speedway. It enjoys excellent airport connections, and is convenient to both the mountains and the beach. Textiles and transportation are key parts of the industrial infrastructure. The moderate climate facilitates various sports, hunting, and fishing.

To apply in strict confidence, please fax a cover letter, resume, & salary history.

SAMPLE AD #3 (INCLUDES LINK TO COMPANY HOME PAGE)

Internet Recruiting Manager - PowerBank, NC

PowerBank

Corporate Staffing, Dept IRM/INT

1500 Tryon Ave

Charlotte, NC 28209

Fax: 800-123-4567

E-mail:	recruiter@powerbank.com
Job Location:	Charlotte, NC
Job Status:	Full Time Position
Salary Range:	$50-$80K depending upon experience.
Benefits:	Major medical, dental, 401K with 6 percent match after 1 yr., standard retirement program, flex-time, health club membership.

DESCRIPTION

This human resources vice president will create and manage a fast paced recruiting and career management operation using the Internet to source top quality job candidates. Our growing operations demand the latest in personnel selection technology to develop an elite staff known for high quality, consistently professional innovation in banking and other related enterprises. The group will consist of between five and twelve persons, and will be fully operational within six months. The successful candidate will report to the Director of Human Resources for coordination, but will have personal responsibility for the group budget and operations. Responsibilities will include career tracking and retention oversight, and service on the compensation policy committee.

QUALIFICATIONS

Must have at least two years experience in both employee selection processes and online job advertising technology. A thorough understanding of major online job advertising services is imperative, and the VP must also have the necessary

Web page management and linking skills to provide technical oversight to services provided the group by our information systems department. A background in I/O psychology, a Five Factor certification, fluency in at least one foreign language, and strong general business experience are highly desired.

COMPANY INFORMATION

PowerBank enjoys a strong reputation for service to the corporate and governmental institutions in the southeastern United States. Conservatively managed, but well invested in regional and worldwide enterprises, the bank supports its customers with excellent guidance and decisive action. We are committed to excellence in everything we do, and meeting the needs of our clients through top quality personnel. Located in Charlotte, North Carolina, PowerBank is an acknowledged community leader in a culture that prizes leadership. <A HREF="http://www.powerbank.com">Click Here</A> to visit our Website for more information.

COMMUNITY INFORMATION

Charlotte is a modern, growing city that strives to maintain its southern charm and manners. It is a banking, distribution, and commercial center that attracts talented personnel from across the United States. Charlotte enjoys a diverse professional mix of bankers, computer specialists, electric utility management, doctors, and human resource experts. Both public and private schools are excellent, the arts are well represented and supported, two professional sports teams have reached early success here, and the region includes excellent educational opportunities. The cost of living is modest compared to that of other cities its size and its rapid growth keeps unemployment low.

To apply please either fax or e-mail your resume.

S U M M A R Y

Writing an effective online job ad requires a distinct change of literary gears. Abandon the terse, deliberate language of obituaries and explore the wide plains of marketing literature. The cold, short lines of newspaper job ads are history now, but a lot of people just haven't caught on yet. The fixed per ad fee makes the online job ad a low cost marketing opportunity for human resources.

You must know a great deal about an open position to sell it successfully. There are good ways for collecting and presenting that data, but no short cuts. A closer cooperation between human resource recruiters and the operations managers will take more valuable time, but can provide a bountiful dividend in more qualified personnel and reduced interview time required. You can't do a decent job of recruiting until you understand fully what the hiring manager really wants. Go for the data, and incorporate it into the job ad.

The online job ad can be a wish list of skills and attributes needed for job performance success. A sound list of requirements attracts good candidates and discourages bad. If your budget is slim, your newspaper ad has to work right the first time every time, but the same budget can provide multiple tries with online job ads. Ask for what the manager really needs, and see what happens.

Use the online job ad to sell the company to anyone who reads it, but focus in those aspects that will be particularly attractive to job candidates for the open position. Inherent in your recruiting strategy should be the concept that every job ad is a promotional corporate ad, announcing to the world the high expectations for progress and the high quality of employees needed to make it happen. Announce to those online job ad readers in both plain and subtle ways that your company hires only the best.

Sell the job location in your online job ad. People live there, and some of them must like it. Find out why and advertise the location. If you invest some extra effort, the Chamber of Commerce will soon be borrowing your text to promote the community where your jobs exist.

Create model ads or ad templates now. They will pay off handsomely later as opportunities to recycle some of your best text become apparent. More talented staff may produce a spectrum of model ads that fit the full range of personality types and preferences represented by your diverse human resource base.

Begin thinking about how the online ad service could fit into your overall recruiting strategy. Later in the book, strategies will be covered in some detail, but you need to creatively consider how the paradigm shifts inherent in Internet advertising affect your recruiting potential.

Don't make writing online job ads too complicated. Simplicity can and should be the hallmark of your online ad process. Online job ads should be clear and functional enough to fit under the umbrella of any effective recruiting strategy.

4

ADVERTISING OPTIONS

Reverend Leroy's Revivals

You may have heard of Penance Peak, North Carolina. The town rests on the west bluff of the Pine River about two miles upstream from where the Cold River joins it to form the Washington River. Penance Peak owes its existence to the Westend Railroad, which built the town as a construction and maintenance housing location. The Westend built the first lines through the mountains in the early part of the century, and very little happened in Penance Peak for years afterwards.

But then Penance Peak became famous for the tent healings of the Reverend Frank Leroy. Before the big war, thousands of folks would jump into their Studebakers, Fords, Chryslers, and Chevrolets to attend the Sunday afternoon hellfire preaching, inspirational gospel singing, and mass healing of the Reverend Leroy. On Saturday nights, folks from as far away as Charlotte, Greensboro, and even Raleigh would start their slow journey on the gravel roads to climb the Blue Ridge Mountains and watch the Reverend Leroy heal sinners.

As you might imagine, all these folks needed a place to stay when they arrived in

Penance Peak, and sleeping in a car was a burden even for the devout. Many roughed it in tents, but for years, the only available good lodgings were Esther Pearls' guest bedrooms, and she favored her Freewill Baptist friends. Even for them, it was not such a good option because Esther was the town gossip.

The local sins that Esther knew about were minor and mundane, but she would not shut up recounting the details until at least thirty minutes after the last kerosene lamp was extinguished. Also, her husband Lazell snored with a sound like a boar hog eating dried corn. The guests who were not very sound sleepers showed up at the tent event on Sunday needing some balm from Gilead, or wherever.

Well, sensing that something needed to be done to accommodate the visitors, the mayor of Penance Peak, Ed Earl Campbell, asked all the church folk to help build lodgings. This created a problem. No new housing had been constructed since the Westend Railroad quit building the railroad. Good carpenters were in short supply, and the main skill sets for the Penance Peak populace consisted of tobacco farming, moonshining, and dirt track auto racing.

For months, the lodging project dragged on. It took several years just to figure out what direction to go, what exactly to build, and how to build it. After three years, ground was broken, but construction progress stalled when the only local plumber began installing bathrooms that featured toilets. The local folk, who were giving free labor and had seldom enjoyed such "high dollar" amenities, objected to building such luxuries for those out-of-towners.

After a few months of stalemate and seeing revenue lost from the lack of lodgings, Billy Ray Kinard had an idea: hire professional builders from the metropolis of Hickory, NC to get the job done quickly. Billy Ray had only finished the 6th grade, but he did understand that free labor and services actually might lose you money in the long run. Billy Ray hired the Byrd Brothers Construction Company, and within one year, the Rest in the Mountains Retreat House was built with nice showers and flush toilets. Money flowed into Penance Peak in general, and Billy Ray's pockets in particular.

Sadly, Penance Peak's economic progress faltered two years later due to a lapse of faith and a shortage of theological healing integrity. Thelma Sue Cunningham's parents brought her all the way from Cooters End, North Carolina to find a cure for what they called "excess passion." The Reverend Leroy was distracted by her assets during the laying on of hands and failed to step back when Thelma Sue followed the standard healing formula and fainted. She tried to catch herself and her right hand caught the Reverend Leroy's often admired mane of hickory brown hair. His top se-

cret Memphis mail order toupee came off as Thelma Sue collapsed in the arms of her parents.

Because the Reverend could not even heal himself of an affliction as simple as baldness, serious doubts developed about the authenticity of the highly entertaining and spiritually uplifting cures he had conducted under the big tent. He was branded a fraud and lost his Southern Salvationists ordination credentials along with his toupee. The devoted stopped coming to Penance Peak, and Billy Ray's Rest in the Mountains Retreat House became as bare as the Reverend Leroy's head.

However, Billy Ray Kinard was saved from an embarrassing bankruptcy by the Reverend Leroy's inspired career change. The denuded and defrocked Leroy started an orphanage and invested his savings from the substantial collection plate proceeds to purchase the facility from Billy Ray for a sum that equaled the mortgage balance that Billy Ray owed the bank. Billy Ray breathed a sigh of relief and switched his membership to the Pennace Peak Associate Reformed Presbyterian church.

The moral of the story is simple: price does not equal value. Billy Ray understood that to get a job done right, you sometimes have to hire folks to do it right. Remember this when you are told about how the Internet is free, how your assistant's sister's cousin can find you employees on the Net for free, or having not taken our advice, you are in your 100th hour of trying to get your Web site online without success. You might not pay in terms of dollars, but you will pay in terms of time and frustration.

REVIEWING YOUR OPTIONS

By now, you probably understand that there are literally dozens if not hundreds of options available for your organization regarding online employment advertising. Most of you have collected scores of brochures by mail, been contacted by phone by online ad reps, heard about how one of your employees has a cousin named Billy Bob who has a friend with a local jobs database, or met some young technogeek in your MIS department who was released from the subbasement long enough to make you aware that he could solve your problems. (We use the masculine gender in this discussion because we are southern gentlemen and do not wish to think of females as technogeeks hanging out in anyone's basement. Please forgive us for our political incorrectness in this matter.) Because the number of venues in which to advertise your jobs seems limitless, it is helpful to break all the options into three main categories:

- Commercial Online Services - these folks traditionally have the most traffic, best-looking Web sites, and most up-to-date features. After all, you are buying service and quality when you place an ad with one of these enterprises, and their success or failure is measured in stark economic terms.

- Free Job-Listing Services - these services range from the free job Usenet posting groups listed in Appendix A, "Internet Job Sites," to the free job-listing services provided by the federal, state, and local governmental agencies, including hobby databases housed on the big mainframes at public universities. Consistency of service depends on the level of commitment of both funding sources and the volunteers manning the system. The free services are more subject to ballooning with stale ads and hourly jobs than the commercial sources, but can be very valuable.

- Your Company Web site - obviously this is an option, but we suggest that it remain as part of a more integrated solution with other forms of advertising. See Chapter 6, "Web Page Warnings," for more details.

COMMERCIAL EMPLOYMENT SITES ON THE INTERNET

Let's begin by defining the concept of a commercial online employment site. Basically, commercial online employment providers place your job ad on the Internet, generally in a searchable database, for a fee. In addition, they might also help you develop ads, provide software to minimize the effort of placing ads online, advise you on supplemental online recruiting approaches, promote the professional database to improve response rates, offer cross links to your Web site, expedite and ease the contact between candidates and your company, and provide premium candidate traffic to your Web site in order for you to maximize your ads' exposure. There is no intrinsic magic to having a job ad online, and most of the value often flows from the supplemental services that are either included in the cost of the ad or are separately contracted.

Many commercial sites also allow candidates to store resumes online in a resume database. In some cases, candidates place their resumes in such a database for free, and you, the corporate recruiter, pay for access to the database. In others, job candidates pay a modest fee to enter their resume on the database for a period of three months to a year. Needless to say, the latter service includes a select group that is more serious about changing jobs. Free placement resume sites attract large volumes of resumes and require good search skills. The better sites offer excellent keyword searching through resumes by city, state, job discipline, and other criteria.

The exchange is simple: candidates find jobs, employers find candidates. The commercial online service provides the mechanism through which this exchange of information is conducted.

Technology, however, never stays at the most basic level. Advances in Internet browsers, in the speed of the transfer of information and in database capabilities, have helped commercial online services evolve beyond just placing an ad online. Some services offer advanced technological features:

- Job seekers can store their resumes online, update them when necessary; and then, with the click of their mouse, instantly apply for a job listed in the database.

- Job seekers can choose to post their resume in either public or private modes. In public mode, an individual's entire resume can be viewed by the wholeInternet community. In private mode, all identifying information about the job seeker is eliminated, with only skills and experience being present. Companies must e-mail the individual about the job opening, and it is up to the job seeker to decide whether to pursue the opportunity. No longer must anyone feel threatened about putting his resume online and having his current organization know of his intentions.

- Integrated scrollbar and keyword search technologies make searching easier then ever and deliver better-targeted candidates to companies.

- Smart search software eliminates the initial problems with keyword searching. For example, if I want an OD (organizational development) specialist. The perfect candidate enters O.D. into the keyword search. In the past, the correct job description would never have been accessed because the perfect candidate used periods in his keyword search. Today, software is able to recognize related terms, which makes keyword searching more usable than ever.

- A candidate's real resume (the pretty ones done in Microsoft Word and WordPerfect) can be stored online and sent to an organization along with the ASCII text one used in traditional resume storage systems.

- Agent technology gives either the candidate or the organization the ability to enter the type of job or candidate they are looking for. The computer does the matching, and continues to search and find long after the candidate has signed off. When the match is found e-mail notifies the interested party.

- Application blanks and initial screening mechanisms can be developed by organizations and used online in conjunction with their job ads.

- Custom Web brochures developed with an emphasis toward attracting candidates to a particular job, company, or region of the country can be interlinked with job advertisements.

- The whole range of Internet technology is available for your use - Java, sound, video, and so on. Web pages can now come alive to present a rich multimedia presentation about your organization to the job seeker.

In addition to offering technology, commercial services offer the most important element: traffic. Some experts quantified traffic in terms of hits, times searched, accesses to the database, and so on, but they all measure the quantity of job seekers who check their ad database for jobs.

Commercial services generally advertise liberally to bring traffic to their sites. This is an important consideration because the hobby based business models that launched many online job services might not hold up in the new Internet marketplace.

Because of the user friendliness, advanced technology, and premium traffic that commercial online services provide, such services might actually cost less in the long run than the so-called free services.

BUSINESS MODELS ARE A CHANGING

In the Net's infancy, organizations that had Web sites containing data were highly regarded. After all, there wasn't much accessible information then, so if your site contained interesting or valuable data, Internet managers who wanted to increase traffic to their sites linked to yours for free. Several online job sites developed a business model whereby for a set fee (approx. $3000 per year or $300 per month), any organization could upload an unlimited number of ads to the job site's database. Still other sites did nothing more than gather up free ads and resumes placed on the Internet and sell organizations banner advertising on their site. These models worked fine in the old environment where links were free and the number of ads were rather sparse.

Times have changed. Such a model must now contend with a growing number of ads. The ad count situation shifts as contingency-based recruiters and similar entities learn how to use the Internet to their advantage by often running hundreds of ads in these services. In addition, some Internet service providers (ISP's) are now demanding big dollars to be linked from their high traffic Internet vehicles.

The increased volume and the need to reach less technically sophisticated Internet users drives the need for higher-quality search engines, and increased bandwidth becomes mandatory to handle the ever-increasing Internet traffic. Meeting those technical needs requires both significant capital and increased sophistication in systems management and marketing.

We believe the services that will remain will be those that charge on a per ad basis. That business model best provides the capital and flexibility necessary to adapt to the ever changing Internet world.

COMMERCIAL SITE EXAMPLES

In the past several years the number of commercial sites has increased dramatically on the Internet. While the number keeps rising, all commercial sites can be categorized into two major areas of operation:

General Sites : These are jobs databases which are national in scope and try to aggregate a huge database of jobs appealing to a broad spectrum of candidates. These are the jobs supermarkets, with a variety of keyword and menu systems to help job candidates find the electronic aisle they want to shop in. These sites will also generally offer resume databases that allow employers to do some active shopping as well.

Niche or Boutique Sites: These sites are built around a specific occupation, ethnic group, or region of the country. While traffic going to a niche site is generally much less than a general site, it is the quality of the traffic (qualified jobseekers) which makes them valuable.

EXAMPLE OF A GENERAL SITE

CareerWeb is an excellent example of a general job site in looks and functionality. It is by no means the only good choice; we suggest you also consider several of the other options located in Appendix A. It is definitely representative of the group, but you may find other features in some other service that are especially valuable to your company. For a more full description of recruiting site options on the Internet we suggest reading the book "Careerxroads" by Gerry Crispin and Marc Mahler. They review over 500 job related web sites.

The CareerWeb site (www.cweb.com) bills itself as a site for "professional, technical and management jobs". On its home page, there are three key features to note. The first is a keyword heading of six options worth exploring, but all are not necessarily obvious to the first time user. They provide quick access for the informed regular user.

The second feature are the banner ads. These very visual and compelling appeals for attention are an up front effort by client employers to capture the attention of job candidates early. CareerWeb also uses banner ads to direct attention to its own bookstore and other site features.

The third feature is the tree structure menu. The person checking out this page must first make the obvious selection of their main interest; if they are looking for career opportunities, they move to the "Find a Job" column, and if they are a human resources recruiter, they go to the "List a Job" column. They also have two more choices at the very bottom, to "File a Resume" or visit a "Career Fair."

An example of what is on the other end of a banner ad is represented in Figure 4.2. When an individual clicks on the IAMS banner on the CareerWeb home page, this is the page that is returned. From this page the jobseeker is presented

Figure 4.1
The CareerWeb
Home Page

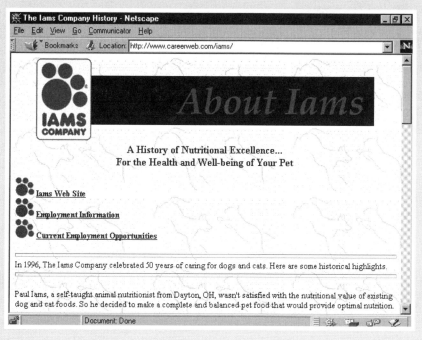

Figure 4.2
IAMS Web Page Linked
From CareerWeb
Banner Ad

the options of reading about IAMS, accessing their corporate website, or viewing current employment opportunities.

When a person clicks on the either the "jobs" or "international jobs," a search page appears (figure 4.3). The search page allows the job candidate to narrow the dimensions of her search quickly and accurately by making some basic choices:

- Job Category- a listing of the major occupational categories covered in the database.

- A two character code of the state one wants to work in (optional)

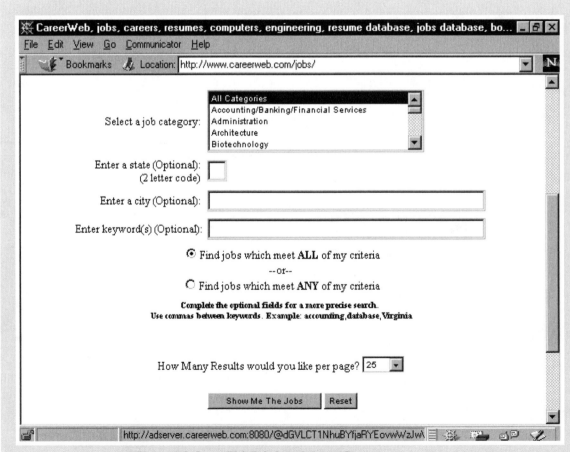

Figure 4.3 CareerWeb Job Search Input Page

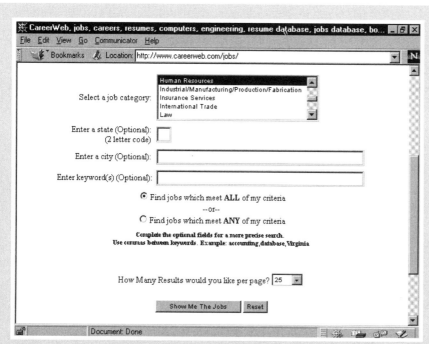

Figure 4.4
CareerWeb Job Search
Input Page

Figure 4.5
Return Screen for
"Human Resources"
Search

- A city (also optional)

- Keywords which more precisely describe the job (also optional)

Then CareerWeb gives the reader two choices, either to require that the jobs presented meet all the criteria, or just one of the criteria. Selecting all of the criteria narrows the selection very quickly, but it may leave out a desirable choice.

The next choice is the number of jobs one wants to preview at one time. The default, 25, is usually a good starting place. Having made that decision, one simply uses the mouse to click on the "Show Me the Jobs" button. The "Reset" button is used to start the choice selection process all over again if the criteria you selected provides either too few or too many results.

To explore a very simple job search, we can select the job category alone, and use the "Human Resources" choice from the table. Then leave all the rest blank except the "all criteria" button and the 25 job default. Figure 4.4 shows how the page would appear just before we pressed the "Show Me the Jobs" button. Figure 4.5 shows the results for the "Human Resources" search.

The first item to be noted about the listing of jobs on the return screen for the "Human Resources" search is that there is a "New Search" button in the upper right hand side of the page, just under the banner ad and the "Job Search Results" heading. This button enables you to go back to the criteria selection page, and modify the criteria you use in the search process.

Note also that this page contains the count of the total number of jobs which met the criteria specified, and in this case the first 25 of those 48. At the bottom of this page, there is a button which takes the reader to the next set of 25 (or a lesser amount).

This listing provides three quick reference pieces of data: the job title, the employer, and the city/state location of the job. Depending on one's preferences, some preliminary eliminations can be made and a first choice made. For this example, we scrolled down to a HR Generalist III job at First Union National Bank, Charlotte, NC. Figures 4.6 and 4.7 is the text of the ad displayed.

Notice that at the bottom of the First Union ad there is a hyperlink which reads, "Find Out More About First Union National Bank". Figure 4.8 is the web page returned when that hyperlink is pressed. CareerWeb has links from all of their ads to additional corporate information if the corporate client is a yearly member.

Another example of an ad hosted by CareerWeb is the Peoplesoft Human Re-

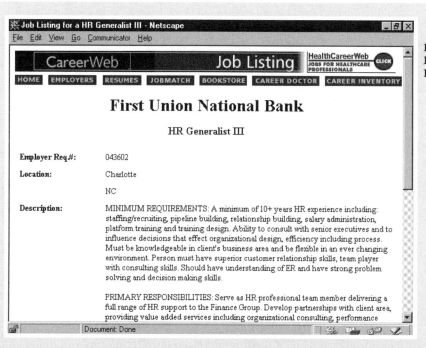

Figure 4.6
First Union National
Bank Ad on CareerWeb

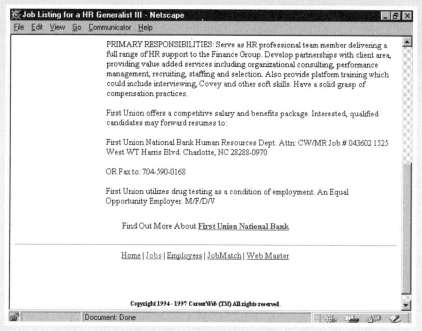

Figure 4.7
First Union National
Bank Ad on Career Web

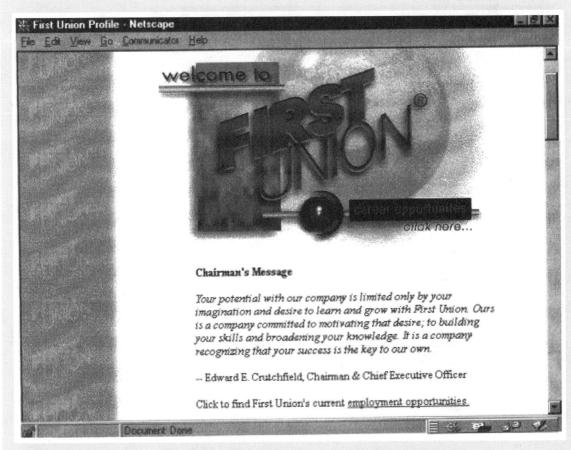

Figure 4.8 First Union Corporate Profile on CareerWeb

sources Education Specialist ad represented in Figures 4.9 and 4.10. Notice that this ad is similar in look and style to the First Union ad just covered with the exception of one area: resume response options. First Union chooses to accept ads via fax and postal mail only. Peoplesoft, on the other hand, gives jobseekers the option of emailing their resumes to "jobs@peoplesoft.com" or submitting resumes using the resumes that jobseekers store on CareerWeb.

The above examples are just one way that a job candidate has to find the big opportunity. Going back to the home page, the job candidate can click on the "Employers" button and obtain a listing of all the employers currently listing jobs with CareerWeb (figure 4.11). The job candidate has the option of simply scrolling

Figure 4.9
Peoplesoft Ad on
CareerWeb

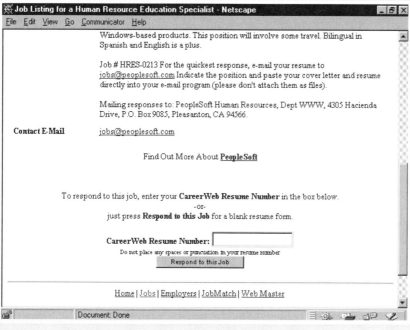

Figure 4.10
Peoplesoft Ad on
CareerWeb

Figure 4.11 Employer profile page on CareerWeb

down the list, or if he has a specific company in mind, click on the first letter of the name in the line between the introductory paragraph and the beginning of the "A" list.

For example, if the job candidate would like to manage a McDonalds and would like to see opportunities there, she can click on "M". Under the "M" listing, she clicks on McDonalds in order to get the McDonalds Employer Profile page (Figure 4.12). This page contains links to all the job information and career opportunities found at this major American employer.

For the job candidate beginning a serious search campaign, the home page provides the "File a Resume" button. The process is begun with Figure 4.13. A

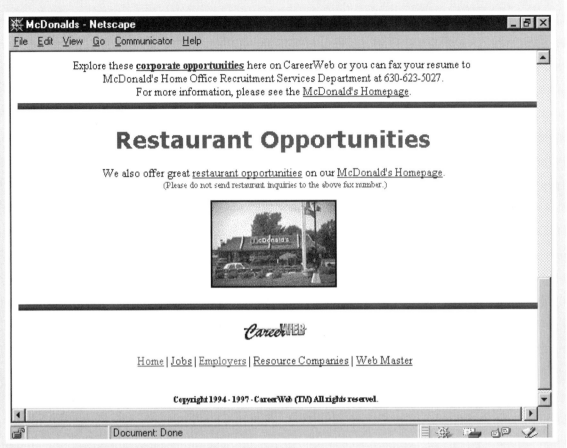

Figure 4.12 McDonalds employer profile on CareerWeb

complete resume can be stored on the CareerWeb system for downloading in response to attractive job ads. The process eliminates the need for entering a resume repeatedly into an e-mail communication.

On the other side of the online jobs market, CareerWeb provides its client companies with an "Account Manager" feature that provides a wide range of options for entering new jobs, changing job listings, reviewing responses, checking job listing statistics, and searching their resume database. This web page (Figure 4.14) is set up to enable the client to be active and engaged in maintaining their jobs online. This hands on approach can be accomplished with basic computer skills (using a mouse and keyboard, for instance).

Figure 4.13
CareerWeb Resume
Input Screen

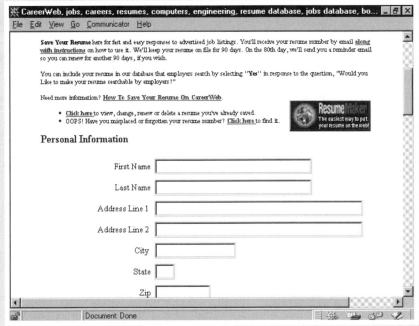

Figure 4.14
Account Manager Page
on CareerWeb

Figure 4.15 displays the beginning of CareerWebs's online rate card. In this example the types of services an organization can receive under CareerWeb's yearly membership option is displayed. Please check the CareerWeb web pages (http://www.cweb.com) or contact CareerWeb direct for a complete and up-to-date description of features and costs.

Each of the major commercial online ad companies scramble to provide a full range of services to both the employer and the job candidate. After all, the essential nature of their business is to maintain a marketplace where buyers and sellers can meet, make deals, shop costs and features, and make economic decisions. They are a supermarket for human resources in one respect, but a much more

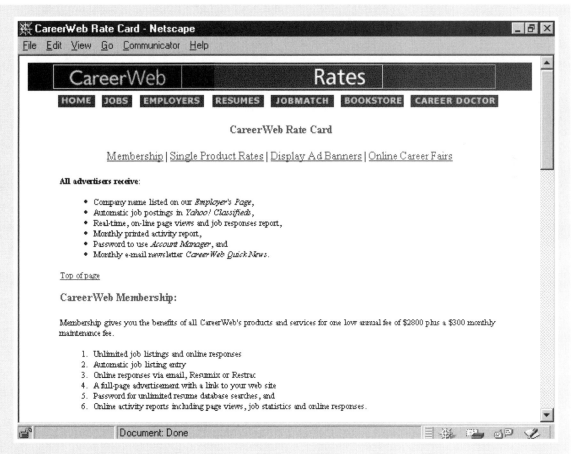

Figure 4.15 CareerWeb Rate Card

accurate parallel is the stock market where the key institution is simply an intermediary.

But the most important insight to retain is that job candidates are not just selling their talent in this market; the companies involved are selling themselves in a highly competitive market. They can use the Internet simply to identify good job candidates, or they can use it to inform and persuade job candidates that their companies are an avenue to a successful and fulfilling professional future. The companies that do not understand the distinction will not find online job advertising as productive as those that do.

THE NICHE OR BOUTIQUE SITES

The niche site offers many of the same services as the regular commercial online ad site, but it has an organizing premise that usually limits the jobs listed to a given profession, or other occupational subgroup. For the job candidates who fit in that category, it is a simple matter of entering that web site to review a significant number of the open job opportunities of interest to them at the time. For the companies who advertise there, it is a focused job market that may attract fewer resumes but much higher quality ones.

The key to niche site success is the quality and quantity of job site promotion that is performed. If the site is advertised in professional publications and discussed in industry articles and if the overall quality is consistent with the image and prestige of the sponsoring organization, a niche site can be successful for both job candidates and employers.

One good example of a niche site is the SHRM web site. The Society of Human Resource Management web site tells a lot about the organization and one of the important features of the site is a job section. Figures 4.16 and 4.17 below are a display of the home page. Please note that there are many topic choices, and a selection box which allows the reader to directly access "HR Job Openings".

A click on the "HR Job Openings" button takes you to the job site where several hyperlinked words allow the job candidate to search for jobs by either geographic location, job title, or date of post. Or she can check all listings. The text explains how to use the service, and describes specific features. (See Figure 4.18.)

The geographic listing provides a map of the United States and the job candidate can limit her search to one state by simply clicking on one of those hyper-

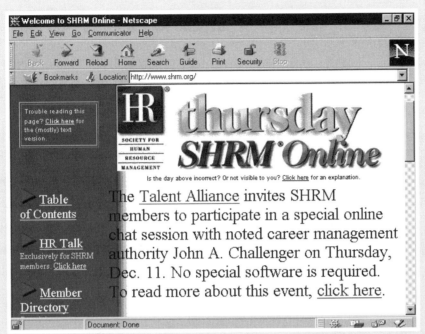

Figure 4.16
SHRM Homepage

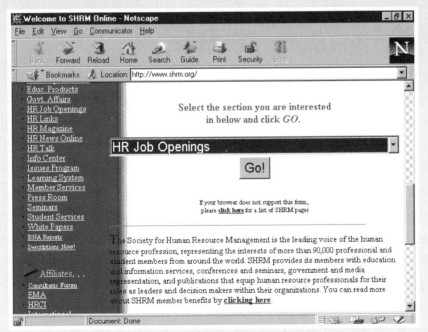

Figure 4.17
SHRM Homepage

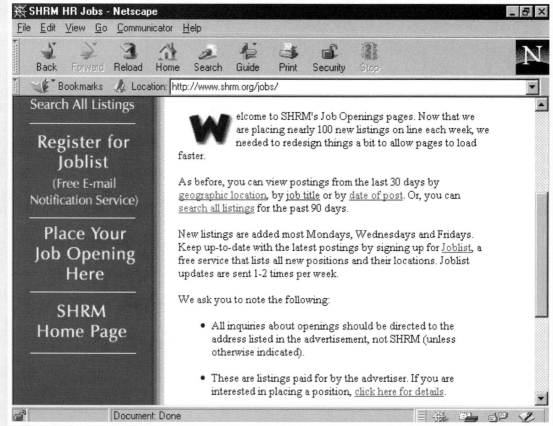

Figure 4.18 SHRM Jobs Page

linked images. Under the map is a state-by-state listing, allowing the candidate to scroll down the complete list if desired. (See Figure 4.19)

By clicking on individual job titles, the job description is displayed (See Figure 4.20). Please note that the job ads in the SHRM jobs database tend to be brief. SHRM's pricing reflects the newspaper paradigm by charging on a per line rather than a per ad basis.

One of the most appealing aspects of the SHRM jobs database is its explicit listings of posting dates as seen in Figure 4.21. It is very useful for a job candidate to know if the ad was just placed, or has been ripening there for 60 days.

Another nice feature is an automated e-mail notification of new listings on the

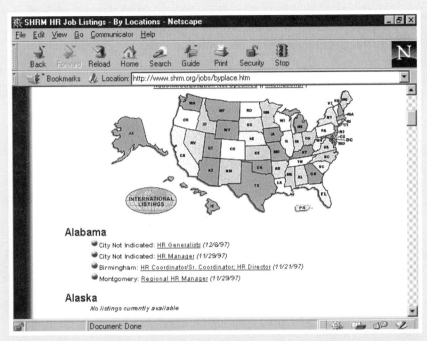

Figure 4.19
SHRM Job Listings
By Location

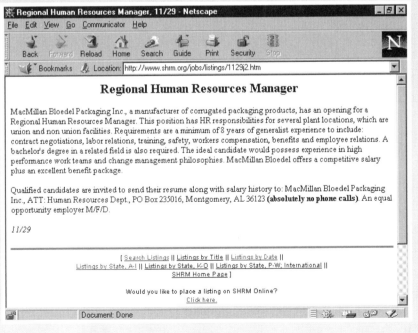

Figure 4.20
Job Ad

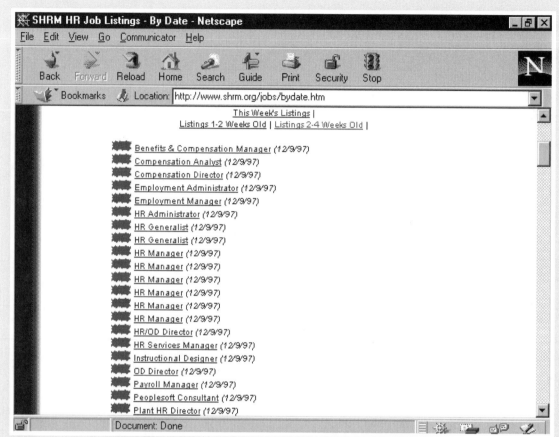

Figure 4.21 SHRM Job Listings By Date

service. That kind of personalized service is very useful to job candidates. See Figure 4.22 for a glimpse of the signup procedure.

The SHRM jobs database also supplies a keyword search capability (Figure 4.23). Jobseekers can enter search words into the input screen and receive a listing of jobs matching their query (Figure 4.24). In our example we do a search on the word "Internet".

Figure 4.25 shows another sample job ad from the SHRM jobs database. As you can see, this kind of online job ad can be productive when an ample number of serious job candidates utilize the resource. It is also obviously targeted at the mid-to-upper level professional with comprehensive career plans.

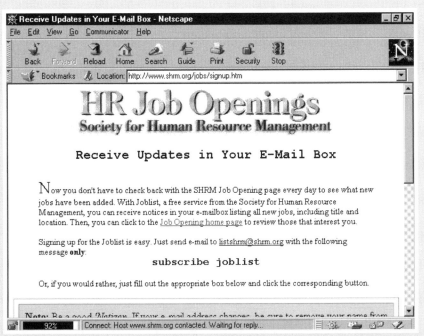

Figure 4.22
SHRM Email Update
Page Screen

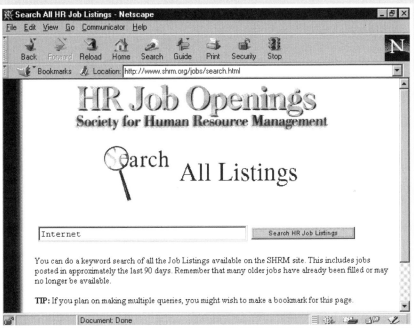

Figure 4.23
SHRM Job Search
Input

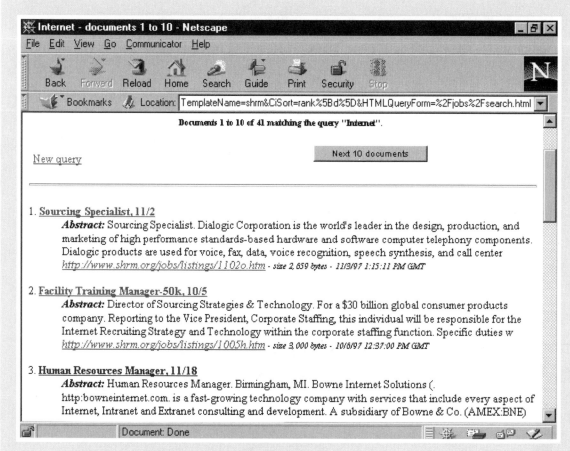

Figure 4.24 Job Search Return Screen

This particular niche site has very straightforward pricing to complement its well-designed, but modest set of features. Please note the link between hard copy and online communications products; the cross promotion is particularly effective. Figure 4.26 displays the advertising rates for the site.

The niche or boutique job ad site has two salient features:

- It is targeted towards a specific audience.

- It is generally linked to a professional organization, mutual interest group, or regional / professional publication.

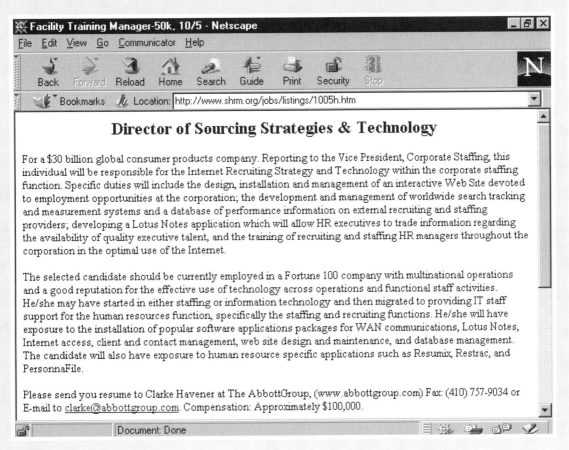

Figure 4.25 SHRM Job Ad

Needless to say, for key human resource requirements, the niche site could be either a sole source or a valuable supplemental site. Review the companies using it currently, and talk to your colleagues in the industry. When you do try one, be sure to utilize tracking tags and source codes in order to evaluate objectively the results.

❑ ❑ ❑

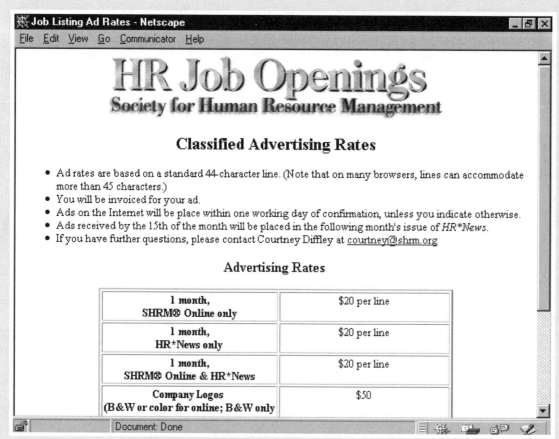

Figure 4.26 SHRM Ad Rates

FREE JOB LISTING SERVICES

Yes, we said free! Dozens of services will post your job ads online free of charge. Today, many types of nonprofit and community-based Internet networks are popping up across America. It's natural for these services to offer job postings as one of their services. Unfortunately, the response rates with most of these services are minimal at best because such sites often receive only a fraction of the Web traffic that a major online employment site receives. You can waste more hours on these free areas than you will on several of the paid services. In the end, it's up to

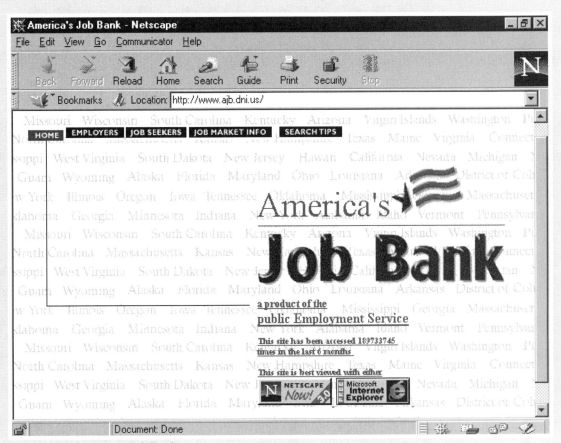

Figure 4.27 America's Job Bank

you. The commercial services offer superior traffic and ease of use. The free services offer, well, free postings.

But there is one stand out organization among such free services. It's called
America's Job Bank.

What is America's Job Bank? Simply put, it is a free service that is sponsored by
the United States Government. It contains all the job listings submitted to your
local job service offices by government contractors as required by law, plus listings submitted by approved organizations via their Internet web site (see Figure
4.27). Currently, more than 150,000 jobs appear online, with the major percentage of positions being submitted via various state employment job centers. Jobs

range from minimum-wage positions to PhD scientist positions.

The vast resources of the federal government allow America's Job Bank to compete with commercial online services. What form this service will take and how much will be invested in it in the future is anyone's guess. On the plus side, such a free service gives organizations a low-cost way of sourcing talented professionals. However, free services are often buried in thousands upon thousands of jobs placed by contingency-based recruiting firms sourcing resumes for current client contracts or perceived future needs. How America's Job Bank handles such growth will determine its future success.

We suggest you go online and give America's Job Bank a try. Remember to use tracking tags and source codes for your ads, and make sure you measure the quality, not the quantity, of the resumes you receive. America's Job Bank can be accessed at http://www.ajb.dni.us.

USENET GROUPS

So what is a Usenet group? Simply put, it is a listing, by date, of thousands upon thousands of comments on any particular subject. You can add a comment to an ongoing list by e-mailing it to the newsgroup. There are thousands of Usenet groups on the Internet, with topics ranging from Elvis to cooking to Corvettes to jobs. Dozens of Usenet jobs groups on the Internet focus on specific subjects or particular regions of the country. Appendix A, "Internet Job Sites," lists several of the major Usenet job groups on the Internet, with the group misc.jobs being one of the most popular (see Figure 4.28). To access a Usenet group, type the group's name after news: in the URL space of your Web browser. For instance, to bring up misc.jobs Usenet group, type news:misc.jobs.

After you access a Usenet group, you are presented with a long list of topics that should relate to the subject of that group. By clicking a topic with your mouse, you can read about that topic in depth.

Several factors make Usenet Groups worthwhile places to post jobs:

- They are free.

- Several services grab the data and place it in searchable databases (such as Career Magazine).

- Little skill is required to post a job opening.

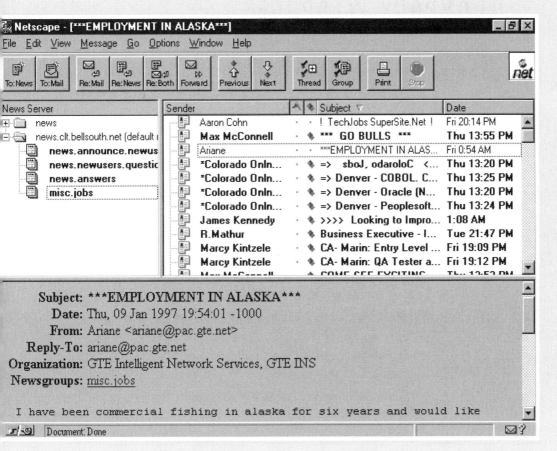

Figure 4.28 Usenet Ad

We suggest that everyone give Usenet groups a try. Search Appendix A for a Usenet group that matches your job opening's area of expertise or your geographical region of the country. Be sure to include tracking tags so you can monitor the results. Also, many major commercial online ad services include Usenet postings in their packages.

❑   ❑   ❑

COMPANY WEBPAGES

The advantages and shortcomings of corporate web pages will be discussed more eloquently in Chapter 6. The primary handicaps are

- Recruiting web pages are frequently under supported technically. Generally the IS Internet staff charged with the creation and maintenance of web pages have other tasks that are often more career building and more technically interesting than web page work for the HR department.

- They are frequently under supported with content. Many IS departments have created technically superior Web pages with a lot less effort than they will admit, only to see their creation left to wither and die from lack of current data. You should make a survey of corporate web pages, and note the number of jobs listed among those that do list jobs. Would you believe a profitable growing corporation with 30,000 plus current employees only has four job openings listed and two of them are already filled? A critical issue in the design and management of successful web pages is that staff in the human resources department should be able to make entries and updates routinely (design issue) and that human resources staff should have the motivation to do so (management issue).

- They are underlinked. The quantity of traffic that is routed to a web page is the major determinant of functional success for online job ads as well as other objectives. If a company web page concept includes the deluded idea that the company is the effective center of the universe, and all of the targeted readers will search them out no matter how long it takes, their web page will languish from lack of attention.

The solutions are simple. If web page visibility is a part of your recruiting strategy, you should consider the following tactics:

- Develop a budget for technical support in terms of hours to create and regular hours to maintain technically.

- Explore a menu of options early, and decide which bells and whistles you wish to have, and which you do not.

- Allow outside sources to compete for the work with in-house IS staff and ensure that specific guarantees protect you from neglect.

- Insist that the package include an easy to use interface that allows the recruiting staff to make routine additions and perform routine editing of your online job ads; and that the training to perform those tasks be included in the package as well. Build in periodic updates and the training of new personnel as they are hired.

- Establish firm policies, timelines, and task responsibilities for making entries to the online job listing web page.

- Coordinate your recruiting element with the other elements and objectives of corporate web pages.

- Develop a master explanation of why your company is a great place to work and feature that data as an integral and early part of your recruiting web page element.

- Create separate location components for each major location within the company, and develop the web page so that job candidates can review the company promotion and the location promotion data in a way that is related to the jobs listings, but not redundant. For example, you might wish to tout the company and the location under a "Career Opportunities" local link and provide a short list of the job openings at that location, and code the job titles so that they are links to individual pages with a full description of the job and the requirements for consideration. At the bottom of each of those pages, provide links back to company and location data.

- Design in cross links from your location data to various community resources. Does the YMCA there have a Web page? The local Board of Realtors? The Chamber of Commerce? The school system? Major sports teams? Professional organizations? Churches, synagogues, and mosques? The Humane Society? Hospitals? Museums? Historical societies? Symphonies? Whatever? You want persons that are looking at that community to take a look at your company as well, and a cross link can provide lots of traffic as well as performing a good service to persons wanting to know more about the place where you have an open career position.

- Incorporate into your planning prompt deletions to your ads from the web page.

- Include both tracking tags and source codes into your web page job ads, make it part of the response address. You want to compare your web page listing expenses with commercial online job ads, newspaper ads, and other media.

- Make it easy for the job candidate to contact you; incorporate an e-mail response form for requesting applications and/or submitting resumes.

- Provide quality of life testimonials from current employees and favorable statistics about corporate growth, turnover, advancement, benefits, and so on.

- Survey the corporate web pages of competitors in the labor market the way your marketing department looks at your operational competitors, and resolve to be a leader in finding and keeping great performers.

If a lot of this advice seems like common sense, you are perceptive.

S U M M A R Y

The Internet is a resource with vast potential for your recruiting needs. There are literally hundreds of options available for advertising your job openings online. Both cost and effectiveness should guide human resource professionals to explore all the options thoroughly, enabling them to make sound business decisions that are consistent with the best objectives of their organizations.

Consider trying all the resources available, including the major commercial sites (4-Work, CareerWeb, Career Mosaic, E-span, NationJob, etc.) and the major free sites (America's Job Bank, Usenet groups, etc.).

Resolve to manage your investments in online job advertising and to incorporate this approach to your overall human resource management strategy.

CHAPTER 5

SELECTING AN ONLINE SERVICE

If the rate of growth in online employment advertising sites and services continues at the current pace, in ten years there will be more online advertising services than jobs!

J ust a few years ago, there were only a few startup online employment advertising services. The Web was new, and few services were equipped technically and financially to offer full-blown keyword-searchable databases on the Web.

Back then, the cost of going online with a quality online employment advertising service was exceedingly high, and the Web was still in its infancy. Not many organizations were willing to invest in such a novel enterprise, especially when the average readers were high-tech computer hackers, and the candidates sought by mainstream America thought surfing was something done on the water in Hawaii.

The initial online employment advertising services included Help Wanted-

USA in the Career Center on America Online, E-Span on America Online and CompuServe, and The Online Career on the Internet. In time, as the cost of computer equipment and software decreased, and as traffic started going online to the tune of 10 million plus users, hundreds of other online job services sprung up across the Internet.

Major ad agencies, such as Bernard Hodes and TMP, now have their own services, as do Uncle Sam and the dozens of newspapers that have begun to publish online. In addition to listing job ads online, several commercial employment advertising providers have developed and introduced new technologies to make Internet job searches easier and more productive. Candidates can now store their resumes online in resume databases, update them at will, and send them to prospective employers with the click of the mouse.

Employers and job seekers can now tell the computer the candidate or job of their dreams. The computer does the matching between available jobs and candidates and e-mails each party about the other. Computer matching is here today, and improving steadily.

As this book goes to print there are over 4,000 employment-related sites on the Internet. Included in this number are commercial and free job databases, company webpages that list internal jobs; newspapers listing all their Sunday job ads electronically as well; and recruiting firm webpages. Dozens of firms, from recruiters to major corporations, are jumping on the Net daily. In addition, elaborate application blanks for submitting resumes are popping up on company sites across the Web.

Today, online advertising is big business, and dozens of organizations are positioning themselves to capture this new marketplace. Recent reports suggest that in 1998 online employment advertising will start to significantly drain revenues away from the traditional print employment advertising methods. The word on the street today is that newspapers are beginning to panic as they see their potential cash cow, the Sunday want-ad section, slip away from them. This is one reason that dozens of newspapers have banded together to deliver their employment ads online via CareerPath. The Online Job Advertising Industry, which was unknown in the early 1990's is expected to generate over a quarter of a billion dollars in revenue by the year 2000. That was billion with a "B."

The marketing of online advertisement has already begun. If you work for an organization of any size, odds are that you have been approached by at least one online employment advertising service extolling the virtues of online advertising.

Some of these services are legitimate and offer real success in meeting your recruitment needs. Other services may seem promising, but are actually operated from someone's spare bedroom with no real capital for future expansion. Still others may be nothing more than a hastily built Web site with no real traffic, and thus no real results.

The cost for entry into the online employment advertising business is fairly small, and many downsized HR folks with some Internet experience are trying to be the next Bill Gates of employment ads. Several of them may have contacted you already.

NET NOTE

In our consulting experience, we have talked to several firms that tell us they have tried "Bob's local online ad service," and stoically inform us that the Internet does not work for finding talent! Unfortunately, these firms were not informed consumers. Had they chosen a reputable online advertising service, they probably would be singing a different tune.

Our goal in this chapter is to provide you with the tools and knowledge necessary to become informed consumers in the online employment advertising arena. After reading this chapter, you will be able to successfully compare one service to another, and to determine which service best meets your current needs.

YOUR FIRST CONTACT

As you read this book and consider your online advertising options, you'll probably place a call to request information from several services regarding their Internet advertising packages. As you read their brochures, you will see a cascade of claims, not particularly original or reliable, but certainly persuasive:

- The World's Leading Online Employment Provider!

- Reach an Audience of over 40 Million Individuals on the Internet!

- Used by 200 of the Leading Fortune 500!

- The First and Original!

- On Prodigy, CompuServe, America Online , and the Internet!

- Our Site Gets More Than 1,000,000 Hits per Day!

- We Have the Largest Online Database of Employment Ads

What should you believe? Unfortunately, like most advertisements, truth is often the modest mortar that holds together the bricks of wishful thinking. We are unaware of any unbiased statistical studies that clearly quantify the response and success rates of ad placements of such services.

Comments on success are anecdotal instead of statistical. In all fairness, the same can be said about newspapers. We have seen no research reports that state "for every 100 ads placed in the Peoria Post, you can expect to get 20 hires." That's not to say that these services don't work - many of them do work extremely well. One thing we do know is that several leading corporations are using several online employment advertising services and monitoring the results to determine the best direction for their advertising dollar. Obviously, it must be working because many more organizations are jumping daily on the online employment advertising bandwagon. Let's face it: The cost per ad for several of these services is so low that even with limited success, online advertising is a much better value than the traditional newspaper ad - and smart organizations and recruiters have figured this out!

NET NOTE

Internet snake oil takes many forms and shapes. In addition to the platitudes about success and numbers of hits, we have recently seen a "research study" about Online Advertising that indicates one online advertising service is hands-down superior than the rest. But a modestly close reading of the research study discloses, in fine print, that the research was conducted from a limited set of respondents from the online job advertiser's customer list

Imagine if the company that made Commodore computers commissioned a study of computer users and gave the company conducting the research a list of their most active users. The results, of course, would show that Commodore outperforms IBM, Compaq, Packard Bell, Dell, Apple, and so on. But would you take it seriously? Just recently, a prominent recruiting industry periodical quoted from the painfully slanted report, apparently without checking the methodology buried in its text. By the way, Commodore was an excellent computer, but just didn't make it in the marketplace over the long run.

THE MARKET

Before you tackle some of the technical aspects of Internet advertising, it is critical that you understand one thoroughly non-technical, three-century-old concept that has more impact on your online job ad than computers, bytes, electrons, and e-mail: the market. A market is nothing more than a location or medium that both buyers and sellers find productive and cost efficient for making exchanges. All the fluff about hits, traffic, links, number of ads, hours online, number of subscribers, and so on are all just rough measures of how well employers find good candidates and how well candidates find good employers.

Adam Smith, the venerable author of The Wealth of Nations, might consider computers a miracle, but he would immediately recognize the free flow of information about jobs and job candidates on the Internet as a classic example of a market. The beauty of online job advertising comes not from the speed of rushing electrons, but from the broad scope of access that raw processing power makes possible.

When making an online job advertising decision, keep the market foremost in your mind. All locations on the Internet are not the same by any means, and the numbers can be very deceptive. The value comes from large numbers of qualified talent sellers meeting large numbers of buyers on a regular basis at select locations. The Internet is different only in that changes can take place very rapidly.

FORGET YOUR NEWSPAPER PARADIGM

In the pre-Internet days, your choices were rather limited: you could place an ad in the Sunday newspaper. The cost for such an ad placement was based on the size of the ad and the newspaper distribution. The larger the ad and the greater the distribution, the more expensive the ad. Your decision about where to place the ad (in the Peoria Post? in the New York Times?) was based on which venue would bring the most success for the dollar invested. If your organization was in Peoria and you needed to hire an administrative assistant from the local talent pool, the

Peoria Post would do just fine. But to hire an investment banker, your best bet would be to undertake a national recruiting strategy, making the New York Times a better choice. The ad in the Times would be more expensive, but worth the cost.

When making such a newspaper choice, the following factors are considered:

- **Distribution** - How many individuals will see my ad?

- **Ad Size** - How big an ad is needed to attract the attention of the reader?

- **Location** - From which region of the country do I need to attract talent?

With Internet advertising, the dynamics of placing an ad are quite different. Ad size is no longer a concern because the cost of newsprint no longer enters the equation. Also, because the Internet is global in nature, ads can be viewed worldwide, making geographical location less of a concern. Your primary concern in deciding where to place your ads, then, is the distribution of the ad, or what we call traffic to the ad.

TRAFFIC

The most important component to consider regarding an employment advertising service is traffic: simply, how many people are actually going to the site to look at the job ads. If The New World Employment Center job site is the most technically brilliant and user-friendly site, it might garner a write-up in Internet News or win an award from a national magazine, but it does nothing to help you get your positions filled!

Getting People to the Site Is What Counts!

As you have probably ascertained, it doesn't take much to place job advertisements on the Web. All you need is a $30 book on HTML programming, a shareware HTML editor, space on a server, and presto! You can place a job advertisement (or basically anything) on the Internet. Great. Likewise, you can write a job ad on a piece of paper and place it on the outside door of your business and hope to catch the attention of passers-by and clients who enter. However, in both cases, the probability of success is slim. Neither method really provides the traffic necessary to sustain a good recruiting effort. Neither a web site nor your front door constitutes a market.

The reason your organization pays for advertising in any medium is based on the traffic that medium brings to your advertisement. You pay dearly for an advertisement in the Wall Street Journal or the New York Times because of the audience it reaches through each newspaper's massive distribution. TV and radio ad rates are based on the audience viewing the event - remember the $1 million, 30 second Super Bowl ads.

Similarly, one of the reasons you pay for online advertising services is because of the traffic they bring to your employment ads. In general, the top quality sites with premium service and traffic charge considerably more than startup sites with less traffic ($150 per ad versus less than $50).

On the Internet, a site's traffic is related to three important components:

- number of links - how many other Web sites point to this one?

- quality of links - is this site linked from any high-traffic sites?

- advertising - does the company running this site purchase additional advertising to get the word out about their Web site?

TARGETED TRAFFIC

The one big caveat is with the case of targeted traffic. If by chance you are searching for a specific skill set or group of individuals then by all means a targeted job site may be valuable. For instance, The World Statistical Association may run a website that attracts Phd statisticians and may be an excellent place to advertise. But BEWARE, we have seen several job sites appear based on specific occupations, regions, and/or ethnic populations that have little traffic yet use their "Targeted Audience" hook as their main selling point.

NUMBER OF LINKS

One of the most important factors that defines success for any Web site or service is the number of links that Web site has obtained. Think of links as calling cards spread across the Internet - the more, the better. Links let people at other sites know about a particular site and instantly access that site with the click of a mouse. All quality general employment ad services have links to their sites that number in the thousands.

Links take a fair amount of time to build, thus making it hard for startup services to compete with long-standing services. Generally, the services that have the most links are the ones that have been around the longest: Career Mosaic, Career Web, E-span, NationJob, and the TMP family.

Links come in all shapes and sizes, and range from a major link on America Online, CompuServe, or Netscape to a mention of the site in Bob Smith's home page. Although links vary in type and quality, a general statement can be made about links: The more links to a site, the better traffic to that site. Other factors contribute to a site's success, but having people pointing to you electronically has no harmful effect whatsoever.

Figure 5.1 The BellSouth.net home page for Research Triangle, N.C.

Figure 5.1 is the startup page that subscribers receive each time they log on to BellSouth's Internet service, BellSouth.net, in the Research Triangle area of North Carolina. BellSouth has nicely organized links to information that they deem important to subscribers in the immediate area. Under the Home and Life section, subscribers can click a link that takes them to the Employment Listing section.

Figure 5.2 shows the Employment Listing page of BellSouth.net. Links are provided to several major national job sites, including Classifieds 2000, Career Mosaic, CareerWeb, E-span, et al. Imagine you are a first-time Internet user, and you passively view the employment section. You click the mouse button and

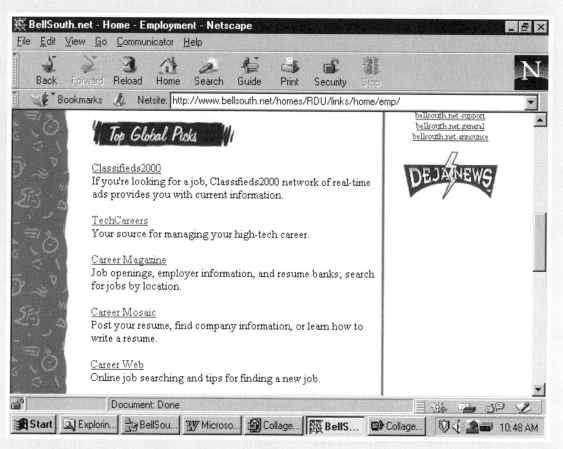

Figure 5.2 BellSouth.net Employment Page for Research Triangle, N.C.

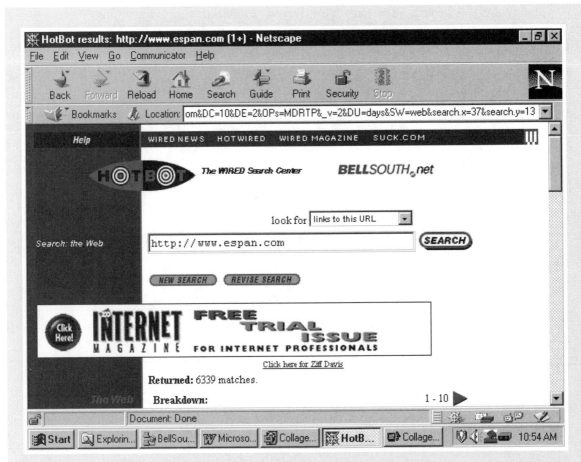

Figure 5.3 Link search for E-Span - 6339 Links Found

come across the dozen or so job services and give each a try, maybe even submit your resume to a few. You may never visit the hundreds of other job sites on the Internet, and you may never miss them.

There are over 4,000 job sites on the Internet. However, in the BellSouth example, only a handful of job sites are noted in BellSouth's site. This is not an accident. The major online advertising services do everything they can to seek out new alliances, build new links, and, in some cases, they pay dearly for them.

❑ ❑ ❑

Assessing Links to a Site

There is a little-known way to roughly approximate the number of links a particular site has to it on the Internet. One of the leading search engines on the Internet, Hot Bot, allows you to search for Web sites that have links to another Web site that the user defines. In essence, you can ask the search engine to tell you how many Web pages in its database have links to the employment site *http://www.jobs.com*. Hot Bot takes a few seconds to search the database, and returns a number to you that specifies how many links a site has, and lists each site that is linked to the site in question. To perform this task, follow these steps:

1 Go to the Hot Bot search engine site on the Internet at *http://www.hotbot.com*.

2 Enter the Web site of the employment advertising site like so: *http://www.employmentsite.com* (employmentsite is a placeholder; actual entries might include *http://www.careermosaic.com*, *http://www.espan.com*, and so on).

3 Select search "the Web" for "links to this URL" from the 2 drop down boxes on the main page.

4 Click search, and an approximation of the number of links to that Web site will appear.

Figures 5.3 - 5.4 display the results of a link search on some major employment Web sites.

The number of links to a Web site is a good way to determine whether the employment advertising site you are considering is a leader in the field. The site should have over a thousand links to it to be considered a major player on the Internet. Use this tool as a quantitative measure of a site's presence on the Internet.

Quality of Links

Please understand that not all links are equal. Although it is nice that Web sites such as the Appalachian State University Career Center links to employment sites such as Career Mosaic, Espan, and 4-Work, it is much better for the online advertising sites if they have direct links from the major Internet access providers or

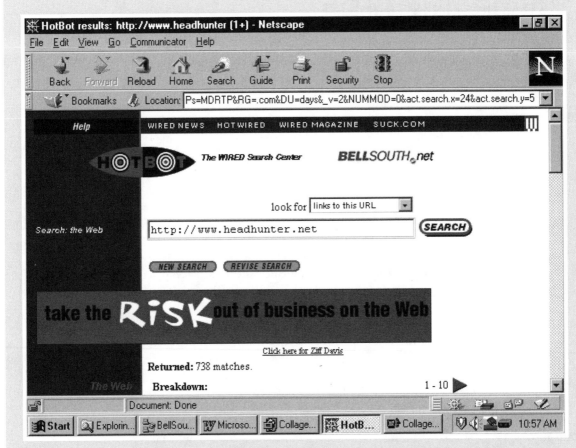

Figure 5.4 Link search for Headhunter.Net - 738 Links Found

from highly accessed Internet sites. After all, traffic on these sites is exceedingly robust compared to traffic on a local college's career site. Important major links include:

- America Online

- CompuServe

- Prodigy

- Microsoft Network

- Netcom

- AT&T

- MCI

- Sprint

- Any of the new regional Baby Bell Sites

- All the major search engines: Yahoo, AltaVista, HotBot, Excite, Infoseek, etc.

Links may be either freely given text based entries on a given website or highly graphical banner ads which are purchased to provide additional flow of traffic to the job site in question.

Figure 5.5 shows the Workplace Classifieds section on America Online. This section of America Online attracts a high number of individuals looking for employment and other information. E-Span has a banner ad link which when clicked with a mouse will access the E-span job site.

Because AOL is the world's largest Internet access provider, these links are worth their weight in gold to online ad services (and they are paying in gold to get them). These links deliver huge amounts of traffic to these Web sites and determine the major players in the job advertising field.

LINKS FOR SALE, LINKS FOR SALE

When the Web was new and had the feel of a community, it was common courtesy to share multiple links between sites and help each other out. As the Web has moved toward the commercial realm, it has become very obvious that links have important economic value. High-traffic sites, such as Netscape and USA Today, and online services, such as AOL and CompuServe, have become well aware of the economic value of the traffic they generate and charge for links to their sites.

These companies used to welcome the placement of links in their sites, often free of charge. Now, however, they are beginning to charge to put information and links in their sites. Extensive negotiations have ensued to establish linkages from specific sites. What were free linkages yesterday have turned into purchased links and banner advertisements today!

Several leading online employment ad services have purchased keywords from

Figure 5.5 AOL's Workplace Classifieds with E-Span Banner Ad.

leading Internet search engine services. When a user enters a specific keyword into a search engine, a banner ad for the online employment ad service appears. Keywords such as career, employment, and job are often linked to specific banner ads on online employment ad services. Figures 5.6 illustrates what happens when the keyword career is entered into the Yahoo search engine. Notice the banner ad that appears on top of the page. This is no coincidence. Sites such as Yahoo often generate ads related to the topic for which a surfer is searching.

❑   ❑   ❑

Figure 5.6 The return screen when career is entered as a keyword in the Yahoo search engine.

ADVERTISING

Not everyone finds an employment site by seeing it listed online. Sometimes people hear about Web sites via advertising in traditional venues such as print, radio, or television. In these cases, job seekers simply go online and enter the Web site address to access the service. Because this is a new medium, leading services are using all sorts of techniques to get the word out, including

- **Newspaper & Magazine Advertising** - leading online employment advertising services mention their sites in such publications as the Wall

Street Journal, Business Employment Weekly, USA Today, Personnel Journal, and leading computer magazines.

- **Radio & TV Advertising** - some online advertising services advertise heavily on local cable and radio outlets in major metropolitan areas across America.

- **Press Releases** - Job sites are continually using every means possible to market the value of their services online. Some have taken to flooding the news wires with information on every statistic and new wrinkle their site may possess. Who is the target for these releases: the media who may use the release to write or broadcast information about the site, and the thousands of Internet users who sign up to news delivery services on the Net.

- **Billboard Advertising** - In major cities across America billboards are popping up with the www.ourjobsite.com plastered across them.

MORE THAN JUST TRAFFIC

Besides traffic, you should consider a few other important factors before choosing an online advertising service. Several sites draw lots of traffic, but not all sites are created equal, nor do all organizations placing ads have the same needs. Here are additional factors you should consider:

- **Ease of Use** - How Web functional and technically informed must you be to use this service? Will the job candidates that you want to reach find it equally appealing?

- **Local Support** - Is anyone available to come in, give a presentation, and help you get going?

- **Special Posting Features** - Are your ads posted to Usenet groups, to Yahoo? Can the service help you post to multiple sites on the Internet?

- **Ad Removal** - Are your ads removed from the Internet in a timely fashion?

- **Database Quality** - Is the database of ads professional in appearance? Are the ads in the database professionally written? What is the level of junk ads in the database? Junk ads are generic blind ads from headhunters looking for resumes to bolster their sagging sales, or ads designed to lure the desperate into acquiring job search services. (These may be hard to spot but usually are evident from their shortness of length and vagueness of source.)

- **Links From Your Ads** - Will the service allow you to link from each of your ads to additional information on your own corporate recruiting web site?

- **Search Criteria** - Can users conduct full-text keyword searches? Are options available to search by state, city, or job category?

- **Response Options** - Can users respond online immediately?

- **Special Upload Features** - Some sites will work with you to upload ads from your internal corporate jobs databases. Others license technology to copy ads from your corporate website and place them on their service. (Be careful, they may upload more than you want!).

- **Service Appearance** - Does the job ad site look professional in appearance and content?

- **Passive Job Seeker Appeal** - Will people who are not looking for a job stop in just for a peek?

- **Database Size and Competition** - How many ads are there in the database? How many will compete with your ads?

- **Statistical Analysis of Ad Visits** - You will want to track how many individuals access each ad you place online.

- **Cost** - Doing a cost benefit analysis, is advertising on this service worth the money?

EASE OF USE

Although some organizations don't mind personally writing and placing their ads online through e-mail or other means, other organizations prefer to fax their ads in and let someone else do the composing and online ad placement.

We suggest that you determine which option is best for you. Clearly, you can surf around the Internet and place your ads online in several services, both free and commercial. If you are comfortable with a word processing software program and take the time to develop familarity with the processes, it will quickly become routine. But is that the most productive use of your time? Probably not. Consider letting an online ad professional do it for you, or delegate this task to a specialist within your organization and spend your time on other aspects of the recruitment process - interviewing, assessing, and negotiating.

If you do choose to take a hands-on approach within your organization, we suggest you look closely at the input interfaces on the particular services you are considering:

- Are they user friendly?

- Do they work? Can you access and transmit information fast and easily?

- Can you convert existing data files (job descriptions, company information, etc.) easily into the format desired?

NET NOTE

We're amazed by how many online employment advertising services provide no fax-based services! It seems strange that in an emerging field with approximately 10 percent penetration of the market, such services eliminate the other 90 percent. Fortunately, we did find some services who do provide fax based services.

LOCAL SUPPORT

Let's face it, not everyone reading this book is Internet trained. If you are uncomfortable with this new technology, it would be reassuring for someone to give you a demonstration and answer your questions face to face. If you are not Internet savvy, your questions might include

- What are the best local Internet services?

- How do I get this e-mail system to work?

In the beginning, almost all major commercial online advertising services operated from centralized offices with no local representation. No one was available to help the client get going. This was a major issue for organizations that were new to the Internet. Fortunately, this is rapidly changing, and a few services now have local representation to provide the support that many organizations need. Still others can recommend training and support for bringing your staff up to speed.

Special Posting Features

Wouldn't it be nice if you signed up with a commercial online ad service and they automatically posted your ads to all those free Internet sites we mentioned earlier? Guess what! Some services do just that. Ask your online ad service whether they can post your ads to Usenet groups, Yahoo, and other sites in your area.

In addition, some services will cross post your ads to other competing services. Because Internet job ads are so cheap, many corporations place their ads in multiple services, but use one service as the exclusive distribution hub for their ads.

Ad Removal

Are your ads removed from the Internet in a timely fashion? This is a thorny issue in the Internet community. In an effort to boost database size, several services retain ads online for an extended period of time. Unfortunately, their customers continue to receive resumes long after the job is filled. Loyalty to such a site by both companies and job seekers will and should dissipate rapidly.

Database Quality

Not all databases are equal. Some have a standard format for the ads, giving the database a highly organized, professional appearance. Other databases accept anything in any order. We suggest that you go online and look at the databases of many online ad services. Put yourself in the shoes of a job seeker, and ask yourself: "Is this a site I would want to return to?" Usenet sites and other free posting areas are notorious for containing low quality ads.

You should also be concerned about the number of junk ads in the database. Several free and unlimited-posting databases contain ads for multilevel marketing opportunities and "get-rich-quick" schemes. Also, some recruiting firms place bogus ads online to source candidates for potential jobs in the future. They even bundle the resumes they obtain from those ads together and incorporate them into sales presentations to clients, touting the quantity and quality of job candidates with whom they maintain contact.

Another negative practice is to run the same ad several times, but to slightly manipulate the title and job description to attract more candidates. Recruiters have learned that the more ads they place in these services, the more resumes they get. We have even heard of a service that places bogus ads in free areas of the Internet, and sells the resumes they receive to other recruiters.

Ask yourself: do I want to pay extra to be in a better database? Or do I mind having my ad among the sites with the practices just mentioned?

Figures 5.7 and 5.8 show the difference between the ways ads are displayed in CareerWeb versus a major Usenet group. Note the professional appearance of CareerWeb database compared to the haphazard way postings are displayed in the Usenet group.

LINKS FROM YOUR ADS

One of the wonders of the Internet is the hyperlink, which is briefly covered in Chapter 3. As your experience with the Internet grows your organization may decide to hyperlink from your ads to additional company information, application blanks, or even assessment questionaires. The simple hyperlink is easy to add to your ads and will greatly enhance your recruitment strategy.

BUT - some online advertising services refuse to allow hyperlinks from your paid ads to additional information. Still others charge thousands of dollars for the privilege to hyperlink to off site information.

SEARCH CRITERIA

You need to determine how job seekers will search for your postings. At the very least, your job ads should be in a full-text keyword-searchable database. This means that any word contained in the body of the ad can be searched. In addition, candidates should be able to search for your postings by city, state, or selected job category.

❏ ❏ ❏

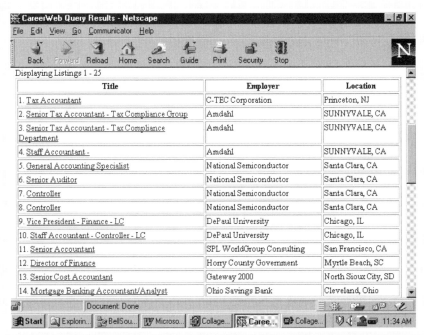

Figure 5.7.
CareerWeb

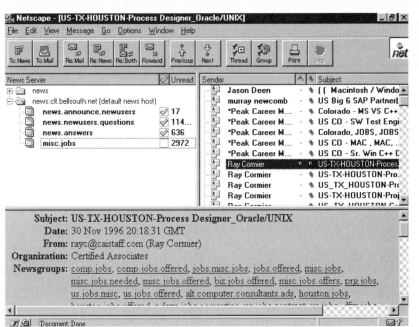

Figure 5.8.
Ads in misc.jobs
Usenet group.

WARNING

Some services offer keyword searches only on the title of the job ad.

Some services even offer keyword searches directly from your company's Web page. Still other services have agent technology, whereby job seekers enter their search criteria into the database, receive all ads currently in the database that match their criteria, and receive new ads as they become available via e-mail. Better search technology means that more candidates will view your jobs, which means that you will receive more resumes from qualified candidates.

RESPONSE OPTIONS

Imagine that a candidate who is perfect for the job you need to fill sees your ad online. Now comes the hard part: getting a resume from the candidate. If candidates have to use the postal service or a fax machine to send their resumes, a sizable portion of these candidates may never make it to the responding phase. Some services allow candidates to store their resumes online and e-mail them to your organization if they are interested in the job you need to fill. This is one way commercial sites boost response rates as compared to free posting areas.

SPECIAL UPLOAD FEATURES

Many organizations have job data stored in internal databases or on corporate Intranets. Some job sites will write special code to aid in automatically uploading your internal corporate jobs databases. Others job sites license technology to copy ads from your corporate website and place them on their service.

SERVICE APPEARANCE

What does a job seeker think when he visits a site with out-of-date links and stone-age graphics? Looks count. Make sure the online ad service you choose has a professional appearance that will attract candidates time and time again. Basic text based websites may have been the standard two years ago, but quality graphics and Java are the norm today!

❑ ❑ ❑

Passive Job Seeker Appeal

One problem with job databases is that they tend to attract large numbers of individuals who are currently unemployed or who are very unhappy with their current job. While many of these people make fine candidates, most corporate recruiters also want to locate people who are not currently looking for a job.

To attract the valuable passive job seeker, some services have set up alliances or co-branding efforts with several major Web sites. The concept is simple: Web users go to a particular site for fun, education, or information and view as part of the site a jobs database. Ask your online employment advertising service what they do to attract the passive job seeker.

Database Size and Competition

How big is this database of jobs? What kinds of ads are it? These issues should be your primary concerns. If you place an ad for a C++ programmer and you find that over 2,000 C++ programmer ads are already in the database, you might not get much of a response. Take a look at the database and see how many ads like yours are already online. Consider calling some of the people placing the ads to gauge what kind of response they have received.

INTERNET SNAKE OIL RISES AGAIN

One trick in measuring database size (number of job ads) is to report one job with several locations as multiple jobs. So if Burger King needs a restaurant manager in 260 cities that counts as 260 ads! Recently one popular service advertised 25,000+ ads online. BUT, when the site was analyzed only about 3,000 individual job descriptions were found!.

Statistical Reports

At a minimum the online service you use should provide you with information as to the number of individuals who access each ad you have online in their database. Make sure you backup all statistical reports you receive with your own solid monitoring.

❑ ❑ ❑

NET NOTE

The word "hit" is a generic term used by many online services to define the number of individuals who view your ads. For instance, you may be sent a report which states your job ad received 300 hits last week (300 individuals viewed your ad).

Recently we discovered one online ad service which counts a "hit" each time the title of the job is loaded on a page vs. when the entire ad is viewed. Clients of this service receive hit reports numbering in the thousands per month yet receive no more resumes than the folks who get reports in the hundreds from other services.

COST

In the end, it all boils down to a question of cost versus benefits. Unfortunately it can be very difficult to consider all options and arrive at a decision. In an attempt to compare one service versus another, we suggest costing out each service based on a mythical model we call "The Corporate Recruiting Solution". This is a total package a medium sized organization will need to meet their yearly online recruiting needs.

The Corporate Recruiting Solution consists of the following dynamics:

- Placement of 200 job ads during one calendar year.

- Links from each ad to a recruiting website which is designed and maintained on the company's webserver.

- Access to a resume database for accessing additional candidates.

The next step is to cost out several services you are considering using based on this model.

	SITE A	SITE B	SITE C
200 Ad Cost	$10,000	$3,900	$5,400
Links to Corporate Site	$5,000	Free	Free
Resume Database Access	$4,900	$800	Free
Total Solution Cost:	**$19,900**	**$4,700**	**$5,400**
Additional Features:			

Additional Features:

Site A: 3,200 links to the site, radio ads in major markets, billboards,

Site B: 3,700 links to the site, banner ads on AOL / Yahoo / Infoseek , major alliances with Compuserve and Engineering News.

Site C: 2,700 links to the site. Initial fee of $2,800 plus $300 per month. Includes professionally designed Corporate profile page and batch uploading of ads. Distribution of ads to Usenet groups, Yahoo.

CONCLUSION: Based on the data gathered Sites B&C appear to be quite a bargain whereas site A appears highly overpriced. A prudent decision for management would be to attempt to purchase trial membership in sites B&C and test out Site A by purchasing a few ads. With this data decisions can be made on whether additional purchases on site A are cost effective.

TWO WAYS TO LOOK AT WEB ADVERTISING

In our years of both selling online ads and consulting with organizations on integrating Internet job ads into their recruiting operations, we have noticed two distinct attitudes towards using online job ads:

- One type of Internet Ad buyer searches for the most cost effective service, pinches pennies, and searches for the most bang for the buck on a per ad basis.

- The other type of Internet Ad buyer considers the broader scope of the predicament they are in: They are losing money every day positions remain unfilled; tens of thousands of dollars are spent on newspaper advertisements and contingency recruiter fees weekly; while the Internet is intrinsically economical and effective. This latter group buys a series of online job ads in various services. So why not use multiple services? After all, it still is a fraction of the cost of competing recruitment options.

What kind of Internet ad buyer are you?

THE PAID VERSUS FREE DEBATE

The debate continues regarding the commercial nature of the Internet. On one hand, you have the free services provided by Usenet groups, Yahoo, and the federal network of state based unemployment security commissions. On the other hand, you have paid commercial services, such as Career Web, Career Mosaic, and so on, that offer paid employment advertising. So why pay? Simply put, if you want superior traffic, service, and response, you have to pay for it.

We are always amazed by the select few recruiters who pride themselves in pinching pennies and don't spend a cent on paid employment advertising on the Internet. We hear stories about how they spend hours posting ads to free areas of the Web, and about the small (by our standards) number of resumes they receive. Sure, there are free posting areas on the Web that have been valuable in the past, but the fate of free Web services follows a consistent pattern:

- Because the service is free, headhunters and other recruiting organizations fill it with ads of every description, diluting the success it could have enjoyed.

- Because the service is free, the content of information going into it is rarely monitored. The quality of information is suspect at best.

- Because the service is free, information is rarely removed from it in a timely fashion.

- Free usually equates with a lack of user friendliness. Often, free services require you to spend considerably more time on the Web posting jobs compared to the time you would spend posting jobs via commercial employment advertising services.

There are two hidden costs of free ads:

- The productive time of recruiters, whose key function is to contact ad respondents, screen for top candidates, and sell them on the job opportunity, is diminished. Having those key people performing routine Usenet uploads, keying in already-drafted online job ads, and performing other routine work is not a wise investment of time, especially when there are good resumes in house that merit a prompt follow-up. Web surfing is habit forming, but not always productive, and human resources management needs to guard against creating Internet junkies and losing good recruiters.

❑ ❑ ❑

- The administrative time of staff, whose functions include sorting and processing incoming resumes, is diminished. If the tracking tags (codes) indicate that a service generated 94 resumes, 91 of which were worthless and 3 of which were only marginally useful, consider rewriting the ad and dumping the service (even if it was free). Useless resumes eat up valuable time.

The best road to success is to give multiple services, both free and paid, a try. Make sure you code your ads and measure the responses.

NEWSPAPERS VERSUS ONLINE EMPLOYMENT ADVERTISING SERVICES

Will your newspaper run a full-featured online version of your job ad on their Web site to complement the three column inch display ad you have purchased for their Sunday want ads? It can't hurt to ask. But remember: Ads gathered by newspapers are designed for newspapers, not for the online world. If your newspaper posts your ad online, that certainly helps, but job seekers won't be able to use the resume posting and search features found in the sites of leading online employment ad service providers.

If you advertise a position in the local newspaper, and if that newspaper posts its help-wanted section online, should you post the job ad in other services as well? Obviously, sites such as CareerPath can direct additional traffic to your ad. However, wait a week or two and measure the response that services like Career-Path provide before you jump solely into the online world. After all, you paid dearly for that Sunday help wanted ad; why spend another hundred dollars if the Sunday ad will produce results?

THE WAR OF THE RECRUITMENT AD AGENCIES

Not since the Renaissance struggles of popes, kings, and emperors in Italy has the competition been so fierce and the lines of battle so difficult to perceive; the recruitment ad agencies have seized on the economic advantages of Internet job advertising with the resolve and restraint of feudal princes. The once calm competition for your corporate job ads has gotten nasty, but a reduced level of cost to you and other clients is not indicated.

Historically, human resource professionals turned to a recruitment advertising agency to help place effective media advertising. The agency staff helped clients develop effective job ads and select the most effective venues for the job ads. Newspapers and trade journals were often the primary choices.

The agency received 15% of the ad costs for those services. The media selected delivered the ads.

But the Internet disrupts this cozy, conventional relationship.

If an agency places your online job ad with a typical commercial job site, your cost will be less that 10% of the cost of a comparable newspaper ad. Of course, 15% of 10% is 1.5%, and if they provide equally professional guidance with the transaction, their profit margins will become cramped if not negative. Needless to say, whether the ads are successful or not for the corporations buying them, this business model simply will not work for the ad agencies.

The ad agencies have reacted with a two pronged response. The first is to assure their loyal clients that online job ads are a passing fad, like hula hoops and CB radios. This approach is their best option, for as long as they can get away with it.

The second is more innovative - they create their own online commercial job sites to handle the job ads of their clients. As you can imagine, if an ad agency began routing a significant fraction of their clients' business to a newspaper that was a wholly owned subsidiary of the ad agency, some of the clients might have questions about getting adequate value for their money.

The collateral businesses also accept job ads from corporations who are not agency clients, but they quickly become prospects. Whenever possible, clients new and old are switched to the old standby hard copy media where more profits are available for the agencies. The captive jobs databases do not just generate prospects, they also deny other agencies income by placing the ads online. Ad agency A would rather that a company buy an inexpensive but effective online job ad from their subsidiary than buy either a newspaper or online job ad from ad agency B.

The situation is dynamic and the press releases tend to confuse as much as enlighten clients. Some picture it as an added service, others saw Internet gold, but the truth is your trusted ally may in fact own the media they now recommend! But the industry hasn't mentioned the obvious potential for conflict of interest.

Two major problems are developing:

1. Your trusted ally, the person you hire to make wise and unbiased decisions about your recruitment dollar may be pressured to push their own organization's affiliated service (recruitment advertising account coordinators have complained, very discretely about such pressure).

2. Even if your recruitment advertising agency has no Internet Connection, they may be reluctant to recommend an online service which is owned by another recruitment advertising agency - but can you blame them ? - they don't want to both lose you and give your business to a competitor.

S U M M A R Y

The most important factor in choosing an online employment advertiser is the amount of traffic that advertiser's site receives. Traffic is the result of three key factors:

- The number of links to a given Web site

- The quality of links to a given Web site

- The amount of advertising for the Web site through traditional means such as print, radio, and television

Other factors to consider when choosing an online employment advertiser include

- Ease of use

- Local support

- Special posting features

- Ad removal

- Database quality

- Links from your Ads

- Search criteria

- Response options

- Special Upload Features

- Service appearance

- Passive job seeker appeal

- Database size and competition

- Statistical Analysis of Ad Visits

- Cost

If you don't use source codes to assess your success, a continuing evaluation of effectiveness will be impossible. Put the " m" in human resource management.

CHAPTER

WEB PAGE WARNINGS

BILLY BOB'S BARBECUE BILLBOARD

As soon as William Robert Hampton mustered out of the Army with his Vietnam combat pay and other accumulated life savings in hand, he returned to Cooters End, North Carolina, to fulfill two long term ambitions - to open up his own barbecue restaurant and to marry Wilma Sue Cunningham. Because her family doubted that he would ever amount to anything and she insisted on getting their permission to marry, the restaurant came first, and he named it after himself. "Billy Bob's Barbecue." The Hampton family's secret recipe for barbecued spare ribs (see Appendix G) and the location at the intersection of I-90 and NC 44 guaranteed the enterprise would be a modest success, but there was nothing modest about Billy Bob.

After some negotiations over a quart of Jack Daniels with his Uncle George, they agreed on a long term lease of some property along I-90 for the installation of a billboard to catch the eye of tourists and beach goers. Then he contracted with two of his cousins to build it. The collaboration of the county's best shade tree mechanic and a Chapel Hill visual arts major was a sight to behold when installed three months later.

The Billy Bob's Barbecue billboard was 40 feet tall, 110 feet wide, and rested on a 70 feet tall, two pillared steel platform. It featured a rocking chair (rocking) and a 30 by 60 feet rack of well illuminated barbecued spare ribs with pink neon accents. The lacquer painted spare ribs, in 20-inch thick bas relief, almost smelled good. With five hidden aerators generating a moist head of steam over the spare ribs, they looked fresh from the grill and ready to eat from two miles away. The fluorescent lights attracted attention from much farther away and pulled enough amps to entice Carolina Power and Light to install a second local substation. Business boomed.

The folks who came in once tended to come back. In addition to the tasty spare ribs, there were five kinds of eastern North Carolina barbecue, succulent fried catfish, Angus steaks, okra fried and boiled, chittlins, homemade biscuits, banana pudding for dessert, and a variety of other southern eating delights. When customers had to wait for a table or were too full to walk to the car just after a meal, they relaxed in rocking chairs overlooking a low country lake and fed the oversized cooters lolling below in the water.

Everyone admired the sign. It became a scenic attraction all by itself; families traveling late at night developed a standard ritual for passing the site. At about six miles away, parents would wake up the children so they would not miss it, and at one mile the driver would slip on sunglasses to prevent impaired vision. Some tourists claimed it was more inspirational than the PTL Club and more relaxing than watching the North Carolina General Assembly at work. It was a cultural innovation for the state; you could enjoy the sign and the barbecue without being preached at.

The business prospered. Wilma Sue and Billy Bob got married.

But Uncle George, whose ethics and taste had been developed long before he retired from moonshining, was distressed that Billy Bob was making so much money at his restaurant and the annual lease payments for the billboard property failed to cover Uncle George's sporting expenses. Other local entrepreneurs had also noted the billboard success, and over barbecue spare ribs at Billy Bob's, they cut their own billboard deals with Uncle George. His swampy 1/2 mile strip along I-90 otherwise produced little except weeds and road kill.

Soon there was a billboard every fifty yards along the property, and the Billy

Bob Barbecue billboard, while clearly still the aesthetic best and brightest, no longer ensnared nearly as much traffic. The combined and concentrated lights piqued the interest of astronauts passing overhead and raised concerns at the FAA because of the distinct resemblance to a series of landing lights.

Business dropped off seriously and Wilma Sue threatened to go home to Mother when Billy Bob suggested she make fewer shopping trips to Walmart.

NOTE

As you may have gathered, the point so far in this rural epic is that an overused advertising resource loses its effectiveness very rapidly. Web pages are more fashionable and less expensive than billboards ever were or will be. But, the hot new software for creating Web pages makes them a commodity, and even if you buy or create your own electronic diamond, it can get lost in the sandy expanse of the information beach. Even the most interested parties may never find your Web page on the Internet.

In desperation, Billy Bob pulled his last quart of Jack Daniels out of the cabinet and drove to Charlotte to see his cousin Johnny, who had just gotten his MBA at UNC Charlotte. His mother, always proud, claimed Johnny was a wizard at marketing, and Billy Bob hoped that Johnny had forgotten who introduced him to the disappointments of snipe hunting. The Jack Daniels and a sunny day helped.

After some discussion on the deck, a new marketing plan was devised. Billy Bob had to trade in his Ford pickup for a used Yugo and sell his Rolex, but he went home with a plan. Billy Bob had some discount coupons and promotional literature printed up. With them in hand, he cut deals with other retail merchants along NC44 and I-90 to exchange promotional materials and jointly promote each others' enterprises. Billy Bob began pushing the products of 17 other entrepreneurs, and they started promoting Billy Bob's Barbecue. (If you want the details, cut your own deal with Johnny.)

NOTE

The next point is that a key element in the success of Web pages is linking. Web page managers reach agreements with each other about having a links on each others' Web pages, promoting a cross-fertilization of traffic and commerce. Nothing else will be as certain or have anything close to the impact of a good linking strategy (more about this later).

Billy Bob's Barbecue once again became a sound success. Wilma Sue resumed driving to Wilmington to have her hair done once a week. Billy Bob bought a brand new pickup and a bass fishing boat to boot. He stayed away from Rolex watches thereafter, however. They tend to get in the way when you are cooking barbecue in 100 lb. lots, and don't tell time any better than a drugstore wrist watch.

NOTE

This brings up another point: The quality of Web pages varies a lot less than the prices charged for them. Perfectly functional and highly effective Web pages have been designed by outsiders for a cost approximating the price of a case of Jack Daniels, while six figure investments have been dismal failures. A George Foreman, "I'm not going to pay too much for a muffler," attitude is your best guide if you buy a Web page for your recruiting efforts.

This is not to say that the Rolex is not a better watch than the Timex, but if all you need is a reliable timepiece and you are not in a business where you can take the additional prestige to the bank, save your money. If you don't know enough about HTML programming to create a quick and simple Web page of your own, you don't know enough about the technology to be investing four or five figure sums in someone else's learning curve.

A SUPPORTING ROLE FOR WEB PAGES

Before you make a Web page the focal point in your recruiting strategy, seriously consider creating your own local and long distance telephone company to handle all your telephone communications. After the wires are laid and the system is functional, assess your remaining funds and plan your Web page. A Web page is not the answer to your recruiting needs, but it can be a part of the answer. The Billy Bob billboard still attracts customers, but it alone couldn't keep the doors open.

In the stark cold world of Pareto analysis, Web pages fall into that 80 percent of recruiting activities that produce less than 20 percent of the results. Just as a good brandy should follow a fine meal, your recruiting Web page should follow the successful implementation of other recruiting strategies, including online job ads and resume searches. Limit web page expenditures to 5% of your external online ad budget.

The Web page tragedy that continually repeats itself is that Web pages are sold as the only way to recruit on the Internet, the buyers invest bundles before finally giving up, then resolve never to use the Internet in recruiting again because it did not work for them. Those victims deserve our compassion, but they should at least warn others of Web page pitfalls.

THE WEB PAGE DELUGE

A few short years ago, Web pages simply did not exist. The marvelous Internet was text based, UNIX driven, and hacker friendly. With the exception of weather maps and other creations of mainframes and expensive software, the text constraints held the system in a technology straitjacket of single-font, black-and-white visuals. Ingenious programmers with only personal computers wrote hundreds of lines of code that would draw pictures with a combination of ASCII characters.

Until fairly recently, placing appealing pictures on the Internet required the use of exotic, expensive custom software that allowed the use of colors and a broad variety of textures and density (if your mainframe was big enough to handle it). The software cost big bucks, required skilled artists who were also programmers, and demanded much more time than most people wanted to invest. Even when it was possible to create beautiful pictures, the 2400 baud rate of most non-institutional modems severely limited how much could be shared.

But we adjusted. IS departments bought first class computer science talent to program splendid works of computer art. We could even send our computer files to a custom print shop to produce excellent copies on their four color presses. Really good computer graphics cost more than a first class billboard (but less than producing a third rate movie), but we got used to the expense and became comfortable with the awe we felt for their works.

Then we were ambushed by the rapid advance of computer technology. With very little warning, a select few discovered that anyone who could operate Windows, afford $2,500 for a decent Pentium, spring for $500 in software, wasn't color blind, and had the fashion sense of a local florist could very quickly develop excellent computer graphics.

Almost simultaneously, Netscape and Mosaic invented the Web, and everyone with a $50 book (with software under the back flap) could become a fair Web page artist and import those neat graphics into her own private showplace. Even storing it on an Internet provider's server (big computer) became dirt cheap with the slow motion crash of hard drive prices.

The early adapters created beautiful Web pages, which attracted tons of attention and some commercial success. The media touted Web pages as the wave of the Internet's commercial future, and the gold rush to become rich and famous with one's own corporate Web page began. Some people even hyped Web pages as ideal locations to place job ads for corporate openings.

Across the nation, thousands of companies now direct their IS departments to create corporate Web pages for public relations, in-house announcements, product and service promotions, quality bulletins, annual reports, seasonal greetings, and recruiting. The IS manager assigns his best systems analysts and buys the latest Web page software to expedite the creation of a high quality, immediate product.

Meanwhile, hundreds of thousands of technically savvy personal computer owners have bought the book and the software and are creating their own Web pages. However, the very egalitarian Internet has taken its toll, and most Web pages are buried in an electronic field of anonymity. The typical readership is sparse, the majority of readers are current employees, and the second category are stockholders who suspect the Web pages cost ten times more than they actually do (and that is substantial).

But do Web pages work for recruiting?

Seldom. Most companies do not have enough job opportunities of a given category to maintain an adequate selection, creating much too small a market to be effective. Just as buyers and sellers of stocks like to trade in a large market of informed and competitive participants, most eligible job candidates choose to invest their career searching in one or more large commercial jobs databases. And most companies haven't the slightest clue about promoting their Web pages.

Individuals who have a career commitment to winning the big job in their favorite company may discover that it has a Web page of open positions and check it regularly, but they represent a small fraction of the candidates eligible for those positions. They are also often local as well, and the recruiting Web page may well be redundant to the perfunctory display ad in the local regional newspaper. The prime local candidates have networked around the job of their dreams and will know of the opening before anyone tells the human resources department.

Somewhere out there is a corporation that has had considerable and continuing success recruiting through their Web pages, but:

- We haven't heard about it yet.

- We doubt that they have determined the per recruit Web page costs, and if they have, we don't think they will tell you.

- We suspect that they don't use tracking tags and source codes to help them identify the contribution that the Web pages make to their recruiting effort.

Let us introduce you to an online emotional ailment. It is called "Web page envy," and the symptoms are feelings of inadequacy, emotional distress, and inordinate concern with the features on someone else's Web page. There are adolescent overtones of the condition and the cure requires a careful combination of information and maturity. We will provide the information needed about Web pages and personnel recruiting. Maturity is another matter.

Despite the questionable motives behind many of them, Web pages do have a function in recruiting, but it is essential that management make some informed decisions about prices and priorities:

- Your Internet Web page can rapidly become lost in hundreds of thousands of other Web pages on the Internet. Imagine Billy Bob's Barbecue Billboard squeezed into a square mile with 100,000 others. Just finding it would be a challenge unless you had a special interest in seeing it and knew just where to look.

- A good Web page design has very little to do with exotic graphics and slick design, and a lot to do with utility.

- The quality of Web page design is not necessarily linked to Web page cost.

- The recruiting utility of a Web page depends on it being an integral part of a complete Web page strategy, often including other corporate objectives.

- Egos are the most formidable barriers to a good Web page strategy.

You can place an unlimited number of job ads for a year with a commercial online ad service for less than it costs to employ a systems analyst for one month.

A number of companies did enjoy initial successes with their recruiting Web pages, but consider the perspective of the qualified job candidate looking for a better job. Using the keyword approach discussed in Chapter 1, "Internet Job Advertising - The Future is Here Today," you can enter the CPA designation in a variety of Web pages, including some leading online ad databases. The results of

Table 6.1. Searching for CPAs.

COMPANY/SERVICE	NUMBER OF CPA JOBS	WEB ADDRESS
Microsoft Jobs Page	12	www.microsoft.com/jobs
IBM Jobs Page	1	www.empl-ibm.com
Online Career Center	728	www.occ.com
Career Mosaic	482	www.careermosaic.com

this survey are shown in Table 6.1.

Consider the plight of the eager job candidate who only has a few hours to spend looking for a better career opportunity. Would he try to peruse all the jobs databases? Or would he pick a few of the biggest and best who have a large number of jobs that match his career interests?

If any modest successes exist in corporate Web page recruiting, you can count on the company to be a household name with a strong reputation for needing the kinds of professional jobs that dominate their jobs listing. For example, if you are a systems analyst, you might find an IBM listing of job opportunities to be all you need. On the other hand, mechanical engineers, human resources compensation specialists, and quality engineers might logically chose to focus their efforts elsewhere even though IBM hires those kinds of experts as well. That raises an excellent question: If you are a major corporation and know that commercial online job ads are dirt cheap, would you limit your posting of jobs to your own Web page?

We will address broader issues of recruiting strategies and online ads later, but if you already have a Web page, you might want to make a preliminary and confidential assessment of the motives that fostered its creation and maintains ongoing support. The approach is simple: List a significant feature and take a guess about why it exists (either some logical and cost justified reason or "because our competitors did that," "our systems people wanted to create something new and different," and so on). You might even chose to review some of the corporate and organizational jobs databases and hazard a guess about the motives behind them. We have set up a blank form in Table 6.2. Just use a check mark in whichever of the last two columns is appropriate, and be careful about who sees the results.

LOCATION, LOCATION, LOCATION = TRAFFIC, TRAFFIC, TRAFFIC

Yes, the three most important factors in real estate are location, location, and location. And the three most important factors in Web pages (especially online job ads) are traffic, traffic, and traffic.

Whether the motives behind your current or future Web page is rational or ego centered, you must understand that the page's effectiveness will be based largely on how well it is linked or connected to other related Web pages and associated media. One example of Web pages is revealing: Microsoft's.

Microsoft is already a universal computer presence, and has deep pockets and

Table 6.2. Web page assessment.

#	WEB PAGE FEATURE	RESULTS DRIVEN	EGO DRIVEN
1			
2			
3			
4			
5			
6			
7			
8			
9			
10			
11			
12			
13			
14			
Totals			

an aggressive marketing posture. In addition to enough systems people to produce 100 good Web pages a day, Microsoft Explorer is integrated into Windows 95 and is expected to be in all future editions of Microsoft's operating systems and related software. The company has an obvious commitment to the future of the Internet and a lot of logical reasons to make it easy to reach Microsoft's Web pages. If you use newer versions of its software, contacting its Web pages is a few clicks away. Microsoft also is experienced in maintaining online software updates and other online services.

It helps to have a good balance between results and ego, of course. For example, Microsoft's human resource recruiters have actually placed ads on several commercial services for persons to staff their help desks. In addition, they have run banner ads to attract job seekers on several of the leading commercial sites.

Are you likely to attract more attention to your Web sites than Microsoft attracts to its? Not likely, but not necessarily essential either. You may never catch up with Microsoft in the number of software connections to Internet-armed job candidates, but you can create links to related Web pages. The technology is described in Chapter 3.

There are two levels of linking. The first is low tech, easy to do and understand, but nothing to brag about over a cold beer: When you run an online job ad in one of the big online ad databases, simply include a bit of text in the corporate section of the job ad. You might say: "Discover more about our company and other career opportunities by visiting our Web page at *http://www.ourcompany.com/company!*" Or, in the location section, say: "Find out more about scenic and sophisticated Charlotte at *www.ourcompany.com/community!*" Or, in the job description section, say: "For an overview of our career management and advancement training program, survey our Web page site at *www.ourcompany.com/career.*" Or, just invite job seekers to explore your Web site (*www.ourcompany.com*) with a complete menu of information options.

Include your Web site address when you run an ad in the newspaper, in your annual report, and in trade journal ads for your products and services. In short, use your Web site as a focal point for public information, recruiting and otherwise, about your company. But don't forget to tout the other information resources on your Web pages; linking is a two way street. You can create a special link to enable readers to order a copy of your annual report or refer your Web site readers to special articles and company ads in trade journals.

The second kind of linking is more technical, faster, and a key feature of the Web environment. It is called a hyperlink. The "how to's" of hyperlinks, discussed in Chapter 3, are not nearly as important as the "whys" and "whens." Besides, the technology is so widespread, you will easily find a technical person to help, so put any concerns about the technology out of your mind for now.

The short, non-technical explanation of hyperlinks is simple. Have you ever read a document, newspaper, periodical, or instruction manual when the text caused you to ask one of these questions:

- What is the definition of that word?

- Where can I find more information about that concept?

- How does that process really work?

- Can that directive have any impact on my department?

- Who is an authority on that topic?

- How do I talk to the author of this article?

Your standard response, time allowing, is to check the dictionary, find a reference manual, ask a colleague down the hall, or make a quick telephone call to an informed professional colleague. In many cases, the research is more time consuming than rewarding, and your train of thought can be fractured in the process.

The answer to this dilemma, and the biggest advance in reading since Gutenberg invented the printing press, is the hyperlink. Those wonderful programmers have devised a way to identify key words of text that might prompt the kind of questions indicated above, and to allow readers to quickly jump to a wealth of background data that explain the word, phrase, or concept. But the real beauty is not in the speed, but the conceptual ease of the process.

For example, if this book were on an Internet Web page, the term Chapter 3 could be underlined or highlighted in color, and the reader could move to that location in the book not by turning pages, but by simply clicking on the words Chapter 3 with her mouse. To return exactly to her original location upon completion of the digression, the reader would click again, but this time on a left pointing arrow marked "Back". The use of this technology is limited mostly by the imagination of the drafting skills of the writer and her familiarity with the available online resources.

And you haven't heard the half of it yet. What if you don't find all the data you need in Chapter 3? A well designed Chapter 3 will not only tell you a great deal about writing the code for Web page linking, but will also have hyperlinked text to allow the faint of heart to define some of the basic vocabulary in an index, and allow advanced computer users to go much deeper into the topic than the average reader would ever dare. Any source they find on the Internet would have subsequent and diverse levels in which to explore the reader's interest.

But could the reader find his way back? Yes, the software leaves electronic bread crumbs to help find the way home. The reader repeatedly clicks the Back button until she reaches a level that suits her, even to the very beginning of her research adventure if desired. The reader can travel far away from any topic, or deep into it, providing the topic and the pages it is linked to has adequate hyperlinks. Equally valuable, the reader can leave bookmarks behind to help her return directly to a choice information site in the future.

The next pleasant surprise is that these hyperlinks are not limited to the current Web page document. If the Web page designer/writer/author knows the Web page address of a data source, she can attach it to the Web page hyperlink, empowering the reader to easily reach other resources. To carry the book example one step further, you could jump from this book to another text, perhaps covering HTML programming or Visual Basic. Or if the Billy Bob Barbecue story intrigued you, you could hyperlink to a map of eastern North Carolina and jump from there to a list of real restaurants that cook up barbecue spare ribs. You can jump to and from anything anywhere that has a hyperlinked Web page on the Internet.

NOTE

If you can reach it on the Internet, you can hyperlink to it.

But what does all this have to do with online job advertising and using the Internet as a key recruiting tool? Using hard copy corporate resources to publicize your Internet Web location is a useful and dynamic strategy, but it needs a strong, single medium (Internet) strategy to complement it. Begin the strategy making process by asking three major questions:

- Where on the Internet are the people who I want to read my Web page?

- What kinds of data and other content will they expect to find on my Web page?

- What kinds of Internet locations might they choose to find by linking my site to others?

Your objective should be to cross link to as many recruiting related sites as possible, and to integrate your recruiting efforts with complementary corporate Web page applications. Do not delude yourself into thinking that you can make the information highway a one way street that brings all prospective employees to your Web page door. Modestly proficient Web users will do a lot of bouncing around between resources whether you like it or not. You just want a select few hitting your site with interested regularity, and cross linking creates that potential.

Cross linking is a mutual exchange of addresses. You can always reference some other Web site's address without permission, but your key goal is to build up your Web traffic (number of visitors), not theirs. If you do it solo, the benefits are mostly one way, with the only benefit to you being that a special population uses your site as a gateway to others and sometimes visits along the way. If you create a hyperlink to their site in exchange for a hyperlink from theirs to yours, both should receive increased traffic.

Prospective cross linking partners include:

- Suppliers - Unless a supplier is a captive source, it has lots of industry contacts with a direct interest in your business. Improving your visibility can have a significant impact on parts of your business other than recruiting, but ready access to a good Web page where job openings are included in the menu can also attract experienced professionals with skills and motivations that could be of substantial and immediate benefits to your company.

- Corporate customers - For the same reasons as suppliers, corporate customers can be excellent cross linking partners.

- Significant stockholders.

- Colleges and universities who specialize in the professional training that enable your organization to function - Check into the individual departments; they could have their own Web pages. Check your personnel files to see where your organization's stars received their training.

- Trade organizations and professional publications - Most of these organizations are creating Web pages, and cross linking can have mutual benefits. Their clientele tends to be hardworking, ambitious, forward looking, and overachieving. Need we say more?

- Local, state, and federal governments that have significant interaction with your company - This is a valuable back door, and governments are reluctant to decline services to taxpayers, especially corporate. Accept a simple text reference to your site if necessary.

- Any site for which your management and professional staff have created a bookmark to help them find it quickly, excluding those personal interest excursions that they shouldn't be making on company equipment during business hours.

- Commercial or noncommercial online job search and recruiting Web sites - Any kind of link can be very useful.

In addition to looking for sites that appeal to the kinds of people with whom you wish to communicate, you should select those that have enough readers to make the exchange worthwhile. If your site averages 500 readers daily, and the potential partner readership ranges between 0 and 3, the exchange is the equivalent of giving the partner a free hyperlink to their site - unless those 3 people happen to be really key to your recruiting efforts. Don't count on it.

One of the desirable options to look for when working with a commercial supplier of online job ads is an active hyperlink from the job ad to your Web site. Giving a prospective employee your Internet address is one thing; enabling her to instantly access it is another. Both are valuable connectivity options worth exploring. Evaluate the cost of any hyperlinks in the light of your immediate recruiting objectives - it may be cost effective sometimes and too expensive others.

PURCHASING LINKS

Obtaining crosslinks from other sites and major search engines takes time and as we mentioned, often provides less than satisfactory results. In the new economic business model of the Internet many major corporations are outright purchasing links to their job information. What is happening is a trickle down effect:

1 A major site on the Internet gathers a multitude of traffic with information relevant to the population (Search Engines, Magazines, etc.).

2 This major traffic site sells targeted banner ads to job sites which direct traffic to the job sites.

3 The job sites in turn sell your organization banner ads which hyperlink directly to your corporate home page or job information.

While this option is definitely feasible consider several problems with such a model:

1 There are only so many places to place a banner ad on the Internet that are worthwhile. With over 100,000+ employers in America there is not enough space to meet all their needs.

2 Limited space has driven up the cost of such banners out of the reach of most small to mid-size organizations. The going rate for Banner Ads is $40 to $120 per 1,000 impressions. That means, 1,000 people have seen your banner. Once a banner is seen, the individual must click on it to access information. The industry average for individuals who "click thru" to a site from a banner ad is about 1-2%. This would cost you in the neighborhood of $2 to $12 per Visitor! This option is out of reach for many organizations.

The Microsoft's, IBM's, and Nationsbank's of the world may be able to justify such an option, but not the majority of American employers.

S U M M A R Y

A corporate Web page should <u>not</u> be the focal point of your online recruiting strategy. The track record of Web page recruiting is marginal because there are so many Web pages competing for the attention of qualified job candidates. It is very difficult to develop consistently productive, low cost recruiting Web pages, but very few human resources departments will reveal the scope of their failures in this area.

The secret of making Web pages successful is linking. First, coordinate with other in-house corporate Web page opportunities whenever possible. People interested in products and services can also be candidates for careers, and vice versa. Second, be sure that hard copy resources identify your Web page clearly and often, and where possible, reciprocate the courtesy. Third, cross link to a broad number of contacts on the Internet. This is a more technical, but very productive approach for developing your online visibility.

Don't expect your recruiting Web page to start paying off in less than one year, even if you link well and promote it effectively. Two years is a more typical break even point.

The cost of a good Web page can vary dramatically, making tight fisted prudence a good operating plan. Whether your resources are in-house IS personnel or outside vendors, link your understanding of the technology to your investment in it. You can have a productive online recruiting program without any job listing or other Web page presence at all, enabling you to insist that any Web page development and maintenance meet your requirements at a reasonable cost.

Not only are there obviously better sources for job candidates than a recruiting Web page, there are also more pressing and productive demands for your scarce recruiting dollars. One of the outstanding opportunities is the management of the responses that you receive from all resources - online job ads, resume databases, personal referrals, walk-ins, nepotism, and Web pages.

Remember the 5% Rule:

Your expenditures for a recruiting web page should never exceed 5% of your total online recruiting expenditures.

CHAPTER

MANAGING THE RESULTS

O nline job ads can be so successful in terms of quality results and so inexpensive in comparison to other modes of communicating career opportunities that there is a real danger of failing to effectively manage the results. This chapter is a collection of ideas on how to responsibly and effectively manage the results of all communications to job candidates, not just the online job ads.

OUR HERO HARRY

Back in the dark ages of human resources, when it was just called the personnel department, a daring innovator named Harry introduced the "subject matter assessment test" at his company. He had heard about it at both ASTD (American Society for Training and Development) and SHRM (Society for Human Resource Management) meetings. He liked the concept. This relentless revolutionary had despaired at the nodding heads and poor attendance at many corporate training programs, and felt only a modest level of anger toward those who failed to show up, or who mentally departed long before the vital training was complete.

After all, many of the attendees knew almost enough about some of the topics to teach the course themselves and he understood when their minds began to wander. The personnel director insisted that all the relevant details be covered in each class, irrespective of the participants' expertise. The director suggested role playing, overheads, film clips, poster supplements, feedback exercises, discussion groups, progress testing, and learning performance reports (for their bosses). It all sounded good, but enjoyed limited success.

Harry was frustrated but determined. When the director of personnel departed on a three-week vacation, Harry was ready. He managed to have the fifteen persons scheduled for a three-day course in Detoxifying Widgets come to the training area on the preceding Monday for the one-hour subject matter assessment test he had developed. Five of them tested so well that he issued them certificates the next day and told them to report to their regular work stations Wednesday morning instead of coming to the class. He brought in two persons for a remedial review Tuesday afternoon in preparation for the class and the full ten person group managed to cover all they needed to learn on Wednesday and pass the comprehensive exam with flying colors at 3 p.m. that same day.

All fifteen students were pleased, the ten gave Harry glowing evaluations, their managers were delighted with the reduced time away from the job, and the test grades received were significantly above the norm. The CEO heard about Harry's success and telephoned congratulations to his golfing buddy and personnel director, who was at the beach.

The personnel director still had sand in his shoes when he got back from the beach on Friday, and his wrath fell on Harry like a hot stove. The director's background was in training, and he had always taught a course from start to finish. Only the CEO's kind words kept Harry from being fired on the spot; the personnel director liked to hedge his bets. But the subject matter assessment test died a quick death at the company.

Harry was demoted three notches to a personnel recruiter position, but he did have high hopes that the work would be more refreshing. It was, but he noted that every open position resulted in a brand new campaign to find skilled persons interested in working for his company. After two years of agony, he resigned in disgust and took a job working with his brother-in-law in a small recruiting firm.

Harry was stunned by two revelations:

1 The little two man shop retained extensive hard copy records of every qualified job candidate contact, and knew exactly how they had found him or her.

2 By the end of the first year in the business, his junior partner share of headhunter income not only exceeded what he had made the previous year at the other company, but was more than the salary of his old boss, the personnel director.

The moral to this story is that innovation is seldom honored, but good job candidate record keeping will go a long way toward guiding you to recruiting success.

FORMATS FOR RECEIVING RESUMES AND FEEDBACK

In our eagerness to receive some evidence that real, qualified persons are interested in the jobs that become available, we sometimes overlook the mundane necessity of managing the resumes received when our advertising and promotion work is successful. Some preliminary planning will pay off handsomely in both money and time saved.

TRACKING TAGS AND SOURCE CODES

Tracking tags and source codes are vital tools in managing your recruiting campaigns. Specifically, a tracking tag is a short piece of text used in electronic and other communications with job candidates that identifies both the job and the recruiting campaign related to an open position. The source code, on the other hand, identifies the media used to communicate with job candidates. The tracking tag is a recruiting campaign control, the source code tells you which resources were successful. They are both an integral part of the return address which job candidates send back to the employer, automatically indicating the mode of communication that was effective in reaching the job candidate.

For example, you have a job opening for a Total Performance Training developer in the human-resources department, and your internal job code for that job is HR501 (the 501 might tell you something about the pay scale, education requirements, or whatever.) This is the 3rd recruiting job in 1998, providing you with a tracking tag of R98003 to use in general progress and results tracking. Those codes identify the job and your recruiting effort. The internal job code is not needed in the ads, and the tracking tag for future openings for this position could be R98085, or R98015.

The source code, on the other hand, is specific to a communications media. For example, an online job ad in CareerWeb could have the designation - Dept. A. The online job ad address would contain "Dept. A, Job R9703." A Wall Street Journal job ad for the same job would be "Dept. F, Job R9703." The actual coding system you use is not as important as its consistency and flexibility.

The critical source code identifies the mode of communication that generates the response. In planning the promotion of the open position, you select those advertising venues that have worked for that job or type of job in the past, or have real promise for being effective this time. Examine the career opportunity and select from the multiple communication venues those that will be most effective for reaching good job candidates and, at the same time, will be prudent investments of recruiting funds.

The decision process is complicated by volume pricing considerations. Individual job ads have a set cost, but all advertisers create special deals for volume business. For the volume agreements, it is prudent to estimate the total number of persons to be recruited for the period covered and pro-rate the individual ad costs for comparison purposes.

However, because of the price compression in a highly competitive job-ad market, serious attention should be given to the issue of staff time investments. Because of labor overhead and opportunity costs of a competent recruiting function, the hourly cost (annual compensation and overhead divided by 2,000 hours annually) should be multiplied by the number of hours required. In other words, if a staff person costing $30,000 a year takes one hour to place a job ad in a no-charge job-listing service, your effective cost is at least $15.

That sum may be a waste or a bargain, depending on the ad's response rates. If the ad was placed in a commercial online ad service for $150 and an hour was used, the total cost would be $165.

Some care is required to avoid charging job ad development (drafting) time to each and every placement. Writing the great job ad should be a separate function, and only customization time, entry time, and site monitoring time should be charged against an individual advertising medium.

The recruiting progress and results form shown in Table 7.1 is also a tracking document that records when the decisive steps were taken to advertise and promote the job opening. Using the dates, you can determine how quickly the staff was able to complete the initial stages of job publicity and also measure the turn-around and response rates.

An advertising resource (online or otherwise) that produces good candidates within a few days is obviously more valuable than one that requires weeks or months to flush them out. If response data is collected and summarized throughout the hiring process, the accumulation of recruiting progress and results forms will enable recruiters in the future to make more deliberate and cost effective decisions about where to advertise identical or related job openings.

Any summarization process should be tied into existing corporate categories for management and professional jobs.

The Research rows are for online searches of selected resume databases. Low cost or free services are available for the recruiting staffs use to check for qualified job candidates. See Chapter 8, "Did We Mention Resumes?" for more details.

Even if a database is maintained, a hard copy of this form might be valuable as a location to record the approving initials of senior personnel. This form is a road map of how the promotion and communication of this career opportunity will be managed.

A recruiting specialist examines the job description details, the recruiting effectiveness reports for the same or similar jobs, the urgency level of the hiring manager, and the recruiting budget for the year in order to make the best decisions.

The Date Filed column should be used to document when a job candidate could first discover the career opportunity, not when some intermediate step was completed. For example, if you send the job details to a local public-service jobs database that utilizes volunteers to upload jobs to their files, and the average delay is ten days. In such a case, the date filed is 10 days after you turn in the ad.

In your job ad, ask the interested job candidate to send her response to the address specified. The address specified will include the department designation, which is your tracking tag for that communication or promotion medium. When the job candidate sends in her resume and cover letter, the staff can quickly record

Table 7.1 The recruiting progress and results form

JOB CODE: **HR501** *   TRACKING TAG:**R97003** **

PROMOTION SOURCE	APP CODE	SOURCE CODE	DATE FILED	# OF L1 RESPONSES	# OF L2 RESPONSES	TOTAL RESPONSES
CareerWeb	B	Dept. A				
OCC	A	Dept. B				
AmJob Bank	A	Dept. C				
Career Mosaic	B	Dept. D				
Howling Herald	C	Dept. E				
WSJournal	D	Dept. F				
Web site	A	Dept. G				
Newsletter	A	Dept. H				
Local network	A	Dept. I				
ESC	A	Dept. J				
Post Alpha	A	Dept. K				
Post Beta	A	Dept. L				
Post Charlie	A	Dept. M				
Post Delta	A	Dept. N				
Bulletin boards	A	Dept. O				
Internal e-mail	A	Dept. P				
Research A	A	Dept. Q				
Research B	A	Dept. R				
Research C	A	Dept. S				
Research D	A	Dept. T				
Other	A	Dept. U				

APP (APPROVAL) CODES:

A - automatic, no special authorization required for ad approval

B - any recruiting specialist can approve

C - recruiting supervisor must approve the expense

D - department head must approve expenditure

* *Job Code: HR501 represents your internal job coding number.*

** *Tracking Tag: R97003 signifies Recruiting Dept., 1997 hiring campaign, 3rd hiring initiative.*

this and route those documents to the person responsible for processing them.

A group of separate database tables (linked to the recruiting progress and results form) could look like Table 7.2.

The only complicated aspect of this table is the option of checking either Level 1 (L1) or Level 2 (L2). The rest of the form is a primarily clerical identification of when the response was received, who the job candidate is, what kinds of data were included in the response, and the transmission method of the response.

To determine whether the candidate is categorized as Level 1, 2, or 3, the recruiter reviewing the resume must determine how closely the resume matches the job. The triage approach is discussed in considerable detail in Chapter 9, "The Integrated Solution - Success in Online Recruitment" but the short version is simple. Level 3 describes the easily discarded response because the job candidate information is obviously unrelated to the open position. Level 3 communications result from job candidates who are so eager for new employment that they send cover letters and resumes for any job opportunity that remotely relates to even one of their skills or aptitudes, or interests.

Table 7.2 Source Management report

SOURCE: **CareerWeb**   JOB CODE: **HR501**   TRACKING TAG: **R97003**   DATE FILED: **2/18/97**

DATE RECEIVED	L1	L2	CANDIDATE'S NAME	COVER LETTER	RESPONSE TYPE
————	————	————	————	————	————
————	————	————	————	————	————
————	————	————	————	————	————
————	————	————	————	————	————

After the Level 3 decision is recorded (by the absence of input in both the Level 1 and Level 2 columns), a form letter saying "thanks but no thanks" is sent to the job candidate.

The Level 1 candidate is on the other end of the spectrum because her response data indicates a clear qualification for most, if not all, aspects of the open position. Level 1 candidates are definitely keepers, and merit a positive and speedy response.

The Level 2 candidate has skills that the recruiter knows to have obvious and substantial value to the company even if she is not a prime contender for the position currently open. These candidates get a less encouraging but still positive response, the data on them is summarized for quick retrieval, and the raw data is filed for follow-up and review after a set period of time (six months to one year). The Level 2 candidate is someone that the company may well need within a three year window.

Having levels enables human resource professionals to roughly quantify the quality of results received from each advertising or promotion medium used. Table 7.3 is a brief illustration of how such a summary could look.

Table 7.3 Source management summary

SOURCE: **CareerWeb**   DATE: **January 15,1997**

TRACKING TAGS	JOB CODES	CW L1	CW L2	SOURCE TOTAL RESPONSES	GRAND TOTAL L1	GRAND TOTAL L2	TOTALS ALL	AVERAGE RESPONSE
R97001	IS615	2	17	95	5	31	215	6
R97002	AC411	0	1	18	5	15	65	11
R97003	HR501	2	8	45	2	10	70	8
R97004	PR311	4	11	44	10	15	111	19
R97005	PR405	3	8	15	8	25	76	5

Needless to say, this summary report could be expanded to include percentages and other clarifying data, not to mention illustrative pie graphs for each of the recruiting codes. But even a cursory glance should indicate which resource is most competitive for the five jobs indicated to date.

There are other productive ways to examine the same data. Table 7.4 provides a breakdown of how the different advertising venues performed. The departments are source codes that refer to specific job promotion venues.

The obvious application of the source review summary is to conduct a periodic review of overall effectiveness of individual advertisers or other recruiting resources. If a single job ad location has been consistently unproductive across

Table 7.4 Another source review summary

Effective March 11, 1997

SOURCE CODES	TRACKING TAGS	L1	L2	L3	TOTALS	PERCENTAGE TOTALS (L1)
Dept. A	R97003	2	8	35	45	4%
	R97005	0	3	95	98	0%
	R97006	1	4	15	20	5%
Totals		3	15	145	163	2%
Dept. B	R97001	3	8	20	31	10%
	R97007	1	5	24	30	3%
Totals		4	13	44	61	6%
Dept. C	R97002	0	8	15	23	0%
	R97008	2	4	44	50	4%
	R97009	1	3	16	20	5%
	R97010	0	1	3	4%	0%
	R97011	0	2	2	4%	0%
	R97015	2	3	5	10	20%
Totals		5	21	85	111	4%
Dept. D	R97012	3	5	14	22	15%
Totals		3	5	14	22	15%
Dept. E	R97013	2	4	96	102	2%

multiple categories of job openings, and the L1 successes have been modest compared to the total volume of responses received, it might be prudent to take your business elsewhere, removing the company from the list of eligible advertisers.

Another option would be to increase the approval level to a D, flagging the resource for management decisions about the quantity of time and money invested for low returns. Surveying hundreds or thousands of resumes for rare job candidate jewels is not the highest or best use of recruiting staff time.

Information systems staff with a modest level of proficiency with any popular database software can create and maintain a database incorporating these four tables and link them to minimize data entry time, and also generate summary calculations for management reports. We recommend Microsoft Access or Lotus Approach to allow the maximum flexibility in updating the tables and provide customization whenever necessary. Ideally, someone in the human resources area would have the skills to develop and maintain the database with no assistance from the information systems staff.

The technical help one gets from outside the department or company tends to spend an inordinate amount of time developing a database and then freezes the structure of the database indefinitely. A more local technical person can also be of great assistance in managing some of the more challenging aspects of making online job ads work for your company.

All this database reporting is much simpler in execution than it is to explain. And any experienced recruiter can probably enhance and customize the approach into a more effective tool for her company. The work comes down to answering the question "Who delivers in producing good job candidates for our job openings?" With source codes, the question is easy to answer. Without them, you must rely on nebulous feelings and last minute data collection.

Simply, the source code helps you determine which online or hard copy job ad company was most successful in producing the following:

- Large quantities of responses

- High quality responses

- Faster responses

- Fewer trash responses

- Hires

- Lowest cost per quality response

To minimize difficulties in managing recruiting results, be sure to create a category for every possible source of job candidates, whether they are online job ads, or referrals from a current employee. You want to track even the resources that cost you nothing and that you can't take credit for. Even nepotism generates good job candidates.

Equally important, some discipline is necessary when using the source codes, especially when the source is less than conventional. You must track the resumes by their origins. If you start working with resumes and cover letters that seemed to have appeared by magic, your ability to justify internal and external recruiting costs, and to manage the overall process with some confidence, will be compromised. You should know how much it costs to find the good candidates, whether the expense is in salaries, advertising costs, or other resources.

FAXED RESPONSES

The faxed response has two virtues - it is a quick, easily accessed communications resource; and the response arrives in the same format and style in which it was dispatched to you. Any Level 1 response should be followed up with a request from the company for a mailed or emailed (with attached std. wordprocessor format) cover letter and resume, and an application form can be dispatched as well. Key persons within your organization may expect the feel and visual impact of a traditional package, and a request for this supplemental format is unlikely to alienate serious candidates.

On the other hand the ubiquitous availability and ease of use that characterizes fax equipment make shotgun distribution of cover letters and resumes an onerous fountain of less-than-serious responses. The problem is complicated by the ease with which currently employed persons can use corporate facilities to distribute their responses and avoid long distance telephone charges.

In any case, it pays to capture the arrival date and source of the response as indicated in the tracking forms described previously. The receipt of mailed data supplementing the fax should be filed with the rest of the job candidate's response and processed simply as another piece of relevant data. For Level 1 candidates especially, a complete review of the data is justified.

Another fax consideration is electronic storage. Most of us tend to think about faxes as slick paper flowing out of the back of a desktop machine. But there is software (Winfax Pro is an example) that will receive faxes automatically and store them electronically on your hard drive.

A simple OCR conversion allows the fax to be stored in a data file. Depending on the size of your recruiting operation and the links between office computers, it might be productive to harness such software and capture the incoming fax responses in an electronic mode. It can be printed out as well, but one obvious advantage to having electronic files on a central server is that one or eight persons can be examining a candidate's information at any moment.

E-MAIL

E-mail shares the speed virtue of facsimile transmission. The e-mailed message will lack most of the format clarity of the original and will possibly be distorted due to differences between e-mail software used by senders and receivers. However, the e-mailed document can easily be searched electronically and forwarded to other parties with the e-mail software installed on their computers. The sender can transmit it much more discreetly than making a trip to the facsimile machine, and can store the text for transmission to hundreds of other prospective employers.

Two cautions are obvious duplicates of the fax management advice: Remember to enter the data into your recruit-tracking database and ask for a mailed version of the data sent, or a resending of the emailed message with an attached resume — in a standard wordprocessor format which can be easily printed.

A standard e-mailed resume might look awkward because of the difference in e-mail software used and the appearance deficits of all e-mail software, but the text can be easily downloaded into compatible word-processing and database software. Unlike faxed responses, no scanning is required. And if you have lots of space on your hard drives, storing responses electronically represents a savings in physical space as well as in faster retrieval and search times.

A major challenge with email resumes is the management of hundreds upon hundreds of e-mail messages with resumes embedded. Several software packages are currently available to aid in managing the process (see Appendix D - Tools You Can Use).

THE POSTAL SERVICE

Even the postal service, popularly referred to as snail mail, has its virtues. The main benefit to the recruiter is that the job candidate has considerable control over the appearance and style of her response as well as the content. If communications skills and good taste are significant skill sets for the open position, the response you receive in the mail will tell you volumes about the candidate. Smart candidates will send you a good cover letter with a neat resume in a 9x12 inch envelop, even if not requested, as long as they have your address. If they have both e-mail and postal addresses, they may send those documents to both.

And no matter what the final hiring authority says, she will like having a presentation quality resume in hand when beginning the interview. Whenever a manager is making a high-risk decision such as a personnel hire, she likes to have a good package as well as a good candidate.

Because it is an important decision, please limit human resource department attachments to the bare minimum necessary for the manager's decision. The excellent forms you use to manage the recruiting process can be maintained without handing a messy pile of hard copy documentation to the operating manager performing the big interview.

The hiring folder should contain the cover letter, the original resume, a list of critical skills or core competencies numerically cross referenced to a working copy of the resume, the job application, and an interview schedule if the job candidate will be seeing more than one interviewer. If those items are included in a consistent pattern in the interview folders delivered to hiring managers, you will earn their quiet appreciation.

TELEPHONE CALLS

Telephone calls have an immediacy that is usually a better indicator of interest level than a useful supplier of hiring related data. Except in the case of Level 1 candidates, telephone contacts are best handled by administrative support staff briefly and cordially.

Communications with Level 1 candidates should be tracked consistently and the record should become a part of a permanent file that is retained for a considerable period beyond when the hiring decision is made. If a given candidate is hired, the record can serve as a useful review of successful recruiting campaigns. For the ones that were not hired, careful attention should be given to the courtesy and timeliness with which their services were declined.

The Level 1 files, retained for at least three years, should be your first resource when a new job opening develops in the same or a related area. The work invested in the recruiting process is only wasted if you throw it away.

Storing Resumes Electronically

Despite a good deal of technical evidence to the contrary, there is the lingering suspicion that storing data on a computer costs a lot of money. A reality check is in order.

- The going market rate for a 4 gigabyte hard disk drive is approximately $200.

- A gigabyte is equal to 1,000,000,000 bytes; 1,000,000 kilobytes; 1,000 megabytes.

- Dividing $200 by 4,000MB results in $.05 per megabyte.

- You can retain a fairly complete record, even allowing for database overhead, using fewer than 10KB per job candidate

- Dividing 1 megabyte or 1,000 kilobytes by the 10KB per candidate results in 100 candidates per megabyte. If you divide that into the nickle per megabyte, the cost is one twenth of one cent to store the recruiting record for a job candidate. You should perhaps allow for backups, which will increase your cost to 0.1 cents per job candidate.

The point is simple: Every Level 1 and Level 2 job candidate you receive resumes and other data from represents a significant expenditure already invested by your organization. Those persons will not cease to exist or suddenly lose all future potential for employment at your company because you did not hire them for the current open position. But, however your company came to their attention, you cannot be certain that their interest will duplicate itself in the future when your company has a more pressing opportunity for an employer/associate relationship.

If you can store and manage 200,000 job candidate records on a PC in a corner of your office when the only significant cost is the data entry time (and most of the data entry time is integral to your recruiting management process anyway), why shouldn't you make the investment? We don't include the cost of the computer and the software because both would be available for correspondence, spreadsheets, and database applications.

Let us introduce you to a useful human resource management statistic: the Mc-

Carter Index. It is easy to compute. Divide the number of new hires your recruiting staff made from existing recruiting files during a given period (a calendar year, for example) by the total number of persons hired for the same period. In other words, if the recruiting staff took job orders and checked your files for likely candidates, and that process resulted in 3 of the 30 hires made during the period reviewed, the McCarter Index is 10 percent. Needless to say, the higher the better.

We recommend computing the index for 1996 and 1997 to evaluate current procedures and the recruiting utility of existing hard-copy and/or computer-maintained files.

S U M M A R Y

In all your recruiting efforts, whether they are by Internet, newspaper, or internal company bulletin boards, source codes that identify job candidate response origins are vital. They will enable you to manage the process more effectively and to make important time/cost decisions about recruiting operations.

Do not rely simply on the number of resumes received. Instead, make sure you quantify the quality of resumes received. It is our experience that the number of top-quality resumes received from any advertising source will represent less than 10 percent of the total resumes received, and many times will represent less than 1 percent. You will be lucky to receive as many as 30 percent combined of first- and second-quality resumes from the best of advertising placements. Even on the Internet.

The rest are a significant labor expense as well as an administrative burden. Any review of advertisers used will look at hires, first-quality resumes, and second-quality resumes as well as total resumes from any source - with an emphasis on the number of hires and first-quality resumes.

Online job advertising can add significantly to your capacity to attract good candidates, but a lot of the value is wasted if the ancillary results of the search campaign are discarded after the hire is made. Each search campaign should feed two related databases:

- An advertising (communications) media evaluation database that guides future campaigns.

- A job candidate database that minimizes the need for advertising expenditures.

The bottom line benefits of these two databases will grow exponentially with time if they are maintained and utilized consistently.

Did We Mention Resumes?

Gordon's Luck

One of my favorite good old boys carried his bad luck and ignorance with him like a small boy's blanket. Gordon was always late for lunch, close to the scene of the crime, tongue-tied with women, and stubborn with bosses. The pinnacle of his academic achievement was to take to heart his second grade teacher's admonition to smile often and always say "thank you." He dropped out of school shortly thereafter.

His boyhood friend, Benny, kept up with Gordon's misadventures through his mother, who stayed on the family farm in Honeysuckle, South Carolina, despite his frequent invitations to come north and live with him in Pittsburgh. Gordon, however, took Benny's invitation more seriously, especially when Benny said that money was "growing on trees" in Pittsburgh. When Gordon got fired for setting $18,000 worth of chemicals and raw materials on fire with a discarded cigarette (in a non-smoking area), he decided it was time to see Pittsburgh. He started hitch-hiking north without even collecting his last paycheck.

By the time Gordon reached Pittsburgh, he was too broke to use a pay telephone, hadn't eaten for two days, and had a bad cold. As he clutched Benny's address in hand and resolutely began walking the 30 blocks remaining to his destination, he noticed a $50 bill laying under a tree near the street. Gordon dashed over, started to bend down, and then stopped.

Gordon smiled and said, "I guess money really does grow on trees in Pittsburgh, but I'll be damned before I strain myself with anything resembling work on my first day here."

Gordon straightened up and continued walking.

RESUMES DO GROW ON TREES

If you think this tale of woe is improbable, consider the tactics discussed in this chapter and ignored by all but the most savvy employers.

There is a bizarre bias in human resource recruiting for hiring job candidates only from the pool of earnest supplicants who rush their fresh resumes with cover letters directly to the employer upon discovering the open position in online or hard copy job ads. But one of the underrated talent gold mines is the resume database.

A resume database is simply the other side of the online market for human resources. In the same way employers list their open positions in anticipation that some eager job candidate will be overwhelmed by the career opportunity, individuals post their resumes in various resume databases with the hope that an informed and interested employer will contact them with a great job offer.

This chapter explores the "whys and hows" of using resume databases.

RESUMES FOR THE ASKING

Many of the good folks who sell online job ads are more than a little reluctant to talk about resume databases. Not that the databases are an always adequate substitute for announcing the job opening to the civilized world, but that they are often a valuable and price competitive alternative.

WHY USE RESUME DATABASES?

The single best reason for checking out a resume database is that the people who post their resumes on the Internet are looking for new career opportunities. Their level of excitement may vary dramatically from mild market curiosity to financial desperation, but the effort required to create credible resumes marks them as being at least modestly open to making an employment change.

Will this population have more currently unemployed people than the population at large? Yes, but the odds of finding and recruiting excellent performers from this group is still markedly better than the odds of discovering and capturing some reticent industry star.

Internal and outside recruiters love to tell you that they don't want the person who is looking for a job, they want someone who is happily at work and will be a challenge to lure away from their current position. But, what they usually get is someone who can play the job trading game better than they can, and who will switch jobs again when they can negotiate another $4,000 per year pay increase. The resume database addresses two major recruiting challenges simultaneously: finding well-qualified candidates and persuading them to make the move. If their resume is there, they are open to a move.

The talent market has three main groups. Members of one group have listed their resumes on the Internet somewhere; members of the second group are generally passive about career advancement and are pleased that the boss, their spouse, or some recruiter is managing their future for them; and members of the third are both proactive and subtle about managing their progress up the career ladder. You can find good performers in all three groups, but don't look for a dynamic, high-visibility innovator in the second group.

A second reason for exploring a resume database is economics. Some commercial services do charge companies for access to their resume databases while providing job candidate access for free, others do just the opposite. But under either option, the cost per qualified candidate is modest compared to an ad campaign and the net results can be equally satisfactory.

Your major investment in resume searches, whether the source charges for access or not, is the staff time involved. If the process is well managed, the cost per qualified candidate or job hire will be modest. Proactive corporate recruiters pursue both an online ad campaign and a resume search process simultaneously to expedite the process.

The first step to a successful resume search is the selection and training of staff to perform the necessary tasks in a cost-effective manner. A job description for the resume search specialist is found in Chapter 9, "The Integrated Solution - Success in Online Recruitment." Some fine-tuning may be necessary to incorporate the responsibilities of this position into your organization.

One of the responsibilities of the resume search specialist is the development of succinct but comprehensive keyword profiles for representative corporate jobs. To clarify this process, let's use a model job ad from Chapter 3, "Writing the Online Job Ad," to create keyword profiles and test those profiles with the free Career Mosaic resume database. Following is one of those model resumes. Note that we have underlined some key words to use in the search process.

INDUSTRIAL ENGINEER, NEW SITE PLANNING MANAGER – WALNUT ENGINEERING, NC

Walnut Engineering
Recruiter, Dept. IEPM/HWUSA
1 Tarheel Drive
Charlotte, NC 28210

Fax:	800-123-4567
E-mail:	recruiter@walnut.com
Job Location:	Charlotte, NC
Job Status:	Permanent Position
Salary Range:	$60 -$70K plus bonus potential of 10 percent of salary.
Benefits:	Major medical, dental, life insurance, 401K with 4 percent matching, retirement.

DESCRIPTION:

The I.E. **planning** manager will work with client management and engineers to design, plan, install, and implement high-speed **machining** and injection-molding production and assembly operations. The work involves equipment selection, plant layout, materials planning, incentive standards design and implementation, production simulation, just-in-time systems, and quality planning. The planning manager will travel forty weeks per year to client sites in the Americas, with 4-5 days on site each week average. Excellent project planning, communications skills, teamwork orientation, and goals orientation is necessary for satisfactory performance.

QUALIFICATIONS:

Requirements include an advanced degree in management or engineering; applicator certificates in **MOST**, MiniMOST, and MaxiMOST with at least 200 hours of work standards documented; MicroStation drafting qualifications with a portfolio of **industrial** design; superior Microsoft Office skills; 2 years experience with a leading simulation software package; and an **ISO** 9000 background. Candidates with a fluency in **Spanish** and extensive consulting experience will receive special consideration. A familiarity with Okuma and other leading brands of industrial machine tools will be valuable, as will any plans-to-production manufacturing construction.

For the Career Mosaic resume search engine, the search string must have "and" between the keywords to be searched. Search engines used by the various employment advertising services vary in the requirements for entering keywords. Some require no separator words such as "and"; others require semi-colons; while the newer technology contains integrated scroll bar and keyword-search technology. Be sure to read the search engine directions about how to conduct a search.

In the case of the industrial engineer example, several words that might find the best match have been highlighted. In this case matches with the words Industrial, Engineer, Machining, MOST, planning, and ISO would indicate the most suitable candidates. Figure 8.1 displays the resume search screen with several keywords entered. Figure 8.2 displays the results from the search.

When entering keywords to be searched, the most effective approach is to rank your keywords by placing the most important word first, the next most important word second, and so on. Then enter the whole set and initiate the search process. While the computer compares the keywords with the database, the resume search specialist can make initial entries in a resume search form. The form identifies the job or job type for which the search is being initiated, the date the search is conducted, the search database used, the name of the researcher, and the keyword profile.

Having obtained a reasonable number of resumes from your search, start at the top of the list and examine the job title descriptions that the job candidates have placed on their own resumes. If the job title is not obviously relevant, move to the next one. You might pass up a real star by accident, but it is highly unlikely, and you can waste a great deal of time reading resumes with content completely unrelated to the job you wished to fill.

Figure 8.1
The Career Mosaic
resume search
input screen

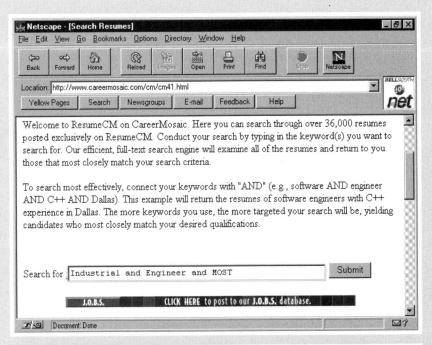

Figure 8.2
The return screen
from a resume
search in Career
Mosaic.

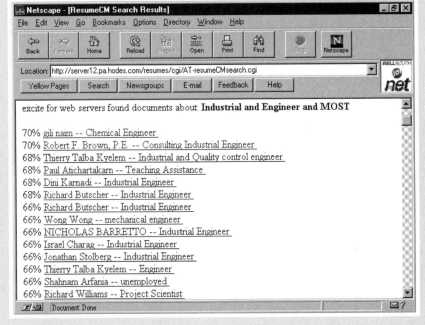

By clicking the resume identification, you can pull up the resume. If the information indicates that the job candidate is a likely candidate, the resume search specialist clicks the print button and/or saves the resume to their computer hard drive and records the name on the resume search form with an L1 notation. Some of the resumes that fall short of the criteria specified for the job being reviewed but display skills of obvious interest to the company should also be noted. The resume research specialist records those names with the L2 notation, but should not print a copy of the resume.

The resume copies can be used directly in a job-candidate search process or, if this search is a preliminary evaluation of the market, the copies can be filed for future reference with the source and date indicated on the resume. One of the manpower issues that human resources departments often face is the proper utilization of recruiting personnel during periods of slow staff growth or hiring freezes.

A good solution is to assign resume search specialists and other staff the task of acquiring at least three good resumes for each staff position of obvious importance to the corporation. The process of developing this backlog also develops the database search skills of the recruiting staff specialist.

The human resource director can direct the recruiting manager to focus on the jobs with large numbers of incumbents, with frequent turnover, with escalating salary demands, with a history of payments to outside recruiters, with a special relevance to growth plans, with specific salary levels, or any other combination of prospective corporate requirements. Also, instead of three resumes, they can specify five or ten.

The idea is that the recruiting staff, should not just look busy when demands for their services are low, or wait for cutbacks that will have a long-term impact on the group's operating potential. Instead they can lay the groundwork for future recruiting successes. The plan is simple. When a job order comes in, the recruiting staff first targets L1 resumes received from people who previously expressed an interest in working for your company. The staff can re-energize the relationships that the recruiting staff has quietly maintained since the job candidates first expressed an interest.

A quick telephone call and/or standard template letter can quickly determine the prospects of recruiting qualified personnel without the time and expense required for an online job ad and other position promotion processes.

A sample letter follows:

Dear Ms. Johnson:

Thank you for your past interest in working for our company. We have kept your resume on file because of your impressive credentials, and a related job opportunity has developed.

A complete job description is enclosed for your review. I will be available to answer your questions about this career opportunity. My telephone number is (704) 555-1212, and Alice Smith will be able to help you if I should be temporarily out of the office.

We have not advertised this position yet. If you are interested, please send me an updated resume and job application promptly. Copies of our most recent versions of those documents are enclosed for your convenience.

I look forward to hearing from you.

Sincerely,

John Doe

Recruiting Coordinator

The obvious next step is to target those L1 resumes from earlier job ads. They will require a slightly different letter content and telephone call contact process, but you are still working with pre qualified job candidates instead of initiating a blank slate search campaign.

Running the risk of redundancy, we must point out that the process outlined previously is an accurate representation of the sequence followed by successful, well-compensated, outside contingency recruiters. They start their job search process with their files and send corporate employers a bill for 20 to 30 percent of a job candidate's first year compensation whether it took fifty minutes or five months to locate the job candidate and sell her on working for you. And when outside recruiters are not telephoning you for job orders, they are trolling the job market, including resume databases, for candidates that you will likely need in the future.

Recruiting isn't just another task for which they are paid, they are in the recruiting **business**.

Your first targets for keyword profiles and resume database searches should be any intermediate-level jobs that you filled through outside resources during the past 30 months.

Table 8.1 A sample resume research form

JOB TITLE: **Process Development Manager**   JOB CODE: **BKOPS64**
TRACKING TAG: R98051   RESUME RESEARCHER: **Jane Doe**

RESUME DATABASE USED	KEYWORDS USED	TOTAL RESUMES FOUND	L1 COUNT	L2 COUNT
American	operations process planner	10		3
Talent Bank	banking operations	75	1	5
	Banking operations IE	20	3	6
CareerWeb	banking operations IE	6	1	2
	banking operations planner	4		2
Carolina	banking operations IE	3		
Talent Bank	banking operations planner	6		2
	banking operations	55	1	5
NationsJobs	banking operations planner	2		
	banking operations	6		1
IECentral	banking operations planner	15	2	5
	banking operations IE	17	3	7

Your resume research form should look something like the form in Table 8.1.

The headings define the job and the talent search campaign, and the person doing the search identifies herself for future reference. Most of the columns are self-explanatory. The first one records where the search was conducted, the second one the keywords used. When there was a change of keywords, a subsequent line was used without changing the name in column one. Column 3 records the total number of resumes found, while columns 4 and 5 record the number of L1 and L2 resumes respectively. As Jane Doe is conducting the resume search, she will save the two levels of resumes to a database with a brief annotation that identifies this search - the R98051 tracking code, and possibly today's date. The table below is a supplement with two applications; it enables the resume researcher to easily track which L1 resumes she has already placed in the database and records how often a given job candidate appears in the various resume databases. It is also a quick reference for pulling up resumes for the top candidates for the job for

Table 8.2 The L1 Name List

L1 NAME LIST

NAME	NUMBER OF TIMES FOUND
John McCarter	5
Billy Bob Wilson	2
Frank Hines	3
Dilbert Williams	1

viewing or for printing out. A series of check marks in the second column may be the basis for entering a numeric total. Please note that the total number of L1 resumes in both tables is identical.

In order to manage the process on a long term basis, some summary statistics for management is essential (Table 8.3). This process pulls data from the resume research forms to give some good hints about where to look for staff. But please note that the summary form recognizes ad results for different media, resume searches, and personal contacts.

As you can see, Billy Bob is tracking not only how many current incumbents there are, but how many likely candidates there are in the marketplace. He even directed his human resources, payroll, and recruiting staff personnel to track the availability of qualified general managers - which is his own role at the restaurant. If he gets a little crazy on his birthday and is bitten by water moccasins while swimming across the Cooters End reservoir, Billy Bob wants Wilma Sue to be able to find an adequate replacement - in restaurant management anyway.

Please note that this form isn't limited to Internet resources only; in addition to ads and resume databases, there are some lines for walk-ins, the Raleigh News & Observer, and the Wilmington Times. Some in the eastern North Carolina labor market haven't caught on about the Internet yet, and Billy Bob runs an ad in the hard copy publications four times a year whether he needs to or not. His

Table 8.3 Billy Bob's Barbecue resume research summary

DATE: **February 2, 1997**

JOB #	JOB TITLE	POSITIONS	SEARCHES/DATES	AVG COST	L1	L2
101	General Manager	1	1	$50,000	4	11
	Career Mosaic				1	3
	Monster Board (resume)				1	5
	Walk-ins				2	3
102	Bookkeeper	1	1	$24,000	2	6
	Career Mosaic				2	4
	N & O				0	1
	Family				0	1
103	Cashier	2	2	$21,000	3	4
	Family				3	2
	WTimes				0	2
104	HR/Payroll/etc.	1	1	$16,000	3	7
	WTimes				1	3
	Career Mosaic				2	4
201	Chief Cook	1	1	$40,000	2	5
	Raleigh N & 0				2	5
202	Pork Cook	1	1	$17,000	2	9
	Walk-ins				1	5
	Family				1	4
203	Chicken Cook	1	1	$28,000	0	4
	Family				0	4
204	Fish/Critters Cook	1	1	$29,000	2	6
	WSJ				1	4
	Walk-ins				1	2
205	Salad/Greens Cook	1	1	$25,000	1	4
	Monster Board (resume)				1	4
206	Dessert Cook	1	1	$26,000	2	5
	Raleigh N & O				2	5
209	Dishwasher	3	3	$14,000	3	5
	Walk-ins				1	4
	Family				2	1
301	Service Manager	1	1	$29,000	3	5
	Career Mosaic				1	2
	Family				2	3
302	Waiters, Inside	8	8	$11,000	4	11
	Walk-ins				1	4
	Family				3	7
303	Porch Service Waiters	3	3	$10,000	3	7
	Walk-ins				3	7
304	Parking/Guard	2	2	$15,000	2	5
	Walk ins				2	5

cousin Edna, who fills the HR (and other) jobs, conscientiously adds at least two names to her recruiting file weekly, although this work precludes extensive at-the-desk manicures and keeping up with the soaps on the office television.

RESUME SEARCH SUMMARY

Like the corporate recruiting Web page job ads, resume searches are an optional element in a human resources recruiting strategy, but a much less expensive one. It is a task that requires a modest skill set and considerable patience, but the annual cost of a staff person working full time should be less than contingency payments to an outside recruiter for one mid-level executive placement and the payoffs much more substantial. With some up front investment in learning the process and developing backlogs of resumes, maintaining a good recruiting staff can be justified if their work assignments are flexible. The recruiting manager will find that the optimum utilization comes from building up the collection of resumes of highly qualified people on a full time basis, and placing a special increased emphasis on resume database searches when the workload on direct recruiting lapses for seasonal or corporate policy reasons.

The biggest challenge is to put the number of resumes received from all sources into perspective. There is a wealth of resumes out there, but the number of people who can make both immediate and long-term significant contributions to your organization are a finite group. Because of their skills, attitudes, and experience, they are a scarce, highly desirable resource, and knowing who they are is the first big step toward recruiting them for your organization.

Developing the systems and procedures to manage your recruiting effort is more of an operational ordeal than an exercise in innovation; discipline is more crucial than inspiration.

RESUMES NEXT DOOR

During a recent consulting assignment we were in the office of a frantic corporate recruiter; she needed job candidates with a critical, advanced skill set. This recruiter had tried advertising in national newspapers, had done all she could through networking, and had canvassed similar professionals at their company to locate these elusive skill sets. In a last ditch effort, she hoped that the Internet could be the source for suitable job candidates.

Later that afternoon we met with another corporate recruiter, a colleague who happened to be located right next door. This person was less frantic and more confident about their success potential for placements. We found out why shortly - this person had a personal stash of resumes. Good ones, that all the recruiters in the department could have used, BUT the organization that these recruiters worked for recognized recruiters based mainly on individual placements made, not on cooperation internally in the department.

This second recruiter was anything but desperate. He wanted to use on-line job ads to fill current jobs with a broader range of candidates and to build his personal hard copy database of high quality resumes. His goal was to have three or four potential candidates any time a key job opened within the corporation. He routinely met his recruiting objectives.

The resumes our first recruiter needed were only 15 feet away, but a poor management reward system created an environment that made them practically non-existent.

Is this your organization?

TYPES OF RESUME SITES/SERVICES

As you might expect, all resume sites are not created equal. While some sites offer free access to thousands of resumes, others only offer access to member companies. With still other services, a corporate recruiter must purchase a membership for access to the resume database. Resume databases can be categorized as follows:

- **Free to Post/Free to Access** - The job seeker freely submits his resume online to the database and anyone can freely search and find his resume. The system is popular because no fee is involved from either party, but such systems tend not to be as well maintained or technologically current as the paid systems; after all, no revenue is generated from offering such a service for free.

- **Free to Post/Fee to Access** - This is one of the options currently offered by many of the leading online employment advertising services. Job seekers are allowed to store their resumes on these job sites at no cost, and client companies can purchase access to the resume database for a set fee. Several sites offer the job seeker the ability to hide her identity, allowing her the luxury of storing her qualifications online for hiring companies to see while still being able to keep her job-search intentions secret from her current employer. Another feature of several fee to access sites is agent technology: you develop keyword profiles of the candidates you wish to hire and every morning resumes that were submitted to the service the day before are inserted into your e-mail box.

- **Job seeker Pays to Post/Free to Access** - This type of service generally involves posting to one national talent bank on the Internet plus a resume distribution service. The job seeker's resume is distributed to hundreds of companies and recruiting firms nationwide. Job seekers pay for the convenience of having their resumes formatted and distributed to actively recruiting companies.

CONTACTING CANDIDATES OF RESUME SEARCH

You have just done your searching and have found dozens of well qualified candidates in regions all over America and now you sit down at the phone to begin calling, right! Wrong. One of the biggest mistakes we have found is using the telephone to initially contact candidates received from resume searches:

- They may have no desire to relocate to your part of the country

- Their spouse may not be able to find gainful employment in your region of the country.

- Your local school system and other key amenities may not be to their liking.

- They may not be home or at the office when you call.

Using the telephone as an initial contact mechanism can result as a labor intensive, time draining activity that leaves the recruiter looking at their watch at 5 p.m. wondering where did the day go and how did they waste the entire day and achieve so little. Such a process works so poorly because the job candidate is not given the chance to self-select out of the employment process at this point. Two of the major benefits of any job advertisement is that they give the candidate the ability to self-select in (send in a resume and cover letter) and self-select out (move on to the next opportunity). Candidates who are found by resume banks must still go through this process of moving forward or selecting themselves out. Do you want your recruiters to spend time doing this one by one on the telephone?

We recommend a more streamlined approach:

> Gather resumes that meet your criteria and either print them out or save them to your computer hard drive. Maintaining your own database is the most economical and worry free choice if you establish procedures that make the resumes easy to search and track.

> Aggregate all the e-mail addresses found in the batch of resumes together (yes, most resumes found online do contain a way to contact a candidate via e-mail).

> Prepare a description of the job opportunity as mentioned in Chapter 3.

> E-mail all the candidates on your list the job description. Include in the e-mail your interest in the candidate and ask for an updated resume.

EXAMPLE E-MAIL

To: ITGuy@aol.com,

From: nccareer@aol.com

Subject: Opportunity matching your resume.

Message:

Dear Bob,

My name is Joe Smith. I am employed in the staffing department at XYZ Computer Services. During a recent search on the Internet I found that your skill sets match the current requirements of one of the positions we have open. I have enclosed a full description of that position below along with information about XYZ Computer Services and our region of the country.

If you are interested in this position, please e-mail me back an updated resume and data on your current availability. I look forward to discussing this opportunity with you in the future.

Sincerely,
Joe Smith

Job Title:	Instrument Technician (NC)
Company:	XYZ Computer Services
Department:	Corporate Staffing
Job Code:	IT100-Int.
Address:	2800 Park Dr. Charlotte, NC 28226
Phone:	800-123-4567 Ext. 143
Fax:	800-123-4568
E-mail:	Recruiter@xyz.com
Job Location:	Charlotte, NC USA
Status:	Full-Time Position
Salaries:	$18-$20/hr. depending upon experience
Benefits:	Major medical, dental, profit sharing, and 401(k)

DESCRIPTION:

Successful candidate will work with industrial instrumentation and controls. Main duties include troubleshooting, repairing, and calibrating PLCs. Will use smart communicators and calibration equipment. Good communications skills necessary. Electrical background a plus.

QUALIFICATIONS:

Associate's degree in Instrumentation via either an industrial or technical school program required. Must be willing to travel. 2-5 years experience in the field a must.

COMPANY:

XYZ was founded in 1983 with the mission to service the process-instrumentation needs of industries in the Carolinas and Georgia. We have enjoyed steady growth in volume of business and, at our customers' request, have expanded our services to other areas. XYZ is now organized into four divisions: Engineering Services, Textile Services, Contract Services, and Shop Services. We currently provide technical personnel, both contract and direct, as well as project work throughout the Carolinas and Georgia. Our staff contains engineers, designers, CAD operators, technicians, skilled laborers, and programmers, and provides a broad range of services to the industries we support.

COMMUNITY:

North Carolina offers quality schools, nearby lakes, excellent public and private colleges, a rich history, and graceful residential communities. The beautiful Blue

Ridge Mountains are a short distance from Charlotte, and peaceful beaches are
accessible for a weekend of fun in the sun. The four seasons, with an extended fall
and an early spring, offer diversity and comfort for anyone.
The qualified candidate should submit a resume.

If you manage the resume process this way, marginal candidates will self select
out and you will be left with a more manageable handful of qualified job seekers
who have expressed sincere interest in the position.

RESUME DISTRIBUTION SERVICES

In the ongoing Internet dynamics, new services are persistently popping up. One
of the latest related to recruiting is the resume distribution service. The provider
has two sets of clients. Members of one set, consisting of job candidates, pay the
provider a modest fee to distribute their resumes to a select set of regional- or oc-
cupational-specific companies, which are members of the second set. The companies agree only to accept the resumes for employment consideration, and
frequently get them via e-mail for quick and cost-efficient processing.

The logic of resume distribution services is simple:

- The corporate clients receive a set of resumes via e-mail absolutely free
  (beyond their own internal processing and review costs). The e-mail
  format makes the resumes keyword-searchable, easy to store and retrieve, and the results are easy to track. Most importantly, this venue
  features a select group of job candidates who are committed to making a job change, and are confident enough about their skills to promote them at some cost to themselves over the Internet.

- For the job candidates who find broadcast resumes with cover letters
  less than an optimum job-search process, the resume distribution service makes sense. The cost is significantly less than the postage and
  labor involved in a mass mailing, and the corporate clients are in a hiring mode if they are using the service.

- The mutual self-selection approach pays off for both parties. The typical job candidate who uses this service also pursues job opportunities
  through networking and job ad responses. For her, this service is one

step up from the free resume listing services because there is reduced competition for attention and the generally high-quality resumes found on the service are attractive to the corporate clients.

- For the service provider, the challenge is to obtain a large and impressive set of corporate clients and then produce enough successes for the job candidate clients to create a steady stream of business from word of mouth advertising. After momentum is established, the low overhead costs and the regular turnover of accounts is a good source of income.

A resume distribution service is a low-cost source of resumes, but not always easy to find. The provider typically identifies corporate prospects from online job ads, Chamber of Commerce corporate lists, and newspaper job ads. If you are not actively in the job market or readily identified as a major employer, you might be overlooked. The most likely reason behind a missed participation opportunity, however, is that a provider tried to solicit your company but failed to reach someone who understands and appreciates the service.

A resume obtained through a typical resume distribution service can be processed just like any other resume, but you shouldn't forget to note the source as well. Even if the service is free, the labor expense of process and review merits periodic review of the results. The data will be especially useful if your favorite service changes its operations to require fees from companies as well as job candidates.

Two well-known resume distribution services are examined below.

EMPLOYMENT ZONE
http://www.employmentzone.com/
For $75.00 the folks at Employment Zone take an individual's resume, reformat it for Internet distribution, send it out to over 1,500 companies, databases, and recruiters nationwide, and give each client her own resume web site for one year. Figure 8.3 depicts the Employment Zone web site. We suggest you take a look at the site to determine the current resume distribution number. We know of individuals who have used this service with excellent results.

RESUMEPATH
http://www.bridgepath.com/getajob/index.html
Job seekers are presented with a list of a few hundred employers categorized by industry. Candidates cut and paste their resumes into the web site and choose

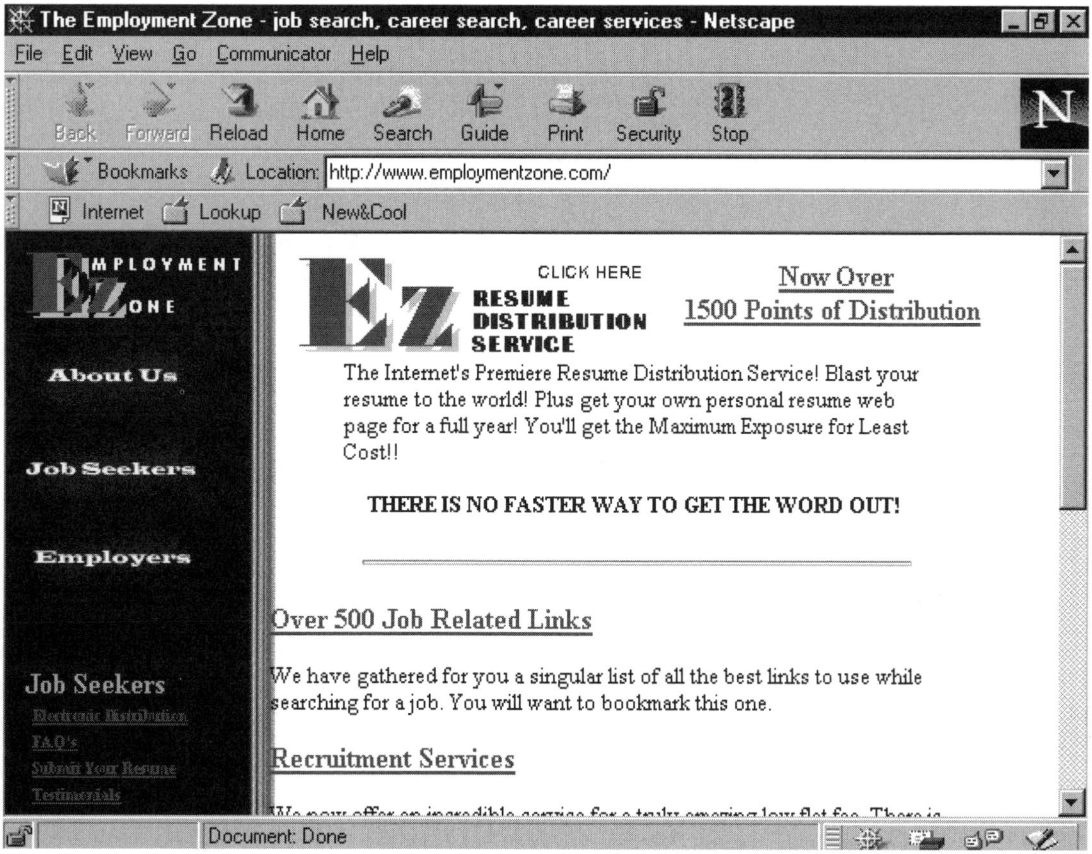

Figure 8.3 The Employment Zone web site

the employers that they wish to receive their resumes. They also have the option of sending a cover letter with the resumes. Figure 8.4 depicts the ResumePath web site. Job seekers will find this service good at targeting jobs in specific industries.

RESUME SITE SUMMARY

Appendix B lists several of the leading resume sites on the Internet. We suggest you first investigate the free services to determine whether you can find suitable candidates. Understand, however, if the service is free, odds are many top-of-the-

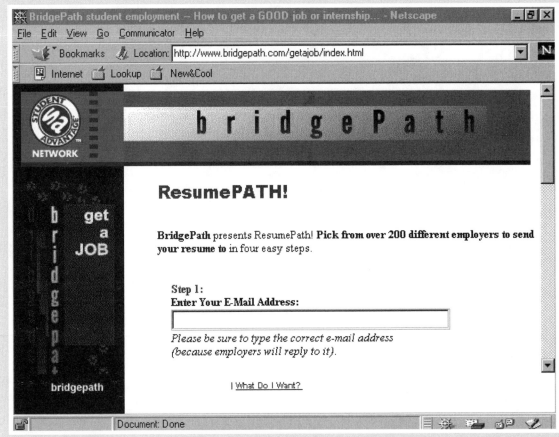

Figure 8.4 The ResumePath Web site

line candidates who are not new to the site have been hired long ago. If there is a fee to search the database, odds are you will find more unclaimed talent.

OUTPLACEMENT

From time to time, companies face the ugly necessity of dismissing good people. The quantity and quality of departure assistance that one can provide varies dramatically, but the Internet job market raises some high results, low cost potential. Consider this process:

1 Deliver the bad news and the various elements of the departure package.

2 Provide refresher training on the creation of great resumes, with immediate and tangible incentives for prompt completion.

3 Place the job candidate's resume in a broad variety of resume databases and resume distribution services that meet your corporate criteria for regular resume searches. Explore others that might also be productive for the person's experience and skills.

4 Have your Internal IS Department, or an outside service create a database of resumes of your displaced employees on the Internet. Send a letter from the company president to all HR managers of regional firms discussing the layoff, the qualifications of the workforce, and the location of the resumes on the Internet.

5 Provide technical support for a personal home page and e-mail on their home computer, and include the necessary address data on the resume listings. Many Internet service providers like AOL include both e-mail and a modest home page in the regular cost of their monthly service.

OUTPLACEMENT SUMMARY

There are a number of local and national outplacement firms that will provide excellent outplacement services ranging from low four to low five figures in cost, and that may be an excellent choice for some of the people that must be dismissed. But many skilled and confident managers will be able to find a new opportunity without the broad array of services that those firms have to offer.

If otherwise competent people only have minimum Internet skills, resume-placement support may be the technical boost that abbreviates their job search without compromising the quality of the new job they acquire. Your resume search specialists will have an excellent background for showing them where and how to place a resume on the Internet for maximum results.

G E N E R A L   S U M M A R Y

A well placed job ad - either on the Internet or in a hard copy periodical - can produce such a large volume of responses that human resource recruiters tend to regard them like a fisherman's boat load of catfish; fun to catch and good to eat, but hell to clean.

The sheer volume of resumes on the Internet create a parallel situation. There is nothing we can say to make resume review and evaluation personally rewarding and spiritually uplifting. However, there are two major sources of relief in this chapter.

One, having a disciplined process allows you to spread resume work over the year instead of struggling with every candidate search as an independent, although redundant, campaign. After a lot of hard work, you can manage the talent market instead of having it manage you. At the same time, an ongoing resume search process can save the company serious money in terms of ad costs and outside recruiter fees.

The second benefit is speed. Although operating departments frequently experience personnel shortages for months before they submit a job order, they want several incredibly well-qualified candidates to interview by Tuesday of next week. If you have already been looking, you can meet those challenging expectations more often. Just don't spoil them.

Please note that what is a less than perfect Internet job market now will in time improve significantly as more job candidates and corporate recruiters utilize the benefits that it obviously has to offer. Every good hire you find in one of these resume databases will become a success story that will be retold whether you publicize it or not. During the next Internet computer generation, the number of obviously excellent resumes on the Internet will probably triple at least. If you are diligent and adventuresome, you can achieve excellent results before many of your labor market competitors become aware of the resources available.

CHAPTER 9

THE INTEGRATED SOLUTION
Success in Online Recruitment

T
he purpose of this chapter is to make concrete recommendations about how a human resources professional can integrate the online recruiting process into a company's overall recruiting strategy in particular, and into related overall human resources policy in general. Online recruiting can function as an ad hoc, bootleg, or renegade process, but the process is much more productive when it is a recognized and coordinated component of a much larger human resources policy.

To avoid a shotgun list of tactics, the chapter is divided into three strategy levels, one task oriented series of staffing options, and a series of HR "to do's" on the recruitment process. We encourage readers to use their good judgment and knowledge to selectively adopt the tactics that will best fit their organization's goals and resources at any point in time.

❑ ❑ ❑

STRATEGY A: LOW COST, LOW RISK, EARLY USER APPROACH

We realize that not everyone will want to jump into Internet recruiting at full speed. Some of you would rather dip your little finger in the Internet pool to test the waters for awhile. Remember while you surf through the low cost/free areas of the Web to consider the time you are spending versus the payoffs. If you get results, great! If not, don't blame the Web; remember what your grandfather told you about getting something for nothing.

Key points to a low cost, low risk, early user approach include

- Search for free resumes

- List job ads in free online services/Usenet groups

- Place job ads on your company Web site (if you have one)

FREE RESUMES

For a given type of job, there should be an established list of free online resume databases to be searched and a list of keywords to use in the initial search process. New jobs and ones not previously reviewed will require some enterprising creativity on the spot. Chapter 8, "Did We Mention Resumes?" covered the availability of resumes in considerable detail and Appendix B, "Internet Resume Sites," lists several free sites on the Web. With some online research, you should be able to pick resumes of candidates who can be very productive for you. Of course, you want to use the databases which usually have the most candidates in the job category required, but some qualifications in terms of ease of use and data capture time are also important.

You can also find good resumes on certain Usenet groups. These tend to be more specific to a given profession and specialties within that profession, or to a particular region of the country. Appendix B also lists several Usenet resume sites.

Free resume databases can contain several talent gems, but remember that hundreds of recruiters have been in line before you. We suggest you track the time spent versus the actual results. If you find you are getting more dead end leads than results, try another strategy.

There is a special resume source of which you may not be aware. Some commercial online ad services have a sideline business or subsidiary enterprise called resume distribution. It works like this:

1 The service contacts a number of companies that have obvious high volume personnel requirements and makes them an attractive offer, "Would you like for me to send you resumes of people who are actively looking for career growth (jobs) in this state? In this profession? There will be no charge and we will simply fax them to you or e-mail them to the site of your choice.

2 The service contracts with resume writing services and individuals to place their resumes for a modest sum on the Internet, the distribution list, or both, depending on costs and resources. Typically, the charge is between $30 and $70, but the jobseeker bears the expense.

3 The service publishes the resumes in the preferred mode once a week, or more often if the volume justifies the production effort.

4 As long as it generates job opportunities, the process is much better for the job seeker than stuffing envelopes for a mass mailing once a week. The experts still recommend that job seekers emphasize networking and research based cover letters to targeted companies, but there are very talented people who are inclined to reduced effort job search campaigns.

Don't rule out resume distribution services until you have tried at least three for three months. The only cost is the time it takes to forage through the resumes, but if you have no more luck than a blind hog hunting acorns, redirect your recruiting efforts to more solid sources. Details on two of these services are contained in Chapter 8.

ONLINE JOB ADS (FREE)

In Appendix A, "Internet Job Sites," we identify a number of sites where you can list jobs free. Be selective, but don't be bashful. Give Usenet groups, America's Job Bank, and the others a try. You should be using the sites that target people whom you want to apply for the job. For instance, if the Web site is a favorite of the nation's new college graduates, and you want to find a mechanical engineer with five years of hydraulic experience (with at least two of those overseas), you may be wasting valuable time with new graduates.

Be sure to use all the tools mentioned in previous chapters: Write quality ads that describe the job, company, and community in detail and be sure to link your jobs to your company Web site if available. Remember to use job templates so you don't have to re-invent the wheel every time a new position must be posted online, and last, but not least, add tracking tags and source codes to all your ads and closely monitor the results.

CORPORATE WEB SITES

Don't forget your corporate Web page if you have one. A modest amount of training will allow one of your clerical staff to place a complete online job ad in the recruiting or career opportunities area of your corporate Web page. There may be a review process before the coded text is actually placed online, but the process will be expedited if you establish with your Webmasters a simple, concrete process for job ad submission and if you take the initiative to accomplish the necessary clerical training.

Make sure that your corporate Web site contains information that is attractive to job seekers. One of the biggest mistakes we encounter is in HR departments using their corporate Web site for recruiting, but failing to provide any information as to why a candidate would want to apply for a job. Does your Web site inspire an "I want to work here attitude!"? Or does it rather convey to the job seekers an unintended message: "I wouldn't consider working here if my life depended on it!"?

EXAMPLE OF LOW COST, LOW RISK, EARLY USER APPROACH

Margie Ledbetter is responsible for the HR functions at a chain of 100 medium-priced restaurants throughout the Carolinas. Margie heard about the Internet from a friend and has done some surfing, and is sold on using it as a tool for recruitment. Unfortunately, management at her firm has not yet given her the option to use her budget to invest in paid Internet recruitment. Margie is creative, however, and relies on several of the free Internet services to find talent. She has obtained a membership on America's JobBank and places several of her new openings there.

In addition, she posts her openings on the local triangle. Jobs Usenet group, which serves as a jobs resource for Research Triangle area of the Carolinas. She consistently codes all her ads with the source codes and includes a link to their corporate Web page so prospective job seekers can find more information. While the ads are running online, Margie makes sure to check the free resume databases on CareerMosaic and Career Magazine, looking for a few gems who may be interested in the Carolinas. Because she enjoys the Internet experience, she considers the work of posting and searching through the free areas of the Net to be fun. She does her recruiting work early in the morning and surprises her boss frequently with good candidates.

THE PROGRESSIVE STRATEGY

This is where most of you with pressing needs will start. Most organizations want to work with professional services that have records of results. Begin by choosing quality services and professionally designed materials. Follow the steps outlined in Chapter 5, "Selecting an Online Service." As always, use tracking tags and source codes, and monitor the results. If you pick a quality online service that is appropriate for the talent you need, you will get results. Key points to the progressive strategy include

- Job ads in commercial online services
- Fee based resume sourcing
- Well designed recruiting Web site linked from ads

ONLINE JOB ADS

Earlier, this chapter discussed free online job listings, and earlier in the book we covered a lot of ground on how to write a job ad and with whom to place it. The typical for fee ad placement is results based, but some preliminary surveys are in order.

The best selection approach is to place yourself in the shoes of what you would consider an optimum candidate for the most common job opening within your organization, and survey each of the major job sites listed in Appendix A. Some things to look for include:

- Would your optimum candidate likely visit this job site in the first place?

- Does she have the requisite skills to find it or the computer interest to venture here?

- Is the search engine interface on the site friendly enough for the technically faint of heart?

- Are the ads listed for competing jobs of sufficient volume to lure attractive clients back on a regular basis?

- Are the advertisers for those jobs true peers in the marketplace? Would you like to attract personnel from them? Have they ever raided you for talent? Is your favorite outside recruiter advertising there?

- Can you be competitive in this job market? Do your salary and benefits packages have enough appeal to bring some of the good candidates to your company?

- Can your staff create online job ads that are as good as the jobs themselves? Are they competitive in appearance and clarity?

- Are the ads in the commercial database stale? Check a few to be sure, and ask about the cancellation (removal) policies. Job candidates are quickly turned off by databases filled with job ads marketing jobs that have already been filled.

- Most importantly — does the site have traffic, traffic, traffic? Be sure to re-read Chapter 5, "Selecting an Online Service," on how to determine this.

Follow all the directions described in Chapter 3, "Writing the Online Ad." Make sure a full job description and qualifications, community, and company information are included. Most importantly, make sure links are included to your corporate Web site or a professionally prepared recruiting site so the candidate can access more information. As always, use tracking tags, source codes, and monitor the results resolutely.

❑ ❑ ❑

RESUME SOURCING

The newest twist in resume sourcing is the online commercial service that maintains a huge reservoir of professional resumes and charges companies for access to them. You are probably inundated with L3 (fireplace resumes), and the thought of adding to that volume may produce a negative gut reaction. But if the special resume database does contain prime candidates for the jobs you have open, the expense may be justified. Instead of posting your ads on the Internet and providing raw intelligence to your competitors about your growth plans, you can simply pay the fee and survey the available candidates.

Submitting a resume on such a database is not only free, some of the companies also provide job seekers with identity masking. That feature prevents the employer from discovering that one of its key players is interested in peddling her experience, talent, and expertise in the job market. The database only provides key details of experience without naming the job seeker or the companies where the experience was developed. If the employer indicates a strong interest, the service compares individual and corporate profiles, and provides a contact if appropriate. While this approach gives the corporate recruiter less power than she might like, it does attract highly qualified professionals who like the cost of the service (at their end).

So why pay for such a service? Simple. These services contain resumes that are not picked over by every headhunter sniffing the Web for talent. Pure and simple, if it is free, someone has been there many times. Some paid resume databases contain over 100,000 records. This might be a good first place to start.

Appendix B, "Internet Resume Sites," provides a list of these services for your review.

WELL DESIGNED WEB SITE FOR RECRUITING

Let's state the obvious right up front: Company Web sites usually make terrible recruiting tools. Why? There are two reasons.

The first is that when used as the sole recruiting tool, even the best Web site takes years to be productive and cost effective — to establish links and traffic — and, in the meantime, interest and efforts wane. The linking and promotion necessary to make the Web site successful are sometimes difficult to justify in a budget when the payoff is a year or two away. A Web site worth having deserves a three year plan, and should be integrated with related corporate objectives. Quality results before the third year, even for a superior recruiting web page, will be serendipitous.

And second, many corporate Web sites are written for primary purposes other than attracting candidates to apply for a position. Consider this: A bank tries to convey an image through its Web site that its organization is conservative, frugal, and responsible. The pictures on the site consist of tall, cold buildings made of marble and steel set in the middle of a large city teeming with traffic. As a job seeker, does this sound like a place where you want to work?

So what kind of Web site does work for recruiting? Simply, one that is linked from job ads in high traffic databases and is designed for recruiting purposes. When used by themselves, Web sites make terrible recruiting vehicles because it takes years to obtain enough traffic to justify their development. On the other hand, if a Web site is used in a supportive role, where it is linked from high traffic job ads on the Web, it can be an excellent tool to further attract candidates to your organization.

You need to have a Web site designed specifically for you, the HR department, with the goal being one thing: to attract quality candidates to your jobs and sell them on your organization. Your Web site should be well designed and include information about why your company is an exciting place to work, how you have the best benefits program in the country, how you care about your employees, how great your local community is, and so on. The key is to attract and sell the candidates, not drive them away.

In the new Internet, creativity will count. Get graphical, use Java, consider sound and video. Remember that quality job seekers want to know why they should work for you. You have the full interactive technology of the Internet to tell your company's story like never before. USE IT! But don't forget the 5% rule!

EXAMPLE OF THE PROGRESSIVE STRATEGY APPROACH

Bob Brown is HR director for XYZ company, a medium-sized engineering consulting firm in Taylors Corner, NC. Taylors Corner is a town the size of 5,000 with XYZ being the largest employer in the area. One of the biggest challenges facing Bob is finding high tech folks who will move to this small rural town.

Bob believes in the Internet. He has developed several ads that he is currently running on several free and commercial sites. Each ad is skillfully written and contains a hyperlink where job seekers can access more information about XYZ and the surrounding area. The Web site Bob links his ads to has been specifically designed for recruiting purposes. It contains multicolor graphics and has pictures of typical engineering tools adorning the site. A profile of the owner of XYZ, Richard Long and his story of rising from depression poverty to entrepreneurial success, is recounted.

Benefit programs are outlined as well as holiday schedules. Several pages contain pictures of smiling XYZ employees telling about their experiences at XYZ and about the friendly, small town atmosphere of Taylors Corner. But there is more than just information about XYZ company: A full color map of the Taylors Corner area is included with several of the local attractions highlighted. With the click of a mouse, the prospective job seeker can see folks skiing down Sugar Bluff Mountain, riding the wild rapids of the Sage river, or taking a stroll down the Woodlands Ridge trail. One gets the feeling from visiting this site that there are great folks in Taylors Corner.

Bob expects huge recruiting success using his approach. His strategy is to place his ads in the high traffic commercial job sites that will generate a large amount of traffic for his Web site. Contained in that traffic are those experienced engineers who are tired of the rat race, who want to get free from the traffic, smog, and pollution of Chicago, LA, and New York. Bob's approach is not only to become much more effective in hiring qualified candidates, but also to become more successful in retaining top performers on a long term basis. His strategy is to use Internet recruiting to reduce the company's high six figure annual budget for headhunter expenses.

THE PREMIER STRATEGY

This is what we live for: to see people using the full power of the Internet for recruiting success. We have seen several firms who have made the leap to using full Internet power and have gained huge success.

At this point, a firm has been using all the resources mentioned in the two previous strategies in this chapter and is now ready to step up and make a serious commitment to Internet recruiting using all the tools. We do express caution with this approach. Make sure before you jump in with any online ad service that you investigate and quantify the amount and type of traffic any advertising venue receives. You may purchase a banner ad in a service that does not attract the type nor the quantity of candidates you wish to draw. Key points of the premier strategy include:

- Use of most, if not all, of the top quality job sites

- Well-designed interactive Web site

- Prescreening using forms and application blanks

- Banner ads on key Web sites

- Integrate print and online advertising

TOP QUALITY JOB SITES

For a fraction of what you spend recruiting for one job using the national newspapers, your organization can place dozens of ads in several of the leading Internet job databases. Why split pennies? Jump into several services at once; after all, the cost is incredibly inexpensive compared to print advertising. Consider this: a 4x5 inch ad in many Sunday newspapers in LA, Chicago, or New York will run at least $5,000 and run for one day. The same size ad run in the top four commercial job sites on the Web will cost about $600 and run for 30-60 days.

When an organization realizes that the Internet has incredible value and jumps in, they can find incredible success. Timidity has no place in any business endeavor, yet we see it all the time in major corporations on the Internet. Choose your sites wisely using the criteria discussed in Chapter 5, and be sure to construct professional ads that contain tracking tags, source codes, and links to an interactive recruiting Web site.

WELL-DESIGNED INTERACTIVE WEB SITE

Let's face it, if you want to be a leader on the Web, you have to portray a cutting-edge image. This means you must provide a state-of-the art Web site, chock full of all the interactive tools, that is linked from your job ads. By interactive, we mean Java, Shockwave, video, sound, the works! Work with designers to make the site as attractive as possible, and be sure you cover in depth all the questions job seekers have about considering a change in employment:

- What opportunities will I have with this organization?

- What types of employee benefits are available?

- What are my co-workers like? What do they think about the company?

- What is the surrounding community like? What kinds of recreational pursuits are available? What is the school system like? What about housing values?

- Will my spouse be able to find local employment?

- Will I be happy working for your organization?

If you construct your job ads and recruiting Web site well enough, you will save a considerable amount of time in both labor and indirect costs. Unqualified job seekers will not apply; job seekers will self screen themselves if there is a mismatch between their desires and what your organization has to offer; relevant company information about benefits will already be covered, and candidates will develop firm insights into company policies and attitudes.

PRESCREENING USING FORMS AND APPLICATION BLANKS

The Web has many uses, and one that is gaining in popularity is prescreening of candidates. Traditionally, an individual reads a job ad online, accesses additional information about a company, and e-mails a resume. Consider a change in the process: Instead of instructing a candidate to e-mail in her resume, have the candidate fill out a prescreening application blank and attach her resume to it. By asking a few prescreening questions, you can sort out all the unqualified candidates, and have more time and resources to focus on the candidates that matter. Your Webmaster or several of the commercial online job ad services can help you design application blanks. When undertaking a complete Web recruiting strategy, give online job applications a try.

❑ ❑ ❑

BANNER ADS ON KEY WEB SITES

Banner ads are everywhere on the Web. You will find them on all the major search engines (Yahoo, Alta Vista, and so on) and all the major job search sites. The idea behind a banner ad is simple; place a banner across a high traffic area on the Web and entice Web users to click the banner to link to more information about your organization. In recruiting, you are interested in attracting candidates for jobs, so the first likely source of obtaining a banner ad is across several of the highly traveled job sites.

Appendix A lists several sites that accept banner ads. If you want to purchase a banner ad, remember that you have to link it to something (either a recruiting Web site with jobs listed or a Web page that can perform a search of your jobs contained in one or more of the commercial sites). The bottom line value of the banner depends on the quality of the location to which it is linked.

If you haven't guessed it by now, the banner ad concept can be a very pricey option compared to other online recruitment means. But, if your organization has a large amount of hires to make or if the organization has a few open jobs that are difficult to fill, a banner ad is something you should consider.

INTEGRATE PRINT AND ONLINE ADVERTISING

No matter how successful your efforts are in the online recruitment arena, most of you will still use print advertising in one form or another. Smart organizations have learned that for maximum success in a recruitment campaign, it helps to include a Web address in your newspaper ads; then job seekers can go online to find more information about your organization or additional available jobs. The Web site can be your own Web site or a recruiting page hosted by one of the commercial services with a search link to all your online job ads.

EXAMPLE OF THE PREMIER STRATEGY

South Computer Company is one of the leading IS consulting firms in the southeast. Headquartered out of the Research Triangle Park, NC, it provides mainframe and PC support for several of the large banks and research institutes in the Carolinas. Successful growth has created dozens of openings for consultants at client sites throughout the Carolinas. In this region's tight labor market, South is experiencing extreme difficulty attracting talented IS professionals. Part of the problem is the local unemployment rate hovers around 3 percent. Additionally, candidates from other regions of the country are unaware of the advantages of living in the southeast: low cost of living, quality lifestyle, excellent universities, and so on.

South devised a strategy of designing a professional recruiting Web site that fully depicts the opportunities in working for South and the benefits gained from moving to the southeast. Additionally, an application blank, which is used to prequalify job candidates, is contained on the site.

Several job packages have been purchased from the leading commercial job sites. Dozens of jobs have been entered that are professionally written and contain links to South's recruiting Web site. Candidates are encouraged to apply online using South's application blank. Banner ads are being run on major job sites to attract additional candidates. Ads are being run in leading newspapers in the southeast and leading IS publications nationwide. Each ad contains the Web address of South's recruiting Web site, where readers are encouraged to go for more information about the company and additional available consulting assignments.

The reason for the increased advertising is simple: Every week that South goes without an additional consultant, it loses several thousand dollars in client billings and risks losing clients if it is unable to meet their current needs quickly.

STAFFING FOR ONLINE RECRUITING

An effective implementation of any of the three strategies or parts thereof will require some innovation in staffing an online recruiting effort as well as integrating it into the larger human resources mission. A common management mistake in beginning projects, implementing new processes, or changing policies, is to simply turn to the current staff and say "Handle it! Handle it!"

Breaking a comfortable, or even an uncomfortable paradigm will require some training and, often, personnel changes. The window of opportunity is always smaller than you think, and a delay in producing results is a powerful fertilizer for the weeds of indifference that threaten to block your vision of what can and should be. You need an implementation plan with benchmarks to measure progress along each major step. And nothing is more important to the success of online recruiting than the qualifications of the staff.

An early theme of this book was the simplicity of online job advertising. It can be straightforward and direct, quickly accomplished, and simply performed. The challenge is to coordinate the effort with the expectations. You can certainly progress at a slow pace and cost justify every step with results, and in many cases, this is prudent and wise.

Some of the pitfalls include:

- An early success that fuels expectations and inspires without educating the staff, leading key people to ignore the changing parameters of a talent market with many competitors.

- Administrative patterns that lock your staff into doing distinctively new tasks while following old procedures that are painfully ineffective.

- Alliances among your staff with outside resources that resist any changes to the comfortable status quo.

The staff descriptions on the following pages are a starting point in your policy making thought process.

RESUME RESEARCH SPECIALIST

Duties and responsibilities:

- Maintains and updates resume source lists for all major job categories as defined by the recruiting coordinator.

- Conducts custom resume searches for open positions using job profiles, keyword lists, and other provided resources.

- Develops and maintains a backlog of L1 and L2 resumes for each position.

- Records, screens, and documents incoming resumes from multiple sources.

- Performs first cut triage on incoming resumes from all sources.

- Recommends additions and deletions to fields on job candidate databases.

- Supports jobs analyst with statistics and profiles of the online talent market.

- Reviews filed resumes on discard date for action decision.

Requirements and qualifications:

- Excellent Internet skills, including World Wide Web, Usenet, listserv, and e-mail communications.

- At least two years of recruiting experience.

- Software proficiency:
    word processing (at least 40wpm)
    spreadsheet (data entry, totals)
    presentation
    scheduling/project

- Keyword search proficiency including Boolean logic skills.

ONLINE AD SPECIALIST

Duties and responsibilities:

- Files online job ads on commercial and free sites, ensuring accurate transcription of data, timely placement, and keyword accuracy.

- Maintains records of ads placed (site, date, time, related position codes, and other relevant data).

- Maintains summary counts of ads placed with various commercial and free sites.

- Researches effectiveness of ads in producing results, tracking quality of resumes, date received, redundancies.

- Researches possible new sites on the Internet, performing studies on the number of jobs advertised.

- Evaluates the online recruiting efforts of key competitors based on the number and kinds of ads placed.

- Files open positions on the corporate Web site and updates general corporate and community data as needed.

- Provides feedback to jobs analyst about the talent market on the Internet.

Requirements and qualifications:

- Good Internet skills, including Web site, Usenet, listserv, and e-mail communications.

- Excellent facsimile skills, able to broadcast jobs to large numbers of specific locations.

- At least three years of recruiting experience.

- Software proficiency:
      word processing (at least 40wpm)
      spreadsheet (data entry, totals)
      presentation
      scheduling/project

- Keyword and Boolean search skills.

JOBS ANALYST

Duties and responsibilities:

- Creates, updates, and maintains templates for online job ads, and composes job ads for other media as required.

- Regularly reviews online job ads for accuracy and clarity.

- Creates special job ads for special positions, and customizes standard job ads for special situations.

- Routinely adds to the collection of standard job ads.

- Maintains a database of core competencies and key skills for major job areas.

- Performs second stage interviews.

- Reports to the recruiting coordinator.

- Works closely with online ad specialist and resume search specialist.

- Coordinates with careers manager about the talent market and long term plans for growth.

- Interviews operating managers on background, education, experience, and skills requirements.

- Conducts/reviews exit interviews to collect relevant jobs data.

- Conducts surveys and other studies on job performance.

Requirements and qualifications

- At least five years of in-house recruiting experience.

- Distinct and complete writing skills, preferably training and at least two years experience in journalism. Must be able to write quickly and persuasively.

- At least two years experience in jobs classification, core competencies, job description, performance evaluation, performance review, and related skills.

- Certified in either the Five Factor or the Myers-Briggs personality evaluation systems.

- Software proficiency:

- word processing (at least 40wpm) spreadsheet (data entry, totals)

CAREERS MANAGER

Duties and responsibilities:

- Works with the recruiting manager to ensure that the recruiting policies and procedures support overall human resource goals for career management and staff development.

- Monitors training, promotions, and compensation policy for overall conformance to organizational goals.

- Conducts long range planning for staffing quality and makes policy recommendations to the director of human resources.

Requirements and qualifications:

- At least five years experience in recruiting.

- At least three years experience in training.

- A strong human resources background in advancement and compensation, with at least ten years experience in human resources.

RECRUITING COORDINATOR

Duties and responsibilities:

- Supervises resume search specialists.

- Supervises online ad specialists.

- Supervises jobs analysts.

- Works closely with careers manager, coordinating recruiting with broader human resource issues.

- Reports to director of human resources.

- Directs recruiting technical support person when providing advice and assistance to recruiting personnel

Requirements and qualifications:

- A sound background in online searches and data entry, able to perform many of the tasks assigned to subordinates.

- At least eight years of in-house recruiting experience.

- A strong human resources background.

❑ ❑ ❑

RECRUITING TECHNICAL SUPPORT

Duties and responsibilities:

- Perform all technical tasks of resume search and online ad specialist.

- Supports recruiting on a regular, first priority basis.

- Creates and maintains recruiting Web page on larger corporate Web page with support from recruiting staff.

- Maintains Internet access and e-mail capacity of the recruiting area.

- Provides technical assistance and training as needed.

- Recommends hardware, software, and links to recruiting coordinator.

Qualifications and requirements:

- As specified by the IS manager to perform the duties and responsibilities.

GENERAL HR STRATEGIES TO REMEMBER

In addition to the three key online strategies mentioned earlier in this chapter, there are several issues that the HR professional needs to keep in mind while conducting her online effort as well as her whole recruiting program. These suggestions will make your whole recruiting effort more effective, independent of which of the three strategies you use.

ADDITIONAL FREE ADVERTISING VENUES

Just because you are presented with a new tool called the Internet does not mean you should overlook some obvious advertising venues currently available to you, but possibly underutilized.

Two resources that should not be overlooked are corporate bulletin boards and newsletters to publicize job openings. That process activates networking in the communities your organization serves, and your managers and professionals will routinely get inquiries from friends, relatives, and acquaintances about opportunities there. Give them some data to distribute for you. Networks sometimes work faster than the Internet.

As your experience with human resource recruiting grows, you will find more and more outlets for job information. Would some of the professors at your favorite academic institution be able to recommend a qualified job candidate from the great folks who've graduated? How many professional organizations might have good candidates? What are the outplacement firms that serve your industry with some frequency? These are all facsimile campaign possibilities. There should be a fax list for each major type of job opening and you should have the fax software capability to distribute them quickly.

RESUMES ON HAND

There are a ton of free resumes on the Internet, but don't forget the ones you already have on hand in hard copy. Besides being close at hand, they represent a class of job candidates that have already expressed a sincere interest in working for your organization. Ideally, they are grouped first by jobs applied for, and second by last names alphabetically. Other approaches can work if they are maintained by a dedicated staff that values the contribution that personnel recruiting makes to the success of the organization.

But resumes are often filed nefariously by submission date to facilitate quick and easy disposal by barely literate clerks after a brief retention period. If a resume is worth keeping, it should be easy for the staff to find and relate to the job at hand. Marginal resumes shouldn't be retained at all. When a good resume reaches your pre-established disposal date, send the once eager candidate a brief form letter like the following:

Dear Mr. Jones:

> *Thank you for your interest one year ago in pursuing a career with PowerBank. Although I have no jobs currently open that fit your special qualifications, I would like to follow your professional development in regard to future opportunities with us.*
>
> *Please send me an updated copy of your resume with a cover letter which highlights your recent development of skills and experience which might be valuable to us. Upon receipt I will compare your data to cur-*

rent open positions and advise you if I recognize immediate employment potential.

I wish you the best in your career.

Sincerely,
William Robert Hampton

MANAGING OLD RESUMES

When a resume reaches the pre-established disposal date, you have three options:

- Form letter sent from recruiter before disposal.

- Disposal without letter upon recruiter review and authorization.

- Routed to a human resource recruiter for a scheduled review.

NOTE

Clerks should not simply toss out resumes once evaluated as worthwhile, simply because there is a new date on their desktop calendar.

If the files are well organized and maintained, you should be able to quickly identify and rank the likely candidates for further consideration. This is a good start in the recruiting process.

MANAGE RESUME THROUGH THE TRIAGE APPROACH

Triage is a French term for a medical management procedure developed in combat medical facilities to handle large volumes of wounded soldiers. All the incoming wounded were slotted into three broad categories. One group had injuries serious enough that immediate medical intervention was imperative to prevent death or other serious deterioration of physical condition. This group was routed to surgery for immediate action.

The second group had wounds that had received adequate first aid, and their condition was stable enough that the medical treatment required could be delayed for hours without any detrimental long term consequences to their health. They were placed in a holding tent and made comfortable.

A third group had injuries so dire that, even with the most heroic medical procedures, had a slim chance of success. They had their own treatment modality that mediated the pain and allowed them to expire in relative peace.

Triage was so successful medically that the concept migrated to the business world and is now a common management term for a systematic analysis of problems to prepare for an economical focus of efforts.

The first level of recruiting triage is the trickiest to handle. Ideally, the resume search and online job ads should produce a number of good candidates for open positions, to be reviewed and investigated in detail. Handling the interviews, final selection, and salary negotiations are topics best left to another book. The trickiest aspect of handling this elite level is not the hiring, but the constructive handling of the remnant that we don't hire. Independent of when we eliminated the finalists for the current open position(s), they were still prime candidates and prudence suggests that we not simply forget the job candidate unless the hiring decision process discovered they had serious defects of competence or character.

First, when those elite resumes and interview records are stored, they should be routed to a special file. That file should be the first file the internal recruiter goes to when a related job order arrives from the hiring manager. In addition, a follow-up protocol is needed to ensure that the file remains up to date. The staff should place these job candidates on a mailing list for annual reports, product and service promotions, and anything else that might be of value in maintaining the prospect's interest in your company. And recruiting managers need to schedule periodic personal telephone calls. In this book, we refer to these resumes as Level Ones, or simply L1.

The second level of triage is related to the first, but just not closely enough. The job candidate may just require a few courses and three years more of experience before she qualifies for the job under consideration, but could represent some long term potential to your organization. These resumes typically go into the files for future review, and are the ones subject to the disposal options we discussed earlier in the chapter. They definitely deserve a nice note of thanks and appreciation, but we seldom have time to advance the process much further. Tracking and control should follow them through that process and be preserved for future reference, even though they merit a lower level of consideration. These are the Level 2, or L2, resumes.

The third category in the resume triage is an L3. This wild, unrelated resume is the bane of every recruiter's existence. Every human resources department should have a fireplace in which to usefully dispose of the mountains of resumes that are submitted with more earnest prayer than simple logic. The archeologist who wants to design rocket engines; the minister who wants to sell mobile homes; the history major who wants to be a medical center administrator; we have seen them all, and our human resources sentiments are not to crush dreams or stomp on baby chickens. But someone must discard that huge volume of unwanted resumes, and it falls to managers unless we can delegate the task and risk losing some real gems.

They are the fatally wounded, not because of any serious personal deficiency, but because they simply do not fit the job that you are trying to fill or any other that you anticipate having available at your company. The resumes are best routed to the fireplace as rolled logs or to the recycling bin, a more ecological end. A well written online job ad can minimize the number of these resumes, but they will still often account for between 40 and 95 percent of the resumes received. If you choose to be nice, send them a post card with regrets and no encouragement.

But we also use the source codes to identify the media that produced those resumes. If an inordinate fraction of those unrelated resumes come from a single source and only a slim fraction of the good ones originate there, we may reconsider our targeting tactics and our ad expenditures. Every L3 resume costs money to process, both regular labor and opportunity costs. Human resource management should assign a fixed amount, at least $2, and incorporate the value in their review of resume sources.

DEVELOPING TEMPLATES

The arduous and creative process of writing good online job ads really can't wait until the job orders come in. Chapter 3, "Writing the Online Job Ad," covers the "how to's," but the when part is covered here. Middle level, high volume jobs should be covered first with well written job ads backed with excellent task and responsibilities documentation. Next target those jobs for which acquisition expenses such as advertising costs, headhunter fees, signing bonuses, spousal hires, and special benefits packages have been substantial. An optimum initial target would be a set of standard job ads that include the job that made up 50 percent of the management level placements or placement costs in the previous calendar year. Beyond that point, a case-by-case development may be adequate.

CAREER MANAGEMENT

Check your own professional library on the topic of career management. It is mentioned here because companies who have a good career management program also have a clearer perspective on the kind and quality of new people they want to introduce to the company, and a better chance of retaining them for many years in the future.

As a result, the online job ads are better written, the online service selection is more precisely targeted, the fostering of new hires doesn't stop when the new hire reports for work, and the human resources department earns a larger measure of respect and confidence from the operating departments.

Our definition of career management is an ongoing human resources project that reinforces corporate goals by playing an active role not just in recruiting, but in the training, mentoring, education, and assignment of corporate personnel in ways that enhance productivity, professional achievement, job satisfaction, and organizational loyalty.

ADVANCED RESUME HANDLING

This strategy calls for sophistication in two interrelated areas: resume databases and core competencies. A carefully designed and assiduously maintained resume database can improve the speed and quality of your recruiting performance. But creating a fully functional database requires an organized approach to core competency issues.

The hard, cold reality of resume management is that a strictly paper based system, even if a rational triage system is used, involves too much shuffling of files. The work tends to be done by either diligent administrative staff who do not understand enough about the selection process to do it proficiently, or by in-house human resource recruiters who do not have enough time to do it well.

The common response to this quandary is adaptation rather than management. The hard copy files are largely ignored unless creative and organized recruiters keep an informal and unofficial log of the high end candidates who were not hired the last time openings were available, and can summon those files from the records by name. This strategy falls to pieces, however, if an aggressive purge policy has already dispatched the named files to the human resources fireplace. Keeping resumes of good candidates in one's credenza should be frowned upon by management.

NOTE

Unless a job candidate has an irrational, emotional attachment to the idea of a career with your company, he will not send a copy of his resume to you more than twice without the expression of some active interest by your recruiters.

The impact of that insight is straightforward. Young, talented managers and other professionals with good backgrounds and excellent educational credentials send you their resumes with high hopes of beginning a stellar career of personal achievement, well earned recognition, and attractive compensation (in the long run). But you lose out if they do not fit the profile of who you want now, and receive the same form letter rejection as the amateur ecologist who wanted to sell construction equipment. They find a good job somewhere else and begin to build a sound record of accomplishment there, discounting the possibility of future opportunities with your organization.

Years later, through a well nurtured network, they learn that your organization is looking for someone with their background and experience. A flurry of superbly crafted cover letters with updated resumes are dispatched to human resources and the hiring managers. But, because management has decided to transfer and train from within, outsource the tasks, or just because you resent their initiative in going direct to hiring managers, you reject their appeals for consideration again despite the fact that they now possess key, applicable, and valuable skills. They get the same dumb letter, and within a short period of time their resumes and cover letters feed the fireplace.

Only obvious desperation will induce them to submit a third resume.

As a result, we guess that between 30 and 70 percent of the qualified candidates for jobs are effectively unavailable to the companies with open positions.

The broad range results from two factors: the company's reputation for treating its employees well and being a good place to work on one hand, and the company's resume management skills on the other. We should look seriously at the latter.

The logic behind the triage approach is that you reduce the overall resume load to a manageable level by dumping those who are obviously a bad fit, and that you recognize that a large fraction of people in the second group who fail to meet the pressing staffing needs of today can be strong candidates in the future. The 23 year old applicant who has an MBA in corporate finance, internships in marketing and communications, and a 3.9 GPA from a good school may not qualify as a bond trader now, but her resume should not be burned.

When determining a resumes triage value be sure your criteria for making the second tier is clear and selective enough. Depending on how attractive the jobs and your company are, this group could account for between three and ten percent of the respondents.

Second, is the applicant's career track promising? If you need someone with CPA status and an applicant's resume shows that he has been working as an accountant for fifteen years without achieving those credentials, you can legitimately eliminate him from the second tier.

Third, does the applicant's cover letter and resume cover a significant number of the credentials you will be looking for in the future and which would be appropriate for the current stage of his career?

CORE COMPETENCIES AND NUMBER FIELDS

In addition to the keyword search capacity of your resume database, you need to develop fields that bracket the core competencies for specific jobs in a way that allows your well-trained administrative staff to catalog the resumes of this second tier group upon their receipt and to update them when newer resumes are received. If your database allows sufficient fields, you should be able to discover when a candidate also has skills of general value to your organization, in addition to the competencies related to the job for which she originally applied.

As much as possible, the fields should be number oriented. From a technical point of view, numeric values are easier to track, store, and compare in a database; but more importantly, job candidates who include figures with their facts explicitly recognize the importance of quantifying their performance. Let those with nebulous qualifications work somewhere else. Some obvious suggestions are:

- Numbers of dollars saved

- Total sales for the year

- Total contribution margins

- Number of employees supervised

- Number of units sold

- Number of articles published

- Marketing campaigns created/implemented

- Number of classes taught/student load

- Hours of standards created (work measurement)

You get the idea. But don't limit yourself to numbers. Credentials can also come in yes/no answers to questions such as college degree, PE (professional engineer) certification, licenses, and so on.

There is also considerable value in having simple phrase fields that identify the record of employers worked for, schools attended, software proficiency, and so on.

CAUTION

This approach is only a winnowing tactic for reducing the number of resumes that must be reviewed by recruiters when sourcing a job order; if all files received have fully qualified candidates, there are probably a few more that should be reviewed. The good recruiter will always know more about the job requirements than can be fully captured by the computer software.

RESUME MANAGEMENT

One of the long term goals of a human resources department should be to provide so much top notch talent to the organization and fulfill the career aspirations of so many outstanding managers and professionals that this job advertising and resume management process gradually slips into oblivion. Your vision should be that all the best talent in the industry knows about the company and routinely sends their fine resumes to you. Can't you just see the rows upon rows of job candidates with splendid credentials, standing with their hats and resumes in hand, waiting patiently at your office door for an interview?

S U M M A R Y   I N S I G H T S

WAKE UP AND MAKE IT HAPPEN!

The toughest part of any new strategy is getting started, with maintaining momentum claiming second place. Here are some general principles

- You have read all the information about job ads, recruiting Web sites, banner ads, and resume databases. Give several services a call, request information, write some ads. Go do it!

- Review your triage criteria at least once annually. Roughly speaking, one-third of your new hires should come from each of the following sources - second echelon people whose skills and files were updated; first echelon people who made a better fit this time; and new resume arrivals responding to either your ads or your reputation. If only 5 percent of the second echelon group become employed with you, your criteria for them may be too tight. The same applies to the first group, especially after you have a complete program for at least one year.

- Track the on-the-job performance of new hires, especially against the pattern of skills and core competencies established as a part of the hiring goals.

- For each major job category, create and maintain tracking statistics on the depth of qualified resumes behind each position. For example, if you have a quality engineer position with your company with four incumbents, having five first echelon and eight second echelon resumes on potential replacements would be much more comforting than having only one and two respectively. Factor any apparent shortages into the online job ad campaign you conduct the next time one of those jobs becomes open.

- Develop automated follow-up procedures for resumes on the database.

- At least twice a year, poll operating managers on the new skills developing and needed in the industry, and incorporate that data into the resume evaluation templates used by the staff. Interview current employees who have those skills to obtain insights into how they are developed and where persons with those skills can be found.

- Maintain an image file of professional and industry articles describing the characteristics and accomplishments of leaders or trend setters in the key jobs that you routinely recruit for. Work with others to keep it up-to-date.

DODGING PARADIGMS

After a human resource process begins to approach real effectiveness, the parameters perversely change. The hardware, the software, the hard copy, and the personnel will invariably become outdated and under optimized, requiring adaptations or sweeping changes. Anticipate and execute the necessary changes without delay.

Recruiting good performers is never routine, and even the Internet cannot make it trouble free or easy. The Internet is just another tool, but there are different levels of precision and sophistication. None of them preclude some thoughtful planning and deliberate execution.

The low end strategy is a good start for any human resource function, but especially appropriate for the inexperienced, under funded, or bashful. You can use it to get your feet wet without hazarding your career, and use your successes as a foundation for growth in effective recruiting. As your experience, funding, and confidence allow, you can move ahead to other levels or simply bask in the glow of achieved successes.

The middle strategy is a real commitment, but doesn't stretch the limits on what many companies are doing. Most importantly, your savings from a reduced expense of using outside recruiters should fund any extra costs involved and provide some resources for growth requirements. You may be content to stay at this level indefinitely and you would be well justified in many circumstances.

The top or premier strategy is the "take no prisoners" approach. With it, the human resources department goes beyond improving the quality of new personnel and reducing the costs of recruiting them to the point of making recruitment an engine of corporate growth and a competitive corporate tool. The premier strategy is not for the unskilled or weak of heart.

A critical decision parameter is the speed at which you choose for your strategy to be realized. Steady growth will moderate costs, creating almost a "pay as you go" process, but will not become a career maker.

The success of online recruiting depends on the skills you and your staff have now, and the pace at which you choose to enhance those skills or recruit key people to supplement your current staff. If you are in a hurry, on-the-job training will be a disaster, especially if your current staff is computer bashful to begin with.

Sprinkled in this chapter are a few advanced issues without a direct link to online job ads, but they are worthwhile to consider as the part of an overall human resource management policy for progress. We especially recommend the following for additional reflection and investigation:

- Core competencies

- Career management

- Five Factor personality evaluation

But the best advice is to get started.

CHAPTER 10

THE FUTURE OF INTERNET RECRUITMENT

The Bell Parallel

"How were sales today, Andy?"

"Awful. Even the most promising prospects refuse to buy our telephone service. They are just not interested, Mr. Bell!"

"Don't they realize how economical telephones will make communications inside the city?"

"Yes, they don't deny the cost figures I supply, but they have long standing relationships with the courier services here and that expense is already in their annual budgets."

"Is there no interest in cutting costs and increasing profits?"

"Yes, but what they really want is a much cheaper courier service. If they could have a penny off every dime spent on couriers, and avoid selling and training their bosses on a new technology, they would be delighted!"

"But telephones represent a cost savings of at least 50 percent!"

"It doesn't matter to them and they find a future reduction in their departmen-

tal budget a real threat. They cringe at the thought of having a budget so small that management would consider consolidating them with another department. Those business communications managers are very territorial."

"Don't they at least consider long distance telephone communications valuable? We have wires strung to Philadelphia, Boston, Buffalo, and Albany now."

" They like the idea, but their IS (intercity services) people insist that their telegraph facilities cover that need very adequately. Four prospects claim that their IS staff can create their own telephone system more cheaply than our service, but none of them have strung a hundred yards of wire yet."

"How does top management feel about telephone service?"

"They are open to change — for the next generation. To them, the telephone is a fad like automobiles, phonographs, moving pictures, and wrist watches. As long as they can make the payroll and take home some profits, they are content."

"Well, Andy, keep trying. When the five percent who are using the telephone successfully start taking business away from the others, sales will pick up."

"Mr. Bell, what will you be doing in the meantime?"

"Andy, I don't know how to start, but I would like to take a page from Dr. Pasteur's book and develop a vaccine that would protect businessmen from willful folly and compulsive cowardice."

"If you do that, Mr. Bell, it will be the greatest invention in the history of humanity, but you will have to hire a crew of salesmen who are bigger and tougher than I am!"

"Why, Andy?"

"Because, for even a free trial, the salesmen will need to wrestle your prospects to the ground and hold them there while the shot is administered!

CHANGES TO THE INTERNET RECRUITMENT INDUSTRY

Although thousands of individuals have been hired using Internet recruitment methods and organizations worldwide are opening up to the possibilities of this resource, most human resource professionals are still at the borders of online technology. The rate of change is so rapid that we can only make one prediction about the future of Internet assisted recruitment: it will dramatically affect how companies worldwide source, attract, and assess talent.

In the past 3-4 years, we have seen hundreds of individuals and organizations with entrepreneurial spirit attempt to make their mark on the Internet in the employment arena. Some have offered services out of the basement of their home or a spare bedroom, others have piggybacked on publicly financed resources at universities and libraries, and still others have marshaled the Internet magic to bolster old hard copy paradigms. In addition, the types of services offered and the business models used have varied as each tried to find the key to success.

As we move toward that hallmark year 2000, we see many major changes in the Internet recruitment industry. Some are global changes that will affect the Industry at large; others will affect how job seekers find jobs and how organizations integrate the Internet into their HR processes.

Among all the uncertainty and rapid change on the Internet there are a few developments that we anticipate:

- The industry will consolidate around 3-4 general job sites and several dozen niche or boutique sites. These sites will offer full services such as job postings, resumes, corporate profiles, banner advertising, and so on. But there will be some turnover in the industry leadership as enterprising new companies challenge with aggressive service levels and better software. The most likely source of new blood will be a company that has the deep pockets and imagination to make a difference without the handicap of ingrained links to print advertising.

- Third party auditing will become prevalent, and client organizations will be able to better quantify the traffic that their advertisements are receiving in different online venues. The current deluge of contracted evaluations will be recognized more broadly as data fraud.

- Newspapers will lose significant revenue as advertising dollars move to the Internet.

- The Internet will gain widespread acceptance as a recruiting tool as millions more Americans get online access and use it to find jobs.

- Worldwide recruitment will become prevalent as major job sites add overseas databases.

- Communications technology will rapidly escalate bandwidth capacity of telephone and cable lines. Multimedia resumes and online interviews will be possible when the standard modem speed exceeds 100kbs.

CONSOLIDATION OF JOB SITES

Currently, there are hundreds of job sites on the Internet offering everything from jobs in Alaska to opportunities in New Jersey. The reason for the proliferation of such sites is simple:

- The cost for admittance is cheap.

- The rewards are great.

That scenario worked in the old Internet business model whereby the technology was not too complicated (generic HTML), the cost for bandwidth (traffic) was rather small, links to the site were easily obtained, and most Internet users were very computer literate (as well as tolerant for the way things were).

In the future, the standard for Web sites will be high graphic content that is interactive, user friendly, fast working, and fun to visit. To design, develop, and maintain such a site will take a huge amount of capital — much more than was needed several years ago for startup job ad sites. In addition, as the Internet model moves toward the purchasing of links from high profile Internet sites, job sites that are built on a shoestring budget will be unable to fund the links necessary. They won't be able to gather the traffic needed to make their service viable. The links that were once exchanged like scarves at a sorority house will come with a Christian Dior price tag.

What will emerge is a handful of well-funded job sites that have high amounts of traffic and dozens of smaller sites with extremely valuable targeted traffic. All will possess excellent graphic content, be user friendly, and offer the job seeker a well-rounded array of jobs that keeps them coming back.

THIRD PARTY AUDITING

Some job services provide performance statistics that remind one more of street corner shell games than management reporting. Better internal tracking methods, site tracking software, and third party auditing of web traffic will finally give corporate recruiters a good idea of the actual traffic (to a particular web site) and the real value to their actual recruiting efforts. As we mentioned in earlier chapters, the number of "hits" a site receives says little about how much real traffic that site receives.

One individual may actually be responsible for a few thousand hits to a site if that one person spends hours in the site accessing information. The slight of hand statistics currently popular forces employers to perform their own tracking and evaluation of results. But computer technology advances allow the ethically challenged to keep one step ahead of the most responsible oversight functions.

NEWSPAPER REVENUE

Today, your local newspaper has a virtual lock on the local job advertising market, and newspapers in general represent one of the most prominent venues for merchants to advertise their products. Estimates have been made that by the year 2000, newspapers will lose over 10 percent of their ad revenue as businesses begin switching more and more of their advertising dollars online. Dollars lost will be in the several billion range in the next decade. Job listings alone will become a quarter billion dollar a year industry by 2002.

INTERNET GAINS WIDESPREAD ACCEPTANCE

- 100 years ago, it was the telephone.

- 70 years ago, it was the radio.

- 40 years ago, it was the television.

- 15 years ago, it was cable.

- Today, it's the Internet

Each leap in technology had its detractors and at the beginning the road was bumpy with all the headaches associated with a new service. Today you look in the yellow pages for a phone number, buy a car at your local car dealership, and look at catalogs to order merchandise. The technology to let you find phone numbers, order cars, and purchase merchandise over the Internet is already here, but many consumers haven't used it yet. In fact, only about 15 percent of corporate America is currently using online job ads. As each succeeding year passes, the Internet will become integrated into our daily lives, not just because it is new, but because of the quantity and quality of communication that it provides for people.

When AOL switched to a flat monthly rate of $19.95, it was inundated with new customers and with old customers using its services more frequently. Within a computer generation (five years), anticipate that we will no longer sign on to an Internet account. It will become a resource like telephone service, electric and gas utilities, and cable television. We will leave it on and flip the appropriate switches to initiate service almost instantaneously.

WORLDWIDE RECRUITMENT SITES BECOME PREVALENT

As the world opens itself up to the new information age, we expect to see the Internet used for more global recruitment. Currently several major jobs sites run overseas versions of their popular U.S. job sites. Eventually, we imagine several worldwide recruitment networks will form with jobs available at the click of a mouse. In the not too distant future, you will be able to read ads and resumes in other languages on the Internet, and be able to click the appropriate button for translations.

If some bandwidth issues are resolved (see the next section), the new employee cross country moves will occur less frequently. If you work with a colleague primarily through e-mail (or intranet), her physical location is irrelevant — she can be three doors down the hall or on the deck of her mountain-top retreat several time zones away.

MORE BANDWIDTH

Many of the advances discussed previously depend heavily on wiring. Not just those mundane copper wires, but fiber optic cable and microwave, and the software to push text, voice, and video at much faster rates over the lines that make the Internet possible. It is an infrastructure issue, both in terms of the capital required and the ability of the connection providers to recapture their investments with handsome profits. The challenge is that geometrically increasing bandwidth will threaten the very linear minutes-on-the-line paradigm that the industry feels comfortable with. The wider bandwidths will come, but non-technical issues will determine how fast.

❑ ❑ ❑

JOB SEEKER PERSPECTIVE

We also envision several changes in technology that will provide job seekers with faster access and easier matching to jobs that fit their requirements:

- Agent technology will be better developed on leading job sites. Providers will attract more and better job candidates by creating more capable and resilient search technology. One approach would be to allow registered candidates to submit a comprehensive and confidential search strategy that would poll each new ad for career fit and provide the job candidate with a short menu of opportunities when she returned to the site.

- Personal job candidate agent technology will become available. This killer application will allow the job candidate to search multiple job sites continuously and report the results on demand.

- Resume databases that maintain the anonymity of job seekers will become more readily available. After that job candidate vulnerability is minimized, you can expect a flood of resumes from people who believe they are not advancing as quickly or being compensated as well as they should. The perceived lack of corporate loyalty to its employees may "byte" a lot more big companies where it hurts.

- More job candidates will be conducting special peer interviews. They work like this: The job candidate finds an online job ad that is appealing, but doesn't know a lot about the company although the material found on the corporate Web page seems promising enough. She turns to the resume database and places the name of the corporation and a few job related keywords into the search string. The search turns up three or four folks who are working or have worked there, complete with their telephone numbers or e-mail addresses. She contacts them for a confidential chat.

❑ ❑ ❑

RECRUITER PERSPECTIVE

New technology will make the recruiter's job much easier:

- Software becomes more readily available and cost effective, allowing recruiters to manage the entire recruiting process with an integrated capability to identify critical abilities, plan long term staffing strategies, place Internet job ads, receive Internet and other resumes, and maintain a comprehensive human resource database with both candidates and incumbents represented.

- Most HR departments nationwide will gain high speed access to the Internet. The larger companies will be hooked up first to the high bandwidth lines with smart terminals for recruiters.

- The training function within HR will become more integrated with recruiting as human resources functions makes more focused choices about whether to buy or develop the skills they need.

- The recruiting funtion will also become more professional and gradually be integrated into a closely related retention policy.

Inside recruiters will have the resources to be more competitive with outside recruiters. The Internet in particular and computers in general are leveling the playing field. Companies will take steps to avoid losing their best recruiters to the headhunter industry, providing compensations that recognize both the cost savings and the broader contributions to corporate success which professional inside recruiters can provide.

SUMMARY

Internet technology not only opens new opportunities for human resource management, it gives them the leverage to be a major source of corporate success. The old recruiting paradigms cruise the human resource ocean like the great battleships of World War I, while the Internet recruiting paradigm works like a modern fully armed, nuclear powered aircraft carrier.

And it gets faster every month.

Appendix A

INTERNET JOB SITES

Currently, hundreds of jobs sites are available to Internet users. We suggest you browse the sites mentioned in this appendix first. When reviewing these sites, remember to review Chapter 5, "Selecting an Online Service." Although several of these sites may seem attractive, in the end the site(s) that are best for your organization are the ones that deliver the largest number of qualified (L1) candidate responses to your advertisements at the lowest cost per response. For a more complete, up-to-date listing of available online job ad resources please go online and visit either the Riley Guide or Job Hunt at the follow addresses:

Riley Guide: http://www.dbm.com/jobguide/

Job Hunt: http://www.job-hunt.org/

4Work - http://www.4work.com

Jobs database:	Yes
Resume database:	Yes
Banner ads:	Yes
Corporate profiles:	No (But can link to corporate website)

Comments: Excellent general job site with very reasonable prices.

AccountingNet - http://www.accountingjobs.com/index.html

Jobs database:	Yes
Resume database:	Yes
Banner ads:	Yes
Corporate profiles:	Yes

Comments: Accounting.Net has teamed up with Career Mosaic to present an excellent example of a niche site supported by a general site.

America's Job Bank - http://www.ajb.dni.us

Jobs database:	Yes, free for employers to post
Resume database:	No
Banner ads:	No
Corporate profiles:	Yes

Comments: AJB contains jobs from over 2,000 state employment offices, plus postings from employers to the AJB web site. This service is available to U.S. companies or foreign companies legally authorized to operate a business in the United States. Generally, over 100,000 jobs are listed in this site. Occupation and skill levels cover a broad spectrum. Job seekers can search jobs by state, occupation, or occupation code.

Asia-Net - http://www.asia-net.com

Jobs database:	Yes
Resume database:	Yes
Banner ads:	No
Corporate profiles:	No

Comments: Excellent example of a niche site with a focused mission: "To provide excellent job opportunities for professionals who speak both English and an Oriental language, Japanese, Chinese or Korean.

Best Jobs U.S.A. - http://www.bestjobsusa.com

Jobs database:	Yes
Resume database:	Yes
Banner ads:	No
Corporate profiles:	Yes

Comments: This service is operated by Recourse Communication — an ad agency. Job ads on the site consist of ads placed in their publication Employment Review, in USA Today, and the direct postings to the Web site. The main purpose of Best Jobs in USA Today is to feature ads that appear in USA Today and Employment Review. The site is now gearing up to accept direct Web advertisements as well.

CareerCity - http://www.careercity.com/

Jobs database:	Yes
Resume database:	Yes
Banner ads:	Yes
Corporate profiles:	Yes

Comments: Has access to several thousand job openings, mainly from newsgroups, plus corporate links, and a complete career center with resumes and career advice.

Career Magazine - http://www.careermag.com

Jobs database:	Yes
Resume database:	Yes
Banner ads:	Yes
Corporate profiles:	Yes

Comments: Every day, Career Magazine downloads and indexes all the jobs postings from major Internet jobs databases and resume Usenet groups. Support for the site appears to come from banner advertising and corporate profile links rather than charges to job listing advertisers.

CareerMart - http://www.careermart.com

Jobs database:	Yes
Resume database:	Yes
Banner ads:	Yes
Corporate profiles:	Yes

Comments: This site is a service of BSA Advertising. This general career site offers job seekers the option of receiving e-mail of new job announcements as they are posted.

Career Mosaic - http://www.careermosaic.com

Jobs database:	Yes
Resume database:	Yes
Banner ads:	Yes
Corporate profiles:	Yes

Comments: Career Mosaic is one of the top employment sites on the Internet, containing thousands of job opportunities worldwide plus a resume database. In addition, dozens of employer profiles are featured.

CareerPath - http://www.careerpath.com

Jobs database:	Yes
Resume database:	Yes
Banner ads:	No
Corporate profiles:	Yes

Comments: Excellent site with job listings from the nation's leading newspapers, including Atlanta Journal, New York Times, Los Angeles Times, and The Washington Post. Great for job seekers, but employers must pay the high bills for print advertising in order to have their jobs listed here. This may change in 1998!

CareerSite - http://www.careersite.com

Jobs Database:	Yes
Resume database:	Yes
Banner ads:	Yes
Corporate profiles:	Yes

Comments: CareerSite has many features available to members, including the capability to respond electronically to job openings as well as to have employers match a job seeker's confidential profile. Several leading firms advertise on this site.

CareerWeb - http://www.cweb.com

Jobs database:	Yes
Resume database:	Yes
Banner ads:	Yes
Corporate profiles:	Yes

Comments: Site is owned and operated by Landmark Communications, owners of The Weather Channel. Jobs are listed by job category, location, and are keyword searchable.

College Grad Job Hunter - http://www.collegegrad.com/

Jobs database:	Yes
Resume database:	No
Banner ads:	Yes
Corporate profiles:	No

Comments: This site is designed for college students and recent college graduates.

Atlanta ComputerJobs Store - http://www.computerjobs.com

Jobs database:	Yes
Resume database:	Yes
Banner ads:	No
Corporate profiles:	Yes

Comments: An excellent example of a niche site. This site covers Information Technology (IT) jobs in a specific region of the country. Their business model has been replicated with Computer Jobs Stores now in the Carolinas, Chicago, and Texas.

DICE (Data Processing Independent Consultant's Exchange) - http://www.dice.com

Jobs database: Yes
Resume database: No
Banner ads: No
Corporate profiles: Yes

Comments: DICE is a service for high-tech professionals looking for consulting and full-time positions. Positions in Information Systems (IS) and engineering are featured.

Entertainment Recruiting Network - http://www.showbizjobs.com/

Jobs database: Yes
Resume database: Yes
Banner ads: Yes
Corporate profiles: Yes

Comments: Lights, camera, employment! The place where would-be and real cameramen, directors, and others associated with the entertainment industry go on to Net to seek employment.

E-Span - http://www.espan.com

Jobs database: Yes
Resume database: Yes
Banner ads: Yes
Corporate profiles: Yes

Comments: E-Span has thousands of links to its site because it was one of the first online employment advertising services. Thousands of jobs and resumes are contained in its databases.

Engineering Jobs - http://www.engineeringjobs.com

Jobs database: Yes
Resume database: Yes
Banner ads: Yes
Corporate profiles: Yes

Comments: Provides hundreds of links to companies and headhunters offering engineering employment.

Funeral Net - http://www.funeralnet.com/classifieds/index.html

Jobs database: Yes
Resume database: Yes

Banner ads: No
Corporate profiles: No

Comments: This is another excellent example of a niche based site offering employment opportunities to a specific job group. (Yes, funeral home operators.)

Headhunter.Net - http://www.headhunter.net
Jobs database: Yes
Resume database: Yes
Banner ads: No
Corporate profiles: No

Comments: Site has an excellent layout and design and currently is free.

HealthOpps - http://www.healthopps.com
Jobs database: Yes
Resume database: Yes
Banner ads: Yes
Corporate profiles: Yes

Comments: Another example of a niche based site, this one for the medical community. A sister site of Career Mosaic.

Heart Career Connection - http://www.career.com
Jobs database: Yes
Resume database: No
Banner ads: No
Corporate profiles: Yes

Comments: Has been in existence since 1993; HEART stands for Human Resources Electronic Advertising and Recruiting Tool. A few dozen employers are listed on the site. Jobs can be searched via company, location, and discipline.

Internet Fashion Exchange - http://www.fashionexch.com/index.htm
Jobs database: Yes
Resume database: Yes
Banner ads: No
Corporate profiles: No

Comments: Contains jobs, resumes, information about the fashion apparel and marketing industry. Search for jobs and candidates by product line and/or industry interests.

JobBank USA - http://www.jobbankusa.com
Jobs database: Yes

Resume database: Yes
Banner ads: Yes
Corporate profiles: Yes

Comments: General Web site listing several employers.

JobCenter - http://www.jobcenter.com
Jobs database: Yes
Resume database: Yes
Banner ads: No
Corporate profiles: No

Comments: Offers online and e-mail posting of resumes from job seekers and employment ads from company recruiters. Job seekers and recruiting clients are notified via e-mail of all matches found by intelligent agent software.

JobDirect - http://www.jobdirect.com
Jobs database: Yes
Resume database: Yes
Banner ads: No
Corporate profiles: Yes

Comments: A college oriented site that has been featured on CNN.

JobTrak - http://www.jobtrack.com
Jobs database: Yes
Resume database: Yes
Banner ads: No
Corporate profiles: No

Comments: JobTrak is oriented toward new college graduates. In a partnership with 400+ college and university career centers, JobTrak provides over 2,100 new full- and part-time job openings on any given day. Employers enter job ads into the database and select the student body they want to view their ads. Students from each university must enter a password and can view only the jobs that have been preselected for them.

Monster Board - http://www.monster.com
Jobs database: Yes
Resume database: Yes
Banner ads: Yes
Corporate profiles: Yes

Comments: The Monster Board is the premium offering of TMP Worldwide. The other major TMP offering being the Online Career Center. Do try both and do a cost benefit analysis on each service.

NationJob - http://www.nationjob.com

Jobs database:	Yes
Resume database:	Yes
Banner ads:	No
Corporate profiles:	Yes

Comments: Quite an impressive general site with over 175,000 jobseekers signed up to receive email notification of new jobs. Also posts to Americas Job Bank, Yahoo Classifieds, and Headhunter.net

Online Career Center - http://www.occ.com

Jobs database:	Yes
Resume database:	Yes
Banner ads:	Yes
Corporate profiles:	Yes

Comments: The Online Career Center is one of the oldest and best-known employment sites on the Internet. It is now owned by TMP Worldwide and is a sister site of the Monster Board. OCC is the TMP value leader.

Online Sports Career Center - http://www.onlinesports.com/pages/CareerCenter.html

Jobs database:	Yes
Resume database:	Yes
Banner ads:	No
Corporate profiles:	No

Comments: The Online Sports Career Center offers sports-related career opportunities and a resume bank for potential employers within the sports and recreation industry.

Saludos Web - http://www.saludos.com/saludos

Jobs database:	Yes
Resume database:	Yes
Banner ads:	No
Corporate profiles:	No

Comments: This Web site is devoted to promoting Hispanic career advancement and education; it is supported by Saludos Hispanos magazine.

SHRM (Society for Human Resource Management) - http://www.shrm.org

Jobs database:	Yes
Resume database:	No

Banner ads:	Yes
Corporate profiles:	No

Comments: This leading Human Resources Organization has an excellent database of jobs for HR professionals with many cross published in their print newspaper.

TV Jobs - http://www.tvjobs.com/

Jobs database:	Yes
Resume database:	Yes
Banner ads:	No
Corporate profiles:	No

Comments: Simply put, this site has employment listings for the TV, radio, and cable industries. In addition, there are links to employment pages for U.S. TV stations, an online resume bank, situation wanted postings, and a list of joblines you can call.

Virtual Job Fair - http://www.careerexpo.com

Jobs database:	Yes
Resume database:	Yes
Banner ads:	Yes
Corporate profiles:	No

Comments: This site lists thousands of high-tech jobs and resumes.

Job-Related Usenet Groups

alt.jobs - Jobs in Atlanta, GA

ba.jobs.misc - San Francisco, CA discussion forum about the job market

ba.jobs.offered - Job postings in San Francisco, CA

balt.jobs - Job discussion area in Balimore, MD

bc.jobs - Jobs in British Columbia, Canada

bionet.jobs - Scientific job openings

bionet.jobs.offered - Biological science job openings

biz.jobs.offered - Business positions (specifically computer)

can.jobs - Jobs in Canada

chi.jobs - Jobs in Chicago, IL

cmh.jobs - Jobs in Columbus, OH

comp.jobs.offered - Jobs in the computer industry

dc.jobs - Jobs in Washington D.C.

dfw.jobs - Jobs in Dallas/Fort Worth

fl.jobs - Jobs in Florida

il.jobs.misc - Jobs in Illinois

kw.jobs - Jobs in Kitchener-Waterloo, Ontario

la.jobs - Jobs in Los Angeles, Ventura, and Orange County CA

li.jobs - Employment on Long Island, NY

mi.jobs - Employment in Michigan

milw.jobs - Jobs in Milwaukee

misc.jobs.contract - Contract job listings

misc.jobs.misc - Discussions about employment, careers, and the workplace

misc.jobs.offered - General U.S. jobs available

misc.jobs.offered.entry - Entry-level job-seeker listings

ne.jobs - Jobs in New England

ne.jobs.contract - Contract openings in New England

nm.jobs - New Mexico jobs and resumes

nv.jobs - Jobs in Nevada

nyc.jobs.contract - Consulting work in the New York City area

nyc.jobs.offered - Jobs in New York, NY

oh.jobs - Jobs in Ohio

ont.jobs - Jobs in Ontario, Canada

pa.jobs.offered - Jobs in Pennsylvania

pgh.jobs.offered - Jobs in Pittsburgh, PA

phl.jobs.offered - Jobs in Philadelphia, PA

phx.jobs.wanted - Jobs in Phoenix

sdnet.jobs - Jobs in San Diego, CA

seattle.jobs.ofered - Jobs in Seattle, WA

stl.jobs - Jobs in Saint Louis

tor.jobs - Jobs in Toronto, Canada

triangle.jobs - Jobs in the Raleigh/Durham/Research Triangle, NC area

tx.jobs - Jobs in Texas

INTERNET RESUME SITES

Like jobs databases, there are literally dozens of options for finding talent on the Internet. The following list contains some of the major places to find resumes. Many are private databases and require a membership fee to search, while others are freely searchable. Additionally, some have a specific industry focus. At the end of this appendix, several additional Usenet resume groups are listed. For a more complete, up-to-date listing of available online resume sources please go online and visit either the Riley Guide or Job Hunt at the follow addresses:

> *Riley Guide: http://www.dbm.com/jobguide/*
>
> *Job Hunt: http://www.job-hunt.org/*

4 Work (private database): General Focus
http://www.4work.com

America's Talent Bank (free search of database): This is the governments nationwide resume bank.
http://www.atb.org

Atlanta Computer Job Store (private database): Atlanta computer/technology focus
http://www.computerjobs.com/

Broadcast Employment Services (free search of database): TV industry focus
http://www.tvjobs.com/

Building Industry Exchange (free search of database): Building industry focus
http://www.building.org/

Canadian Business Advertising Network (public database): General focus
http://www.cban.com/resume/find.cgi

CareerFile (private database): General focus
http://www.careerfile.com/

Career Magazine (free search of database): General focus
http://www.careermag.com/resumes/

Career Mosaic (free search of database): General focus
http://www.careermosaic.com/cm/cm41.html

CareerPath (private database): General focus
http://www.careerpath.com

CareerSite (private database): General focus
http://www.careersite.com/

CareerWeb (private database): General focus
http://www.cweb.com/

College Central Network (private database): College student focus
http://www.collegecentral.com

Dallas Computer Job Store (private database): Dallas computer/technology focus
http://www.computerjobs.com/Dallas/

DICE (private database): Data processing, engineering, & technical writing focus
http://www.dice.com

Drake Beam Morin (free search of database): DBM is a large outplacement firm
http://www.dbm.com

E-Span (private database): General focus
http://www.espan.com

Franklin Search Group (private database): Biotechnology/medical focus
http://www.medmarket.com/tenants/fsg/findcand.html

Future Access Employment Guide (free search of database): General focus
http://205.230.111.12/bhavlice/scripts/resrcsta.idc?

Internet Fashion Exchange (free search of database): Fashion industry focus
http://www.fashionexch.com/candqry.htm

JobNet (free search of database): General focus
http://www.westga.edu/~coop/reslook.html

JobTrak (private database): College graduate focus
http://www.jobtrak.com/

Monster Board (private database): General focus
http://www.monster.com/

National Educators Employment Review (free search of database): Education focus
http://www.thereview.com/rsearch.htm

Online Career Center (public database): General focus
http://www.occ.com/

Recruiters Online Network (private database): General focus
http://www.ipa.com/

Spie's Employment Service (free search of database): Optics industry focus
http://butler.spie.org/employment/employmentforum.qry

Technology Registry (private database): Technology focus
http://techreg.com/

Training.Net (free search of resumes): Training focus
http://www.trainingnet.com/

Virtual Job Fair (private database): High-tech focus
http://www.careerexpo.com/pub/Rsubmit.html

Usenet Groups to Explore

> **us.jobs.resumes:** United States focus
> **misc.jobs.resumes:** General focus
> **alt.medical.sales.jobs.resumes:** Medical sales focus
> **bionet.jobs.wanted:** Biological industry focus
> **ba.jobs.resumes:** San Francisco bay area
> **houston.jobs.wanted:** Houston, Tex.
> **il.jobs.resumes:** State of Illinois
> **nyc.jobs.wanted:** New York City, N.Y.

pa.jobs.wanted: State of Pennsylvania
pdaxs.jobs.resumes: Portland, Ore.
pdaxs.jobs.wanted: Portland, Ore.
pgh.jobs.wanted: Pittsburgh, Pa.
phl.jobs.wanted: Philadelphia, Pa.
seattle.jobs.wanted: Seattle, Wash.
stl.jobs.resumes: St. Louis, Mo.

INTERNET WEB SITE PROVIDERS

After reading this book, several of our readers might want to explore developing a company Web site of their own. If you desire to undertake such an endeavor, you have several options:

- Hire someone to develop the site and host it on a Web server - you do minimal work.
- Hire someone to develop a site and you manage it on a Web server - you do medium work.
- Develop and manage the Web site yourself on a Web server - you do maximum work.

For the sake of this discussion, we are referring to purchasing leased space on a Web server managed by professionals.

In each case listed, you will need to find space on a Web server. Currently there are over 4,000 Internet service providers (ISP's) who host websites listed in the U.S. These services often do more than just host your Web site; many can fully design and help you manage your site, or at the least provide suggestions and recommendations on whom to call for design services. We suggest you use the following sources to find a Web server to meet your needs:

- On the Internet, access *The List at http://www.thelist.com* - Information on over 4,000 Internet Service Providers is provided categorized by state, area code, and so on. With this site, you can easily find out what services are available in your area.
- Read the business sections of local newspapers or business journals in your area. Local ISPs often advertise in such publications.
- Ask folks at your local computer retail outlets for suggestions. They are often aware of who is doing what on the Internet in your area.
- Contact local businesses in your area that are already on the Internet. Ask them to tell you who provided their services, how much it costs, how much maintenance time is required, and so on.
- Have your questions written down and in hand when you begin talking to likely providers. They will appreciate having an informed prospect and you can collect good data for comparison shopping.
- Read at least the first two or three chapters in a Web page how-to book to develop a good perspective on the base line contribution that you must make to Web page design - even if you hire someone else to do the HTML programming. Laura Lemay wrote our personal favorite, *Teach Yourself HTML in 14 Days.*
- Rough out a storyboard and a linking diagram for your Web page, and if you don't know what they are, see the reading assignment in the previous paragraph.
- Start the Web page process with an overall strategy and some basic tactics decisions in place; the Internet is a dynamic, evolving media, but there is little sympathy among readers for companies who are trying to learn and make a big impression at the same time.

Tools You Can Use

Introduction

Online recruiting can be achieved with nothing more than a typewriter and a fax machine. But for ultimate effectiveness your organization will want to fully equip and use all the tools available to find talent and adequately manage the process. In this Appendix we list several "tools" which you, as an Internet recruiter, should be aware of. The only thing they all have in common is an Internet address for more information. Enjoy!

AskSam - http://www.asksam.com

One of the problems always encountered by online recruiters is what to do with all the e-mailed resumes. AskSam provides an extremely low cost solution to instantly import all e-mailed resumes into a searchable database. You have seen all the packages for $20,000+. Take a look at this solution for under $600!

Eudora - http://www.eudora.com

Somewere we have read that over 30 million folks are currently using this e-mail manager as part of their system. If you are currently using the "standard" e-mail managers often supplied with Internet browsers, we suggest you step up to the advanced features of Eudora Pro. Good online resume management begins with a good e-mail management system.

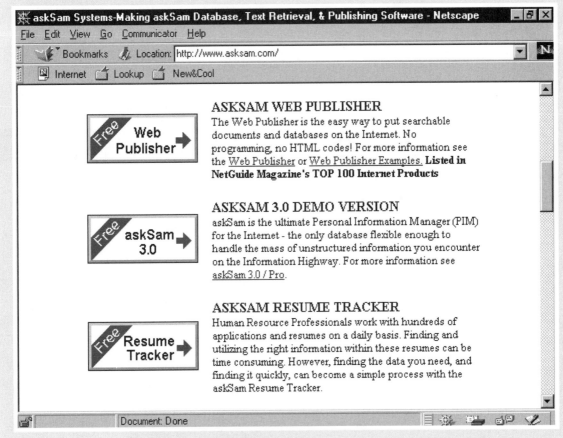

Figure D.1 The AskSam web site

HomeFair - http://www.homefair.com

Home Fair is a real estate / home buying site that has several tools which are extremely useful to Human Resource professionals. Most important is the Salary Calculator: Enter the city/state you are moving from and the city/state you are moving to along with your current salary. Press a button and in an instant you will find the equivalent salary you need to make in order to keep your current standard of living.

Net Recruiter - http://www.joblocator.com

You have heard about all the free Usenet and Yahoo job posting sites. Wouldn't it be nice if there were a software program which could automate the postings to these different sites? Look no further. Net Recruiter is that software program. Software is available for a 30 day free trial and costs $100 for outright purchase.

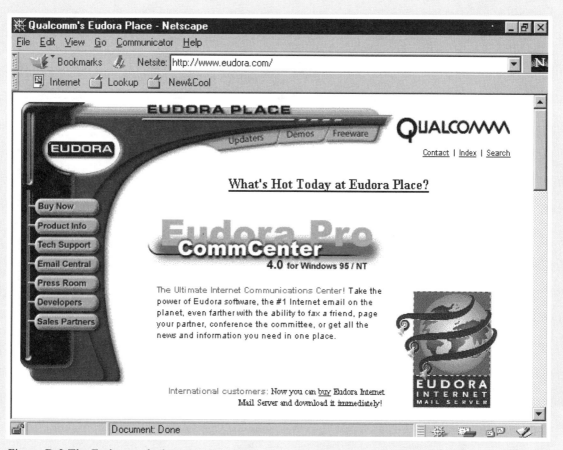

Figure D.2 The Eudora web site

Newspage - http://www.newspage.com

So you are a busy HR professional who would like to keep up with all the news in the recruitment industry but don't have the time! This could be a solution. Newspage allows you to create an individualized newspage which delivers information on the subjects you choose on a daily basis. You no longer need to be uninformed!

Resume Robot - http://www.it-ta.com/robohome.htm

This organization has developed a robot service that goes to all the Internet resume newsgroups, public domain Web sites, and personal Web sites to collect resumes based on the search criteria that you give it. We have not tried this service but the resume collection idea does have promise.

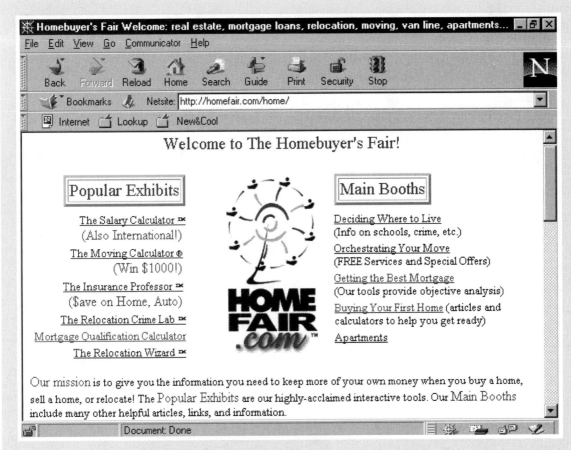

Figure D.3 The HomeFair web site

Search Engines

Just in case you are not aware of the top search engines and directories here they are:

- Yahoo - http://www.yahoo.com

- AltaVista - http://www.altavista.digital.com

- Excite - http://www.excite.com

- Lycos - http://www.lycos.com

- Infoseek - http://www.infoseek.com

- HotBot - http://www.hotbot.com

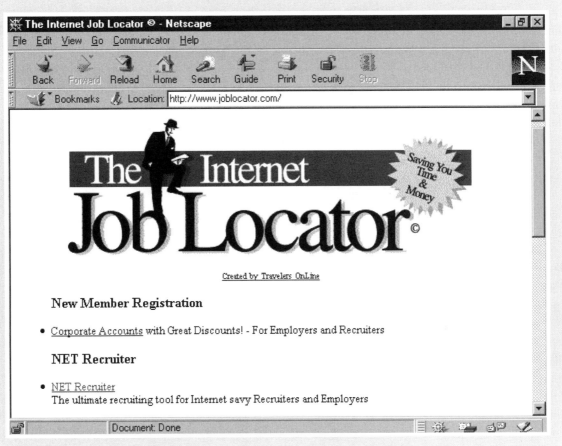

Figure D.4 The Net Recruiter web site

- DejaNews - http://www.dejanews.com

Do go online and learn how to conduct effective keyword searches using these engines. On most sites you will be able to print off specific instructions as to their use. It is very useful to invest a few minutes at the beginning of your "online career" to get the specific search routines down pat.

TUCOWS - http://www.tucows.com

Say What? - It is a strange name for one of the best sites on the Internet. Tucows is the site which lists hundreds of free software downloads of all types and sizes. Most software on the site is usable for 15-30 days after download and then "timesout" unless you purchase a passkey from the software developer.

Figure D.5
The Newspage
Personal web site

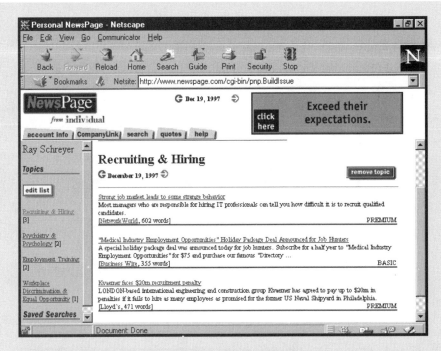

Figure D.6
The Resume Robot
web site

Figure D.7
The HotBot Search
Engine

Figure D.8
The TUCOWS web
site

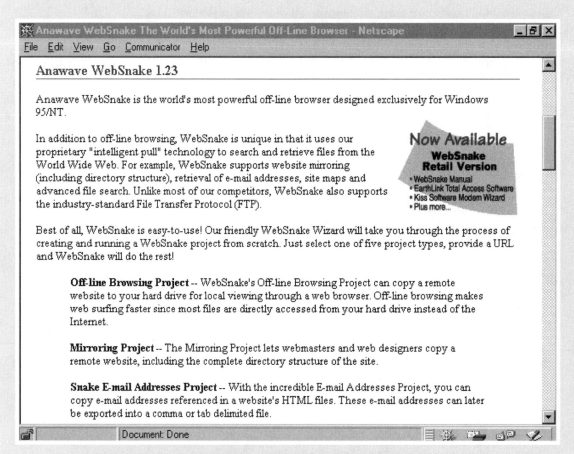

Figure D.9 The WebSnake web site

Every conceivable type of Internet tool is listed on this site for immediate download. In addition, Tucows provides the "5 Cow" rating system to let you know how each particular product stacks up to other competitors in the field.

WebSnake - http://www.anawave.com/websnake/index.html
Anawave WebSnake is a powerful off-line browser designed exclusively for Windows 95 & NT.

There is more. WebSnake uses "intelligent pull" technology to search and retrieve files from the World Wide Web. For example, WebSnake supports retrieval of e-mail addresses, site maps and advanced file search. Give it a look!

EQUIPMENT SHOPPING LIST

It seesms like just yesterday we were uncrating our new IBM PC with the 10MB hard drive and the 360KB floppy disk. What a joy those days were! Unfortunately, early generations of PCs and their subsequent versions (286, 386, and now most 486s) don't have the horsepower, speed, or memory to keep up with today's graphically intensive Internet community. Our recommendations for your system are as follow. You could attempt to navigate the web with lesser equipment, but you will run out of horsepower quickly as the web continues to grow in graphics, content, and speed:

- **IBM-type PC with at least a 166MHz Pentium-class processor.** Any brand of PC will do, such as AST, Compaq, Hewlett-Packard, IBM, or Packard Bell. We're partial to custom-built PCs made with industry-standard components. With industry-standard components, you don't have to throw away your old PC when new features hit the marketplace: you just have your main components changed. Regarding the processor, the Pentium-like versions from Cyrix or AMD will do fine.

- **4GB hard drive.** Sure, you can get by with a lot less, but with time you will fill up your drive with downloaded e-mail. Hard drive space is cheaper than ever, so get as much as you can afford.

- **At least 32MB of RAM, preferably 48MB+.** The Web is highly graphical, and is becoming more so every day. You will need at least 32MB to handle these larger files today and in the near future.

- **At least a 28.8Kbps modem, preferably 33.6 on up.** Anything less than 28.8Kbps, and the Web will seem like molasses in Antarctica.

- **Laser printer.** If you want to print your files, you should get a laser printer. They are inexpensive and have excellent print quality. Hewlett-Packard is a leading brand you should consider.

CHOOSING AN INTERNET ACCESS PROVIDER

These are the folks who will get you hooked up on the world wide web of the Internet from your PC. Internet access is available over most of the U.S. because all the major long distance phone carriers and many local carriers now offer Internet access. Consider these carriers with the following in mind:

- Do they provide a comprehensive Internet package that includes an HTML 3.0-compliant browser and supporting Internet e-mail software that is easily loaded on your PC with minimal configuration problems?
- Are there local access numbers available in your city or the cities you may be traveling? This can be a real problem if you are called away for business and have a regional access provider that does not have a local access line. Add the long distance phone bill up after accessing the net long distance from a hotel room while traveling - YOW.
- Will human beings actually talk with you about problem or do you get placed in a holding pattern for hours? Do humans work at the company or are problems answered by pressing numbers on your telephone keypad? Are training manuals available to help you in your Internet education?
- Do they support ISDN or 56K modem access speeds? Today the standard is

28.8, but tomorrow may be different. You do not want to wait for an ISP to upgrade when the Internet community is cruising at a much faster speed.

- Is a Web page or Web-page service included in your account options? After surfing awhile, you might want to consider putting up a company home page. It is helpful if this service is part of the package.
- Can multiple e-mail accounts be handled through the service? Odds are that your family members may want to use your account or you may desire to have one e-mail account strictly for business and one for personal surfing.

Listed next are some of the best-known Internet access providers. The best way to choose is to ask a friend who uses the Internet; she can at least comment on her own access provider. If you have recently bought a new computer, odds are it is preloaded with several of the services listed below. You might want to give one of them a try before you look elsewhere. These services have a strong national presence with access numbers in major cities:

America Online: 800-827-6364
AT&T Worldnet: 800-967-5363
CompuServe: 800-433-0389
Earthlink: 800-395-8425
Netcom: 800-353-6600
Microsoft Network: 800-426-9400
PSINet: 800-827-7482
Prodigy: 800-776-3449
Sprynet: 206-957-8997

Billy Bob's Barbecued Ribs

The ribs should be polished with Billy Bob's Secret Sauce (details to follow). The pepper water keeps meat juicy and prevents charring.

- Nine pounds spareribs
- Four cups of spring water
- Five dried red chili peppers, or 1 teaspoon crushed pepper

Combine water and chili peppers in saucepan. Heat on grill and keep hot at edge. Trim surface fat from ribs. Place sides of ribs on rack 8 to 10 inches above glowing hickory coals or use small fire if rack cannot be adjusted easily. Heat ribs on both sides until surface is warm and brush with pepper water. cover grill or make a tent with aluminum foil. continue barbecuing and brushing with pepper water for 32 minutes. Brush lightly with Billy Bob's Secret Sauce, turn, and brush lightly with sauce on the other side. Continue barbecuing for 25 minutes, or until juices run clear when ribs are cut near center. Turn every 10 minutes or each time fire flares and brush lightly with sauce. Heat remaining sauce. Cut ribs into serving pieces and serve with Billy Bob's Secret Sauce.

Billy Bob's Secret Sauce
Makes enough for nine pounds of pork ribs. Baste lightly with affection and finesse.

2 cups cider vinegar
3 cups catsup
2/3 cup vegetable oil
2/3 Worcestershire sauce
1/3 cup Jack Daniel's
1/2 cup firmly packed brown sugar
2/3 cup molasses
6 tablespoons prepared yellow mustard
5 cloves of garlic, minced
2 lemons, cut in halves
1 tablespoon dried mint

In a copper-bottomed saucepan, combine catsup, vinegar, oil, Jack Daniel's, Worcestershire sauce, brown sugar, molasses, mustard, mint, and garlic. Squeeze lemon juice into sauce and add one lemon-half shell. Heat slowly about fifteen minutes. Sauce should not reach a boil, but heating enhances flavor.

Use sparingly as a basting sauce, and reheat additional sauce for table use.

Ray Schreyer

Ray Schreyer founded Internet Recruitment Solutions, a North Carolina consulting firm specializing in Internet applications. Earlier he pioneered Internet recruitment at First Union National Bank in Charlotte, NC, where he developed his expertise in Internet strategies. He is currently applying his Internet based skills at Little & Associates, one of the largest architectural and engineering firms in America. He is passionate about integrating Internet technology into corporate human resources and consulting with H.R. professionals on strategies for success.

He received his Graduate training in Industrial/Organizational Psychology from the University of North Carolina and his Bachelors in Chemistry from Elmhurst College. His professional affiliations include The Society for Human Resource Management and The Carolinas OD Network. He lives in Charlotte, NC with his new bride Gayle, where he enjoys cycling, kayaking, and backpacking. He can be reached via e-mail at nccareer@aol.com or via phone at 704-399-7888.

John McCarter

John Lewis McCarter Jr. is the managing director of Internet Recruitment Solutions, a North Carolina consulting firm focused on guiding corporations in human resource based Internet applications.

A native of the Carolinas and a long term resident of Charlotte, John is a twenty year veteran in management consulting. Industries served include textiles, banking, steel, utilities, and shipbuilding. His work experience is a mixture of problem solving management practices, team leadership, classroom training, marketing, and advanced training development processes. John's professional affiliations include IIE, ASTD, and SHRM.

A proud father of three, he writes fiction as a hobby and also tries to maintain contact with his nearly forty first cousins and the associated other relatives. He is a member of MENSA and Common Cause. John received his BA from Clemson University and his MBA from UNC-Charlotte. He can be reached via email at cootersend@aol.com or via phone at (704) 364-6678.

Tell us what you think

As a reader, you are the most important critic and commentator of our books. We value your opinion and want to know what we're doing right, what we could do better, in what areas you'd like to see us publish, and any other words of wisdom you're willing to pass our way. You can help us create strong books that meet your needs, giving you the human resource insights for the 21st century.

Please email us with your comments to nccareer@aol.com.

Index

CAREER RESOURCES

Contact Impact Publications for a free annotated listing of career resources or visit their World Wide Web site for a complete listing of career resources: *http://www.impactpublications.com*
    The following career resources are available directly from Impact Publications. Complete this form or list the titles, include postage (see formula at the end), enclose payment, and send your order to:

IMPACT PUBLICATIONS
9104-N Manassas Drive
Manassas Park, VA 20111-5211
Tel. 703/361-7300 or Fax 703/335-9486
E-mail: impactp@impactpublications.com

Orders from individuals must be prepaid by check, moneyorder, Visa, MasterCard, or American Express. We accept telephone and fax orders.

Qty.	TITLES	Price	TOTAL
Internet Recruitment and Job Finding			
___	CareerXroads 1998	$22.95	___
___	Employer's Guide to Recruiting on the Internet	$24.95	___
___	Guide to Internet Job Finding	$14.95	___
___	How to Get Your Dream Job Using the Web	$29.99	___
___	Internet Resumes	$14.95	___
___	Resumes in Cyberspace	$17.95	___
Career Planning and Job Search			
___	Best Jobs For the 21st Century	$19.95	___
___	Change Your Job, Change Your Life	$17.95	___
___	How to Succeed Without a Career Path	$13.95	___
___	Me, Myself and I, Inc.	$17.95	___
___	The Pathfinder	$14.95	___
___	Up Is Not the Only Way	$28.95	___
___	What Color Is Your Parachute?	$16.95	___
Resumes			
___	100 Winning Resumes For $100,000+ Jobs	$24.95	___
___	1500+ KeyWords for $100,000+ Jobs	$14.95	___
___	Dynamite Resumes	$14.95	___
___	High Impact Resumes and Letters	$19.95	___
___	Ready-to-Go Resumes	$29.95	___
___	Resume Catalog	$15.95	___

___	Resumes & Job Search Letters For Transitioning Military	$17.95 ___
___	Sure-Hire Resumes	$14.95 ___

Cover Letters

___	201 Dynamite Job Search Letters	$19.95 ___
___	201 Winning Cover Letters For $100,000+ Jobs	$24.95 ___
___	Dynamite Cover Letters	$14.95 ___

Interviews, Networking, and Salary Negotiations

___	101 Dynamite Answers to Interview Questions	$12.95 ___
___	101 Dynamite Questions to Ask At Your Job Interview	$14.95 ___
___	101 Dynamite Ways to Ace Your Job Interview	$13.95 ___
___	Dynamite Networking For Dynamite Jobs	$15.95 ___
___	Dynamite Salary Negotiation	$15.95 ___
___	Interview For Success	$15.95 ___
___	What Do I Say Next?	$20.00 ___

Skills, Testing, Self-Assessment, Empowerment

___	7 Habits of Highly Effective People	$14.00 ___
___	Discover the Best Jobs For You	$15.95 ___
___	Do What You Are	$16.95 ___
___	Emotional Intelligence	$13.95 ___
___	I Can Do Anything If I Only Knew What It Was	$19.95 ___
___	Your Signature Path	$24.95 ___

SUBTOTAL --- ___

Virginia residents add 4½% sales tax ___

POSTAGE/HANDLING ($5.00 for first
title plus 8% of SUBTOTAL over $30) $5.00

8% of SUBTOTAL over $30 -- ___

TOTAL ENCLOSED -- ___

NAME _____

ADDRESS _____

_____

_____

❑ I enclose check/moneyorder for $ _____ made payable to IMPACT PUBLICATIONS.

❑ Please charge $ _____ to my credit card:

   ❑ Visa   ❑ MasterCard   ❑ American Express

   Card # _____

   Expiration date: _____ / _____

   Signature _____

On-Line Career Superstore & Warehouse

Hundreds of Terrific Career Resources Conveniently Available On the World Wide Web 24-Hours a Day, 365 Days a Year!

Ever wanted to know what are the newest and best books, directories, newsletters, wall charts, training programs, videos, CD-ROMs, computer software, and kits available to help you recruit personnel, land a job, negotiate a higher salary, or start your own business? What about finding a job in Asia or relocating to San Francisco? Are you curious about how to find a job 24-hours a day by using the Internet or what you'll be doing five years from now? Trying to keep up-to-date on the latest career resources but not able to find the latest catalogs, brochures, or newsletters on today's "best of the best" resources?

Welcome to the first virtual career bookstore on the Internet. Now you're only a "click" away with Impact Publication's electronic solution to the resource challenge. Impact Publications, one of the nation's leading publishers and distributors of career resources, maintains a comprehensive "Career Superstore and Warehouse" on the Internet. The bookstore is jam-packed with the latest job and career resources on:

- Alternative jobs and careers
- Self-assessment
- Career planning and job search
- Employers
- Relocation and cities
- Resumes
- Cover Letters
- Dress, image, and etiquette
- Education
- Telephone
- Military
- Salaries
- Interviewing
- Nonprofits
- Empowerment
- Self-esteem
- Goal setting
- Executive recruiters
- Entrepreneurship
- Government
- Networking
- Electronic job search
- International jobs
- Travel
- Law
- Training and presentations
- Minorities
- Physically challenged

"This is more than just a bookstore offering lots of product," say Drs. Ron and Caryl Krannich, two of the nation's leading career experts and authors and developers of this on-line bookstore. *"We're an important resource center for libraries, corporations, government, educators, trainers, and career counselors who are constantly defining and redefining this dynamic field. Of the thousands of career resources we review each year, we only select the 'best of the best.'"*

Visit this rich site and you'll quickly discover just about everything you ever wanted to know about finding jobs, changing careers, and starting your own business. This rich site also includes what's new and hot, tips for job search success, and monthly specials:

http://www.impactpublications.com